DIVORCE

IN THE PROGRESSIVE ERA

by

William L. O'Neill

NEW VIEWPOINTS

A Division of Franklin Watts, Inc./New York

1973

Library of Congress Cataloging in Publication Data

O'Neill, William L
    Divorce in the progressive era.

    Reprint of the 1967 ed., which was based on the
author's thesis, University of California, 1963; with a
new pref. by the author.
    Bibliography: p.
    1. Divorce–United States. I. Title.
[HQ834.05 1973]   301.42'84'0973   73-3100
ISBN 0-531-06489-1 (pbk)

First NEW VIEWPOINTS edition published 1973 by
Franklin Watts, Inc.

Manufactured in the United States of America

To Henry F. May

PREFACE

This book began as an effort to study the changes in public thinking on a particular social problem during a limited period of time. I decided to focus on the origins of mass divorce because it was one of the first aspects of what we call the Revolution in Morals to become a matter of public controversy. We all recognize the overthrow of Victorian sexual norms as a conspicuous feature of life in this century, but historians have done little to explain it. It seemed to me, therefore, that it might be useful to trace the public discussion of one issue during its critical years to see what light it shed on the problem of moral change.

My first attempt in this direction was my doctoral dissertation, "The Divorce Crisis of the Progressive Era" (Berkeley, 1963). In preparing it I assembled the basic data which I have used in this study, but my perspective was limited to the connection between divorce and the moral revolution. Further study and reflection have persuaded me, however, that the divorce crisis really needs to be examined in several different ways if we are to understand the social and historical functions of such a controversy. Moreover, recent scholarship and my own investigation of the feminist movement have led me to reevaluate some of the assumptions on which I had based my dissertation. I now believe, for example, that "revolution" is the wrong word to use in describing

vii

the changing sexual customs of this century. Women have gained some of the freedoms which once were enjoyed only by men, and Victorian taboos against the candid treatment of sexual themes have largely crumbled. But the social position of American women is not greatly different from what it was at the end of the nineteenth century, and the Victorian family system has demonstrated an astonishing durability. Mass divorce, therefore, now seems to me to have been not the leading edge of a moral revolution so much as the first of a series of adjustments by which the patriarchal family and the Protestant sexual ethic have accommodated themselves to the demands of an urban, industrial society.

In substance, then, because I have revised some of my premises and initiated new lines of inquiry, this study has acquired a more complex character than was originally intended. It will help the reader if he bears in mind that we are concerned with four themes: mass divorce as a chapter in the history of the American family; the influence of ideology on family change; the ways in which groups and individuals respond to this kind of social change; and the insights into the popular thought of a period that may emerge from the study of such behavior.

We know so little about the history of the family that almost any information on it adds to our understanding. I am particularly interested, however, in the process by which criticisms of the family that express a minority point of view become part of a new consensus, how new definitions of acceptable family patterns are arrived at, and the role that criticism plays in determining what is to be worked into the system. Hence I will try to show

how the Victorian family came into being, what its critics thought was wrong with it, and how after a period of intense debate their objections helped establish a new sense of what the family was and where it fitted into the social structure.

As divorce came to be the principal issue over which the old and the new sets of ideas about the family clashed, a study of it gives us an opportunity to examine in detail how the ideological battle lines were formed. The struggle over divorce was in fact a prototype of the kind of dispute that today has become commonplace. It anticipated, in a disorganized and more primitive way, what was to happen when mental health, progressive education, and the like became matters of controversy. Divorce was one of the earliest phenomena to elicit this kind of response. However, the questions it raised were decided before the present ideological alignments had been established, enabling us to see more clearly how we have arrived at our present urgent, not to say obsessive, concentration on the state of public morals.

Finally, since divorce was the cause of much anxious soul-searching by the Progressive generation, it reveals a good deal about the assumptions on which the Progressives' view of themselves and their world was based. Those who were opposed to divorce, and they were, especially in the beginning, decidedly in the majority, greatly exaggerated its importance. But their highly colored rhetoric exposed a conviction as to the purpose of their time that is central to any understanding of what Progressivism was all about. Unlike many of their contemporaries, the enemies of divorce were not primarily concerned with social control or social efficiency so much as with the moral health of the people. A smooth, well-ordered society that did not ultimately stand for individual right-conduct was of no interest to them— even if such a state of affairs were possible, which most of them doubted. The close examination of how Progressives responded to what they considered a vital issue enables us to appreciate better the character of their age.

A few minor clarifications are in order. The exact period to which I have confined myself is partly a matter of convenience. Divorce was talked about before the 1880s and after 1919, but the early years of the twentieth century were crucial, because thereafter it became increasingly clear that nothing would or could be done to control the rising divorce rate. The thirty-odd years on which I have focused mark the outer limits of the time during which a decisive change in the public attitude toward divorce took place. I have chosen to call the critics of divorce "conservatives" and its defenders "liberals" because these are the terms which they most often used themselves. However, I have also speculated on the relationship of this debate to the liberal and conservative political traditions, since the divorce issue cut across party lines. Some confusion may result. Unless otherwise indicated, therefore, the terms "liberal" and "conservative" here refer only to an individual's position on divorce.

Some knowledge of the historian's prejudices are always helpful in evaluating works that deal with subjects of more than academic interest, and it may assist the reader to know something of my own views. No one can grow to maturity now without being touched by

divorce in some way. We all have friends or relatives
whose marriages have broken up, even if ours have not,
and so we can hardly be as cheerful about the consequences of divorce as many of its defenders were a half-
century and more ago. But at the same time we have
come, correctly I think, more and more to regard the
right of divorce as something like a civil liberty. It may
not be wise or just, but easy divorce is the only policy
consistent with the aspirations of a freedom-loving
people. Consequently my sympathies, such as they are,
are with those who defended the right of divorce on
libertarian grounds. On the whole, however, what is
most arresting about the people who engaged in these
polemics is not the degree to which they have a claim
on our sympathies, but the extent to which their arguments were based on faulty judgments and errors in
fact. It is a chastening experience to read through the
literature generated by a heated controversy of the
recent past and discover how much of it was irrelevant
when not actually wrong. If it does nothing else, it
should inspire us with a greater humility when we speak
and write about the moral problems of our age.

I am grateful to the University of California and the
Woodrow Wilson Foundation, which provided me with
research funds, to the staff of the Manuscript Division
of the Library of Congress, and to Professor George
Stocking, of the University of California, for his critical
reading of my original manuscript.
My greatest obligation is to Professor Henry F. May,
of the University of California, who first interested me
in this subject and who, despite his lack of sympathy

with much of what I have had to say, tirelessly advised and corrected me at each stage in the preparation of this work. Every student of the Progressive era will realize how much I owe to Professor May's ideas, but only those who have had the benefit of his energetic criticism can appreciate the full extent of my indebtedness.

With their kind permission I have used material which originally appeared in my articles in *American Quarterly, The Journal of the History of the Behavioral Sciences,* and *Vermont History.*

For their help I would like to thank Dr. Geoffrey R. Elton, of Cambridge University, Professor William R. Stanton, of the University of Pittsburgh, and Professor Robert G. Athearn, of the University of Colorado. To Carol, who gallantly performs the tiresome duties of a scholar's wife, I am more than grateful.

I am entirely responsible, of course, for the opinions expressed in this book.

W. L. O'N.

Madison, Wisconsin
October 1966

PREFACE TO THE
PAPERBACK EDITION

If I were to rewrite *Divorce in the Progressive Era* I would make two changes in it. The first, and least, would be to bring my demographic references up to date. It is more clear now than it was a few years ago that the divorce rate is rising again. The age at marriage is increasing too, and the birth rate falling. The era of togetherness, which temporarily reversed these long-standing trends, now seems over. But later marriages, more frequent divorces, and smaller families do not of themselves mean that marriage and the family are changing greatly as institutions. They have proved, after more than a century of supposed decline, to be enormously durable. Even the current experiments with group sex, group marriage, communal living, and other alternatives to, or variations on, monogamy have had little effect on the domestic habits of most Americans. Every generation in this century has seen the end of marriage and the family proclaimed, yet they go on much as before. I still stand on what I wrote about them here.

The one aspect of this book that most needs changing is the relation between divorce and Progressivism as mood and movement. Like many historians, I used to have too simple a view of Progressivism. We have learned that the movement, and indeed the age, was more various. One cannot speak any longer of *the* progressives. There were different types, some of them not reformers at all in the usual sense. Certain ideas were widely shared, like optimism and faith in progress, which I rightly stressed, but it was wrong of me to imply that the divorce controversy was organically related to a clearly defined entity called Progressivism, about which historians were so much in agreement that no further explanation was required.

I am less concerned now with what was progressive about the divorce controversy, and more with what made it distinctive. It was, for one thing, a purely ideological fight. There were some interested parties—lawyers, merchants—when state legislation was at issue. But mostly divorce was argued by people who had nothing material at stake. This gave the struggle an unusually abstract character. And it is arresting too because what was said on both sides had little or no effect: for reasons explained later, the laws regulating divorce could not be altered enough to change behavior. Thus, while the controversy says a good deal about social thought at the time, it is also noteworthy as a sterile exercise on the part of deeply concerned people who were, all the same, quite out of touch with reality. This was most true of conservatives, who were slow to recognize their helplessness, but also of liberals. They were on the side of history inasmuch as the divorce rate kept rising, yet there was no evidence that what they said made any difference. Liberals did help change the climate of opinion, but as divorces proliferated at a time when nearly everyone opposed them, it is not clear that liberalizing attitudes after the fact mattered much.

This kind of powerlessness and isolation is typical of

debates over morality, sexual morality in particular. Sometimes, as with prostitution, birth control, and venereal disease, these controversies seem more substantial because in theory legislation can produce results. In practice, though, laws strong enough to change behavior can rarely be gotten. Divorce was the first important sex-related problem to be discussed early and over a long time, and also the first to be decided. Not that a solution was consciously arrived at, but a time came when nearly everyone had to admit that little could be done about it. The problem was solved by being dropped. This makes it not so much unique as prophetic, since it showed how Americans would handle similar problems later.

In general, then, I think now that I exaggerated the difference between progressives and moderns. This book was planned before the New Left, the ecology movement, Women's Liberation, and other groups had demonstrated that ideology was far from dead, and that utopianism, rhetorical extravagance, and radical enthusiasms were still part of American life. The Progressive era was unlike our own in many ways, but not so greatly as I used to think. I ask readers to be skeptical of my efforts to play off the dead against the living, and to note instead how much remains the same. The divorce controversy tells us something about the progressives, and also about ourselves. It is worth studying for both reasons, but perhaps for the second most of all.

WILLIAM L. O'NEILL

New Brunswick, N.J.
February 1972

Contents

Chapter

1

THE POLITICAL ECONOMY OF LOVE

Until about the middle of the nineteenth century divorces were rare events in the Western world; thereafter they occurred at such a steadily increasing rate that by the end of the century the legal dissolution of marriage was recognized as a major social phenomenon. While my purpose is to examine the ideological struggles which this development precipitated in the United States, it cannot be accomplished without knowing something about the history and demography of marriage and the family. Their historical adventures and present difficulties were what the public debate was all about, and to make sense of the controversy we need to know not only what was thought to have happened but also what actually did take place.

As is normally the case, there was a standard explanation to which nearly everyone subscribed that went as follows: for a very long time Western civilization had been marked by a stable, patriarchal family system.

Each family had many children and kinfolk who lived together in a big house. Everyone worked hard, for the family unit was economically self-sufficient and performed numerous functions. It was the source of economic stability and religious, educational, and vocational training. The father was stern, reserved, and the ultimate authority on all important matters. Everyone married early, and the young people, especially the girls, were invariably chaste. The parents had a voice in choosing their offspring's mates, and after marriage "the couple lives harmoniously, either near the boy's parents or with them, for the couple is slated to inherit the farm. No one divorces."[1]

Unfortunately, this pastoral idyl came to an end when the snake entered Eden, disguised as the industrial revolution. The force of industrialism tore apart the extended family and reduced it to its nuclear core (father, mother, children). The father dwindled from a majestic authority to a mere first among wage-earning equals as the entire family left the farm and entered the factory. The family unit was thus exposed to unprecedented strains at the same time that its internal resources were diminished. In its crippled form the family, which was no longer supported by the sanctions of religion, custom, and authority, could no longer resist the temptations of unrestrained individualism, and divorces on a large scale ensued.

Individual cases were, of course, complex and different in detail, as Chapter 4 demonstrates, and these

1. This description of what he calls the "classical family ideal" is from William J. Goode, *World Revolution and Family Patterns* (Glencoe, 1963), p. 6.

same points were usually put in a more favorable light. But as a rule everyone who wrote about the family at the turn of the century agreed on its history, and a glance at some recent studies indicates that this tradition is still very much alive.[2] Even allowing for the element of parody which tends to creep into such an abbreviated summary of the conventional wisdom, it now appears that this version of the family's history had almost no relationship with the actual past, but a great deal to do with the nature of Victorian social thought. What seems to have happened was that an idealized version of the contemporary middle-class family was created and then pushed back in time until it became a universal norm to which all the existing discrepancies could be invidiously compared. As William J. Goode points out, the fact that the classical family ideal is always located at some point in the past suggests that it probably never really existed. But this is not to say that the family system has not changed. The Victorians realized that mass divorce constituted one such change, but they erred in thinking, as we still often do today, that divorce was a sign of decadence and that it led to the corruption of a crucial social institution.

Despite the obvious vigor of that domestic life which is daily celebrated by our mass media, the alarmist point of view persists because of the inadequacy of most literature dealing with the family as an historic institution. Until recently almost no history of the family has conformed to the standards of historical scholarship which

2. See, for example, Panos D. Bardis, "Family Forms and Variations Historically Concerned," in *Handbook of Marriage and the Family* (Chicago, 1964), pp. 403–60.

3

are usually taken for granted. Their wealth of detail notwithstanding, most such attempts are scrappy, value-ridden, and present-minded to a degree that would not be tolerated in other branches of the discipline. We must be all the more grateful, therefore, to the French historian Philip Ariés, who has begun the task of subjecting our old assumptions about the family to a more rigorous scrutiny. Ariés was inspired to write his study of the origins of the modern family, *Centuries of Childhood,* after examining the demographic data which, by showing the current popularity of marriage, ran contrary to the accepted idea that the family was decaying:

> It seemed to me (and qualified observers have come to share my conclusions) that on the contrary the family occupied a tremendous place in our industrial societies, and that it had perhaps never before exercised so much influence over the human condition. The legal weakening proved only that the idea (and the reality) did not follow the same curve as the institution.[3]

At the risk of mutilating his subtle and richly illustrated argument, what Ariés discovered was that the family as we understand it did not come into being until about the sixteenth century. Before then the family performed a function by guaranteeing the transmission of life, property, and names, but "it did not penetrate very far into human sensibility." Life was polymorphous, promiscuous, and collective to a high degree. Family relatives, servants, and friends lived together,

3. Philip Ariés, *Centuries of Childhood: A Social History of Family Life* (New York, 1962), p. 10.

4

not only in the same house but usually in the same rooms. Children were unimportant as long as there were enough of them, and were apprenticed out or sent to other families for training as pages at an early age. The upper-class family, at least, was essentially a public institution that made few demands upon its members, who lived primarily not in the family but in society.

In the sixteenth and seventeenth centuries, the modern conjugal family began to emerge in consequence of the discovery of the child. Once it was established that the primary obligation of the family was to train and nurture children, the apprenticeship system was gradually replaced by formal education. As family life became progressively more oriented around the child, privacy and domesticity increased and the family commenced to lose its old public character. Until the end of the seventeenth century real privacy was rare, but in the eighteenth century the family began to push society back. The modern house with its several rooms opening on corridors made it possible to separate the servants from the family, while collateral relatives were banished altogether. Among the middle classes the conjugal family became the normal type, formal visiting was introduced in place of the old casual social relations, and the home came to be marked by the modern characteristics of comfort, privacy, isolation, and domesticity.

Relations between husband and wife grew more intimate, and both became preoccupied with the health and education of their children. The child-centered society was born and the retreat from sociability completed. This movement, which began with the bourgeoisie, spread finally to the other classes and widened the gulf between them. Ariés believes that the old polymorphous social body in which everyone lived in proximity to each other was broken up into big groups called classes and small groups called families:

> The old unique social body embraced the greatest possible variety of ages and classes. Moral distances took the place of physical distance. The strictness of external signs of respect and the differences in dress counter-balanced the familiarity of communal life.[4]

The middle class was the first to withdraw from this society and to begin the process of physical segregation that led finally to the division of all of society into separate and strictly regulated compartments.

The main advantage of Ariés' thesis from our point of view is that, unlike the usual accounts, it explains why the divorce movement began and why it took place in the late nineteenth century rather than at some other time. If we regard the Victorian patriarchal family as an essentially new institution, rather than as the last gasp of a dying one, we can see why divorce became a necessary part of the family system. When families are large and loose, arouse few expectations, and make few demands, there is no need for divorce. But when families become the center of social organization, their intimacy can become suffocating, their demands unbearable, and their expectations too high to be easily realizable. Divorce then becomes the safety valve that makes the

4. Ibid., p. 414.

system workable. Those who are frustrated or oppressed can escape their families, and those who fail at what is regarded as the most important human activity can gain a second chance. Divorce is, therefore, not an anomaly or a flaw in the system, but an essential feature of it. When the modern family came to dominate society in the nineteenth century, divorce became common.

The little knowledge that we have of domestic life in the American colonies supports this contention. The Puritans were among the first to adopt the conjugal family system. It was their rejection of society in favor of the family that helped make them so unpopular in England, and in the New World, with its enlarged opportunities, they created a domestic life that was recognizably modern. They were intensely concerned with the education of children, as their laws reflect, and determined to block the promiscuity and easy manners that still characterized the unregenerate and reactionary elements of society. By the same token, the Puritan colonies were the first to make divorce legally possible, while in England, the old and the new continued unhappily to coexist.

The Puritans attached such importance to the family, which they regarded as the first society from which all else sprang, that they lost control of New England. The Puritans were not completely unaware of the dangers inherent in their preoccupation with their children. They continued the old tradition of apprenticeship for both boys and girls, even when it was not necessary, because, as Edmund S. Morgan points out, they did not trust themselves. Because the Puritans feared that they would lavish an excess of affection upon their children, they

7

bound them out for the good of their souls. But the rationing of love was not enough. The Puritans had come to the New World in large measure to save their children from the profanations of the Old, and when their commonwealth began to fill with unregenerate men, instead of seeking to convert them, the Puritans withdrew into their churches and families. The churches became agencies for perpetuating the gospel among an hereditary religious elite constituting a steadily diminishing percentage of the population. In the end the rule of the Saints passed away because "the Puritans showed more interest in saving their children than they did in saving their religion."[5] They became, therefore, the first American community to be destroyed by a surfeit of domestic virtue.

Conditions outside New England were, however, rather different. Travelers in the back country during the seventeenth century frequently commented on the promiscuous social life that obtained there. Common law marriages were in some places more usual than legal ones, concubinage flourished, and the woman shortage often led to the sharing of mistresses. The promiscuity, intemperance, and extraordinary moral habits of the back settlements were usually understood to be the products of barbaric and uncivilized circumstances. But it is equally likely that the frontier constituted a late expression of the old polymorphous social order.[6]

5. Edmund S. Morgan, *The Puritan Family* (Boston, 1944), p. 104.

6. For a vivid description of life in the back country, see Carl Bridenbaugh, *Myths and Realities: Societies of the Colonial*

If the social devolution of frontier life made it in some respects a special case, domestic life on the Southern seaboard, and especially in Virginia, offered a better comparison. From its beginning the settlement of New England was accomplished by family groups who were affected by the new ideas regarding domesticity and child-rearing. In the South, however, immigration was promoted by chartered companies, who sent only male colonists at first. When women and children began to arrive, they came into a totally different social environment from that created in New England and the middle colonies. The colonists themselves came from either the lower class or the Anglican middle class, neither of which had been as yet much influenced by the new family ideology.

Apart from their origins, the Virginia colonists were greatly affected by the plantation system, which became the standard form of social organization after the collapse of the first semimilitary settlements. The plantation was characterized by intimacy among the family and its slaves and servants. These conditions seemed to have prevailed whether the planation was large or small, for in either case the family was absorbed with the multitude of tasks that the operation of a complex and essentially self-contained socioeconomic organism involved. A dispersed agricultural population lacked the energy, resources, and the will to create the educational system that distinguished the child-centered,

---

South (New York, 1963), Chapter 3. On the mature Virginia, see Edmund S. Morgan, *Virginians at Home: Family Life in the Eighteenth Century* (Williamsburg, 1952).

conjugal family system of the Northern colonies. By way of compensation, when families did visit one another, they did so on a large and generous scale. Visits often lasted for several weeks, no matter how cramped the quarters (the high rank of William Byrd II did not prevent him from sharing a bed with other males on such occasions), and, therefore, the traditions of hospitality and sociability that marked the old order survived longer in the South than elsewhere.

Except for a few families with houses great enough for any emergency, Southerners were accustomed to a degree of intimacy and familiarity that often shocked outsiders. One traveler in eighteenth-century Virginia was astonished to see naked adolescent boys serving white females at table.[7] With privacy such an uncommon state, it is easy to understand why promiscuity was taken lightly. Slaves were in no position to refuse the demands of their masters; the whole society lived so closely together in its separate units that, except perhaps for upper-class white women, chastity was an irrelevant virtue and modesty an encumbrance. Even the pious William Byrd frequently had sexual relations with his servants, and there is no reason to believe that he was exceptional in this respect.[8]

If we accept this interpretation, the pattern of divorce in colonial America is easy to explain. There was no divorce in the South because the loose, easy family system made it unnecessary, while the customs and doc-

7. Bridenbaugh, *Myths and Realities,* p. 10.
8. William Byrd, *The London Diary (1717–21) and Other Writings,* eds. Louis B. Wright and Marion Tinling (New York, 1958).

trines of the prevailing Anglicanism forbade it. In the Northern colonies the situation was reversed. Allowing for local exceptions caused by the peculiarities of each colony's historical experience, the patriarchal family system made divorces sometimes necessary, while the relatively libertarian ideas stemming from the Reformation made them possible.[9]

Divorce remained a rare experience in the eighteenth century, but during the next hundred years, as the modern family system spread to all classes and regions, it became more and more common, until by the end of the century even the Southern states were involved in what became known as "the divorce problem." The nineteenth century saw, therefore, the almost universal triumph of the Victorian family, "founded on the cult of domesticity, a new respect for children, and above all, the sentimental veneration of women."[10] The last feature was made necessary, of course, by the fact that women had lost something of their old freedom, thanks to their increased domestic and maternal obligations, and had to be compensated for the sacrifices that they were now expected to make as a matter of course. The Victorian solution to this problem was to adopt a reverent attitude toward women.

The attempt to ennoble womanhood was largely successful, but it did not obviate the need for escape-hatches from relationships which had now become more difficult and demanding than ever before. Thus the Victorians

9. Nelson M. Blake, *The Road to Reno: A History of Divorce* (New York, 1962), Chapter 3.

10. Christopher Lasch, "Divorce American Style," *New York Review of Books,* February 17, 1966, p. 4.

11

made a characteristic compromise. On the one hand they sanctified marriage to an unheard-of degree, and on the other they tolerated a divorce rate that was unthinkably high by their own standards. Although in one sense they endured a rising divorce rate out of necessity, they were able to make this accommodation because divorce was in most respects compatible with the prevailing modes of thought.

While divorce was superficially the antithesis of marriage—and it was this superficial impression that prevailed in the nineteenth century—in another way it depended upon the same assumptions as did permanent marriage. If the married state was the most exalted to which man could aspire, if it was truly sacred, then those marriages which were substandard undermined the system and made a mockery of the connubial ideals that were the glory of Victorian civilization. Looked at in this manner, divorce was not antithetical to the dominant ideology of marriage, but stemmed, as we shall see, from a literal interpretation of its texts. Moreover, at a time when libertarian, individualist doctrines were in ascent, those who argued for a liberal approach to public questions and an authoritarian view of private affairs were on very weak grounds.

Even though it is possible to explain the emergence of the conjugal family without reference to the industrial revolution, the two have been linked together for so long by social scientists that some attempt must be made to explain their relationship. Two broad lines of argument support the contention that the modern family grew out of the industrial revolution. The traditional position (discussed at greater length in Chapter 6) assumes that

12

the conjugal family took shape during the industrial revolution, and that therefore technological or industrial developments were the main factors in family change. Goode counters this by pointing out that "industrialization in this vague but enveloping sense does 'cause' the modern social and family patterns, but only because it is identical with them. Such an hypothesis is true, but trivial."[11] In other words, it is an explanation that explains nothing.

One reason for the popularity of this hypothesis is that it was formulated in the nineteenth century, at a time when few industrial societies existed and generalizations had, of necessity, to be based on far less evidence than is now available. Today a few sociologists have taken advantage of recent experience to point out that industrialization in the twentieth century has shown itself to be compatible with a variety of family systems. The Japanese stem family survived the industrial revolution, and the French-Canadian extended kinship system flourishes in the midst of urban, industrial Canada. In Brazil the "parentela," or bilateral kindred, has been transmitted intact from the country to the city. In Barbados, on the other hand, the nuclear family and a fragmented kindred have evolved in an essentially non-industrial society. While a number of family types obtain, the dominant one is a "bilateral, structurally isolated, open, multilineal, conjugal" system very much like the American model.[12]

11. William J. Goode, *The Family* (Englewood Cliffs, 1964), p. 105.
12. Sidney Greenfield, "Industrialization and the Family in Sociological Theory," *American Journal of Sociology, 67* (1961), 319.

Having established that there is no necessary connection between industrialization and the conjugal family system, these sociologists argue that the association between the two in the Western world was largely a matter of historical accident. The conjugal family had established itself in Western Europe before the industrial revolution took place, and the industrial system had, therefore, to accommodate itself to the existing family structure. This hypothesis, which is supported by Ariés' more elaborate study, simply inverts the traditional causal relationships. Instead of industrialism shaping the family, the family shaped the industrial system. The area where the two most dramatically intersected was the matter of wages. The level of compensation was determined, inadequately to be sure, by the relatively small number of dependents the wage-earner supported. If the extended family system had survived it might conceivably have forced up the wage scale, with unpredictable consequences.

A more recent contention is that the conjugal family became dominant because it met the needs of the industrial revolution—it "fit" the industrial system as the extended family did not. The conjugal family is compact and mobile and consequently is more easily adjusted to the demands of industry than the less pliable extended family. But Goode points out that

> by definition upper-class families are more in harmony with the industrial economy, since they control it where they do not own it, and can take better advantage of its opportunities and products. Yet their family system is less conjugal than the

14

lower-class family system. Its kinship network is larger, it exerts more control over the social lives of children, exercises closer supervision over dating and schools, wields a stronger hand in choice of mate and so on. Thus the families that seem to be most "out of date" in the modern world are most successful in coping with it.[13]

By the same token the lower-class families that are most firmly integrated into the industrial system owe their position to the fact that they cannot resist the system's demands as effectively as middle- and upper-class families.

Another example of a bad "fit" is that the needs of industrialization do not correspond very well with the role obligations of women within the family system. Improved technology has made housework less laborious than it formerly was, but this has not had the effect of freeing women for productive labor. On the contrary, the increased responsibilities of child care have devolved upon young mothers who no longer have the support of other members of the extended family. The work of child-rearing has increased, while the number of individuals assisting in the process has diminished. Moreover the new technology, instead of reducing the burden of housekeeping, has raised standards, and so while the housewife's productivity has gone up, her hours of work have remained almost constant. The organized activities of children have also expanded, which means that the administrative work of the mother has correspondingly grown. The result is that the percentage of young

13. Goode, *The Family,* p. 84.

mothers who work outside the home has hardly increased at all in recent years, and those who do work are largely lower-class women who have no choice.[14]

This is not to say that there was no connection at all between industrialization and the family system. Industrialization proceeded more rapidly in the West than in the East because it was not handicapped by a patriarchal, polygynous family system, with its harems and arranged child marriages. Historically the Western family had no strong clan system or lineage pattern. Individuals, not families, were held responsible for crimes; arranged marriages were not unusual, but the young had a voice in them. Boys and girls were not segregated, although girls were often chaperoned, while the ideal marriage was the union of two young adults, as opposed to the child marriages common in the East. There was little polygyny or concubinage. These features were all sharpened by the Protestant Reformation with its strains of antitraditionalism, freedom of speech, equalitarianism, political liberty, and individualism. Thus at the onset of industrialism in Europe, peasants were willing to work in factories because they saw no incompatibility between the factory and the family.[15]

In summary, it appears that while the family has changed in modern times, it has changed in different ways and for different reasons than we once thought. The shift has been not so much from an extended family system to a conjugal family system as from a loose, polymorphous society into a tightly segmented social

14. Goode, *World Revolution and Family Patterns*, pp. 15–17.

15. Ibid., pp. 22–23.

order divided into classes that are further subdivided into conjugal families. The extended kin network was not totally destroyed either by this change or by the impact of industrialization, and so it cannot be said that the ties between parents and children have noticeably loosened in the last century. Indeed, on this point Goode goes so far as to argue that "if we consider the difficulties of transportation and communication a hundred years ago, and the numbers of relatives in interaction compared with their frequency of interaction now, common sense suggests that the frequency of social participation between the average nuclear family and its relatives may not have been reduced at all."[16]

The emergence of the modern family has had very little to do with the industrial revolution, which it pre-dated, but instead has been substantially influenced by ideology. The old polymorphous social order was broken up by the discovery of the child and the new modes of thought inspired by the Reformation, while more recent changes, particularly those affecting divorce and education, have been profoundly affected by democratic and egalitarian ideas. The ideology of family change appears before the fact in some non-Western countries, as Goode points out, and this has been true of Western societies as well. The combination of the new family system and the mature liberalism of the nineteenth century created a democratic, conjugal family ideal that appealed to the young, women, intellectuals, and the disadvantaged. It proved to be destructive of older traditions because it asserted "the equality of in-

16. Ibid., p. 75.

dividuals as against class, caste, or sex barriers."[17] It was (and is) highly individualistic, placed great emphasis on romantic love, and maintained that if family life was unpleasant, one had the right to change it.

Within the family the effect of this ideology was to bring the members closer together, to break down the status system based on sex and seniority, and to stress the values of individual uniqueness, warmth, emotionality, and character. It was related to the woman's rights movement and completed the shift in the status of children that transformed them from the least important to, in some ways, the most important members of the family unit. This philosophy originated with the bourgeoisie and has continued to be most influential among them. Hence "lower-class men concede fewer rights ideologically than their women in fact obtain, and the more educated men are likely to concede more rights ideologically than they in fact grant."[18] For example, a middle-class man typically insists that the family not make demands that interfere with his work. He expects preferential treatment as a professional and not as a man or as a head of family. A lower-class man, on the other hand, usually calls for deference because of his sexual or parental status.

Allowing for the possibility that the family is not quite as egalitarian as we like to think, it remains true that a more equal relationship between husband and wife and the frequency of divorce are two features which distinguish the contemporary family from its nineteenth-

17. Ibid., p. 19.
18. Ibid., p. 21.

century predecessor. It is the purpose of this book to trace in some detail how one of these changes, the movement toward divorce, was effected in terms of the ideological struggle which raged about it. If it is true that ideology is an important source of family change, then a study of the public debate on divorce will not only tell us something of the climate of thought in a crucial period, but will suggest how social changes of this type come about.

Before we can fairly evaluate the public debate on marriage and divorce, we must concern ourselves with the actual facts. We need to know as much as possible about the realities of the changing family pattern before we can assess the responses people made to it. Unfortunately the demographic evidence, while plentiful, is not nearly so accurate as we would like it to be. Paul H. Jacobson, who has studied the figures more closely than anyone, reports that the data on marriage and divorce gathered before 1890 is highly unreliable, while the census returns since then, although improved, still contain a large degree of error. Part of the problem has to do with misreporting. Many people do not tell the truth about their marital status when questioned, and the census schedules themselves have often been incomplete. People whose marriages have been annulled are counted as single persons by the census, although annulments are generally thought to be sociologically much the same as divorces. For a variety of reasons, then, the census regularly under-reports the number of divorced persons in the whole population by as much as 20 per cent. When the omissions resulting from incomplete local reports and inadequate methods of gathering data are added to this, we are left with a statistical picture that is more suggestive than precise.[19]

One fact of which we may be sure is that the divorce rate began to increase drastically after the Civil War, as the following figures demonstrate:[20]

Year	Number of divorces	Number per 1,000 existing marriages
1860	7,380	1.2
1870	10,962	1.5
1880	19,663	2.2
1890	33,461	3.0
1900	55,751	4.0
1910	83,045	4.5
1920	167,105	7.7

Although, as we have seen, the change in the family system which this remarkable increase signified was not nearly so profound as has often been thought, the Victorians considered the trend ominous in the extreme. Many of them, as late as 1880, could remember when no one divorced; now it seemed that divorce was becoming almost commonplace.

The gross number of divorces was alarming enough, but even more frightening was their rate of increase. For a long time divorces multiplied about five times as fast as the population, and this growth was so regular that a statistical projection based on the current rate of

19. Paul H. Jacobson, *American Marriage and Divorce* (New York, 1959), pp. 1–19.
20. Ibid., p. 90.

20

increase made in 1891 held up for more than forty years.[21] Since then the rate has changed. The all-time high came in 1946 when the divorce rate reached 18.2 per 1,000 existing marriages. Thereafter the rate declined sharply, and while it began to climb some years ago it has not yet reached the 1946 level.[22] Though in the largest sense the divorce movement was probably caused by the emergence of the conjugal family with its heightened expectations and greater demands, and by the libertarian ideology that encouraged those who failed in marriage to seek relief, there were other, more proximate, causes which were also important.

Near the end of the nineteenth century the *Nation,* in a perceptive editorial, listed the reasons it thought were behind the divorce movement. They included "the increased resort to legal remedies of all kinds, the general uneasiness and discontent with the existing constitution of society, the decay of the belief in immortality and future punishment," the improvement of transportation and the habits created by the new mobility, and the greater independence of women resulting from their enlarged legal rights and greater opportunities for self-support.[23]

The *Nation's* list was by no means complete. But it did point to the great areas of change that affected di-

21. The projection was made by Walter F. Willcox and noted in Alfred Cahen, *Statistical Analysis of American Divorce* (New York, 1932), p. 21.

22. Jacobson, p. 96. It is still too early to tell whether this means that the divorce rate has leveled off.

23. "The Statistics of Divorce," *Nation,* June 18, 1891, p. 494.

vorce—the new ideology and the changing social order. For example, certain legal alterations which had been effected before the divorce movement began helped make it possible. Until about the 1830s, while American divorce laws were more liberal than those of other Western countries, they were not so liberal as to make divorce a real alternative to marital unhappiness.[24] But in the 1830s and 40s many states generously amended their divorce statutes. After the Civil War, Americans began to take advantage of this new opportunity in increasing numbers. In Europe, however, a comparable legal revolution did not take place, and so throughout the nineteenth century Americans annually obtained more divorces than were given in all of Europe. As late as 1905, for example, there were only 821 divorces awarded in the whole United Kingdom, at an average cost of about £40.[25]

When divorces were expensive and difficult to obtain, they were in effect restricted to middle- and upper-class persons. But once the legal restraints on divorce were eased, divorce tended to become a lower-class phenomenon. As a result today the divorce rate among the lower class is more than twice as high as among the middle class.[26] The relationship between the class structure and various social abnormalities is unclear even today: Goode points out that there are a great many

24. Blake, Chapter 5.

25. Hyacinthe Ringrose, *Marriage and Divorce Laws of the World* (New York, 1911).

26. Donald Gilbert McKinley, *Social Class and Family Life* (Glencoe, 1964), p. 114. This is true of most other personal and social problems as well. Lower-class life is generally more dan-

aspects of marriage that are linked to class for unknown reasons. For example, the age of men at the time of marriage rises with their class position; in the upper strata young people have less freedom of mate choice; and sexual intercourse, like divorce, is more frequent among the lower classes.[27]

Of prime importance for our purposes is the fact that, while divorce was generally regarded in the nineteenth century as a product of upper- and middle-class social pathology, it was increasingly coming to be associated with lower-class life. This may have had some connection with the increased employment of women in industry: the number of working women grew from fewer than two million in 1870 to nearly eight million in 1910. However, the woman who worked was almost always a single woman. Studies of working-class neighborhoods in Chicago and New York by the Bureau of Labor in 1893 showed that no more than 5 per cent of the wives were gainfully employed.[28] But of widows under age 55 at about the same time more than half worked, and we can assume that the degree of employment among divorced women must have been almost as high.[29] While comparatively few married women worked at the turn of the century, they knew that work was available if

gerous and lower-class families are more vulnerable than the higher strata. The same study points out that psychosis is about five times as common among the lower class as among the middle class. In this sense money does seem to buy happiness.

27. Goode, *The Family,* pp. 81–82.

28. Robert Smuts, *Women and Work in America* (New York, 1959), p. 56.

29. Ibid., p. 52.

they needed it, and, as alimony was rarely awarded, the new possibility of self-support may have had something to do with the increased divorce rate.

Another related factor may have been the fall in the birth rate. Between 1850 and 1900 the average family declined by one full person—from 5.6 to 4.6 members. Since about half the divorces awarded in the nineteenth century were to childless couples, it seems reasonable to suppose that the fewer dependents one had, the easier it was to divorce.[30] At the same time that the birth rate was declining (and perhaps one of its causes) people were waiting longer before they married. Before the Civil War early marriages were the rule, but by 1890 only 47 per cent of the women aged 20 to 24 were married.[31] Thus by 1900 women who were about to marry were older, better educated, and more likely to have supported themselves than their mothers. When they did marry they had fewer children. These were the "new women" who were so often talked about, and their special characteristics might well have made them more susceptible to divorce.

If the fact that women were going to school longer and finding employment more frequently meant that they were gaining in maturity and self-reliance, this

30. Jacobson, p. 131. This rate has fluctuated a good deal, reaching a low of 38 per cent in the 1920s and a high of 53 per cent in 1955.

31. Ibid., p. 35. This compares with 77 per cent in 1950. After the turn of the century the birth rate rose again and the age of marriage dropped. But it remains likely that because these temporary demographic changes took place during the years when divorce was initially being established, they had some effect on the divorce rate.

would have affected the divorce rate regardless of who usually broke off the relation. Some authorities believe that regardless of which party petitions for divorce, it is almost always the man who wants out. But in the nineteenth century it was believed that women were responsible for marital break-ups, because two-thirds of all divorce suits were filed by them. It was understood, of course, that male gallantry and convenience had something to do with this. It was easier to get a divorce if the woman filed suit, and it was socially more acceptable for a woman to be the plaintiff rather than the defendant. But in either case the new woman might have been a cause of marital disruption. Her strength and self-assurance could have made her less tolerant of a poor marriage and more confident of her ability to survive outside it. Or they could actually have helped bring about a divorce by threatening her husband's tremulous ego and by relieving him of any anxiety as to her postmarital fate.

The new woman may not have been more divorce-prone than her unreconstructed sister, but it was clear that marriages were far less common among the feminine vanguard than for women as a whole. Only about half the graduates of women's colleges ever married at the end of the nineteenth century. Those who did marry were five or six years older on the average than wives without a degree, and they had fewer children.[32] The

32. Mabel Newcomer, *A Century of Higher Education for American Women* (New York, 1959), pp. 212–14. D. Colin Wells, "Some Questions Concerning the Higher Education of Women," American Sociological Society, *Papers and Proceedings, Third Annual Meeting* (1909), pp. 115–23.

25

female college graduate who, for the sake of her professional interests, was willing to defer marriage or evade it altogether was in her way as much a threat to the established concept of marriage as the divorcee. If the divorcee was in effect saying that personal happiness was more important than the institution of marriage, the woman graduate was demonstrating that professional satisfaction was at least as important to her as marital bliss. Victorian society was unwilling to accept either of these propositions.

The law played a crucial role in all this, because divorce was itself a creature of the law. Except for a few obvious points, the exact influence of the law on marriage and divorce remains obscure. If divorce is prohibited, as it was in South Carolina for most of the century, or limited to a single cause, as in New York where until 1966 adultery was the only ground, then no divorce problem exists. Such severe legislation may, of course, lead to other kinds of problems. South Carolina found it necessary, after forbidding divorce, to enact a law regulating the amount of property a man could will to his concubine—the only statute of its kind in the United States.[33] But once the door is opened by the addition of even a few additional grounds, the divorce rate seems invariably to return to its natural level.

Several states unhappily made this discovery when they attempted to repair the damage they believed themselves to have done by making divorce easier. By the

33. Frederick Charles Hicks, "Marriage and Divorce Provisions in the State Constitutions of the United States," *Annals of the American Academy of Political and Social Science, 26* (1905), 745–48.

end of the century a legal counterrevolution was in progress which had the effect of making divorces harder to get than they had been at any time since the Civil War. Samuel Dike, who knew more about divorce than any man of his generation, summarized these changes in 1909 as follows: The residence requirements had been raised from 90 days to six months in almost all states which had had short residence requirements. Twelve states had made divorces conditional for six months, or had forbidden remarriage for one to two years after divorce. These states had refused to recognize divorces obtained out of state on grounds which were not allowable in the state of residence. Some states had made an officer of the court responsible for investigating divorce suits, while others had banned advertising for divorce business. The legal grounds for divorce had been reduced in Washington, D.C., to the single cause of adultery. Several states had repealed their omnibus clauses (i.e. clauses worded to allow the judge maximum discretionary powers). Finally, the residence requirement in the territories had been raised to two years.[34]

But the effect of all these changes was virtually nil. It may be argued, although it cannot be proved, that there would have been even more divorces without these legislative restrictions, but it remains true that the divorce rate increased steadily during the very years when these restrictions were being enacted. Most states never went so far as to reduce the grounds of divorce to a single cause; near the end of the period there were still

34. Samuel W. Dike, "Some Fundamentals of the Divorce Question" (pamphlet; Boston, 1909).

27

a total of 36 different grounds for which divorce was allowed in the country as a whole.[35]

Another indication of the complicated relationship between law and custom in this area is the change in the popularity of the grounds of divorce. In 1867 the usual grounds in the order of their frequency were adultery, desertion, and cruelty. By 1928 the order had been exactly reversed and adultery, which in 1867 was four times as frequent a ground as cruelty, had become only one-fourth as popular.[36] This fact suggests that the legal grounds for divorce do not tell us very much about the real reasons behind them.

The marriage laws were also changing during this same period, and the general tendency was to raise the age of consent, to require that announcements be made before the marriage took place, and to increase the legal formalities surrounding it. Some progressives believed that instead of stiffening the divorce laws, the same end could be reached by firming up the marriage laws, and thereby preventing those unions which would be most likely to dissolve. But no one has ever been able to prove that marriage legislation has this effect.[37]

Another legal aspect of divorce with which the Victorians were preoccupied concerned the problem of migratory divorces. It was widely believed that most divorces were obtained in states other than those of

35. Charles A. Ellwood, *Sociology and Modern Social Problems* (New York, 1913), p. 154.

36. Cahen, *Statistical Analysis of American Divorce,* p. 38.

37. Cahen tried unsuccessfully to establish a correlation between strong marriage laws and the incidence of divorce. Ibid., pp. 83–84.

which the parties were bona fide residents. The divorce mills of Nevada, South Dakota, and other states with easy divorce laws were held responsible for the rising divorce rate. The publication of the Bureau of Labor's report, *Marriage and Divorce,* in 1889, disproved this notion by showing that the great majority of divorces were obtained in the state of actual residence. But the idea that most divorces were migratory persisted long after the fact. Today it is thought that only about 5 per cent of all divorces have been of this character.

The other questions that were raised by the divorce movement did not lend themselves to statistical analysis. It was often held, for example, that most people divorced because they had already found another spouse, and that they were guilty of adultery in thought if not in deed. It is true that today most divorced people remarry, and most of them do so within five years of getting a divorce. Probably the percentage was lower and the interval longer in the nineteenth century. However, usually the length of time from the point when the couple decides to obtain a divorce until it is actually awarded is fairly long. Although evidence on this is scanty, it appears that about two to three years elapse today, while in the nineteenth century the interval was probably longer.[38] Thus, while the first year of marriage is the most hazardous, this fact is not reflected in the census returns, which show that most divorces are granted in the third or fourth year of marriage.[39] These

38. Thomas P. Monaghan, "When Married Couples Part: Statistical Trends and Relationships in Divorce," *American Sociological Review, 27* (1962), 625–33.

39. During the period 1887–1906 more divorces were ob-

two intervals taken together suggest that the time between the decision to divorce and the entry into a second
marriage has been of sufficient length to preclude the
possibility that most people know who their next spouse
will be before they decide on a divorce.

The effect of divorce on children has always been a
source of anxiety, but here again there is little data
bearing on the question. During most of the period with
which we are concerned, about half the couples who
divorced had no children. It was clear that childless
couples were more prone to divorce than couples with
children, but whether barrenness was a cause or an
effect of marital tensions no one knew. Some people
were willing to make a distinction between the divorces
of childless and the divorces of fertile spouses, and
conceded that the antisocial consequences of the latter
were more troublesome. But the law made no such distinction. The ease with which a divorce could be obtained had very little to do with the number of dependents involved.

A final point that should be remembered when
evaluating the controversy is that, while it was usually
assumed that divorce was promoting family instability,
during the 1890–1920 period the family unit actually

---

tained in the fourth year of marriage than any other, while in
the mid-1950s the second year of marriage saw the most divorces. The difference probably is that divorces can be obtained
more expeditiously today, and that the first year of marriage
has always been the most dangerous. Remarriage rates do seem
to be increasing, however. William M. Kephart, *The Family,
Society, and the Individual* (Boston, 1961), pp. 614–28.

became more stable. This paradox is explained by the fact that while divorces were increasing, they did so at a slower rate than the average person's life expectancy was lengthened. In the 1860s the annual number of family dissolutions through the death of the husband or wife was 31.5 per thousand existing marriages. This dropped to 26 per thousand in the early 1900s and to 17.5 in 1954–56. During the same period the number of family dissolutions by divorce grew from less than two per thousand marriages to 9.3. In consequence the combined rate of marital dissolutions from both death and divorce had dropped from 33 per thousand marriages in the 1860s to about 27 per thousand in the 1950s.[40] An almost universal inability to recognize this crucial point was largely responsible for the persistent fear that the family as an institution was on the point of collapse. The divorce rate notwithstanding, it seems apparent that during the very years when the family was thought to be disintegrating it was in reality gaining in stability, cohesion, and, before long, in popularity.

It is ironic, therefore, that the whole divorce question, which generated in some quarters such a crisis-like atmosphere, was based on a fundamental misapprehension. The rising divorce rate was a real social change of considerable importance. But whatever its other implications, it did not signal the impending destruction of the family. Rather it constituted nothing more than a modification of the conjugal family system that had become general only in the nineteenth century. The Victorians were entirely unaware of the social trans-

40. Jacobson, pp. 141–43.

formation effected by the rise of the conjugal family, and so they ascribed to divorce a revolutionary potential which it simply did not have. Divorce was not going to ruin the family, nor was it to usher in a sociosexual millennium, as the more emancipated believed. Instead, in its own cumbersome, painful way it made possible the survival under modern conditions of a difficult and demanding family system.

Chapter

2

THE CONSERVATIVE OPPOSITION

The rise in the divorce rate that became noticeable soon after the Civil War took society unawares. It seemed as mysterious and inexplicable as the plague, and to some, at least, as dangerous. But although allowed by law in most states, and tolerated, mainly for theological reasons, by most Protestant denominations, divorce was considered such a depraved act and the weight of public opinion was so solidly against it that it was hard to see what more could be done to maintain the existing moral standards. Like legalized prostitution, it was at the same time legitimate and immoral, but unlike prostitution, the laws which permitted it could not easily be repealed, because they rested on what were, from a Protestant point of view, perfectly sound theological grounds. Statutes could be amended with considerably more ease than theology, but statutes that were enacted for theological reasons could not be voided without contravening the principles on which

33

they were based. The early opponents of mass divorce were, therefore, baffled by the contradiction between theology and morality which it represented. In consequence their first responses to the divorce movement were fitful, sporadic, and ineffective.

The modern opposition to divorce began in 1889 with the publication of the Bureau of Labor's report, *Marriage and Divorce,* which demonstrated in detail how common the practice had become. The interest created by the report was quickened by the staid *North American Review's* series on divorce, which followed hard upon its publication. The magazine's first symposium, "Is Divorce Wrong?" appeared in November 1889, and even as it initiated the drive against divorce, the article demonstrated a truth of which moral conservatives were in time to become painfully aware.[1] It was one thing, they would learn to their sorrow, to mobilize public opinion against an admitted evil in a homogeneous country like England and Spain, where religious uniformity prevailed, and quite another thing to do so in a great, sprawling country like the United States, where sectarian diversity made the moral consensus much less susceptible of translation into law.

The *Review's* three contributors represented the main divisions of American thought on divorce. On the left was Robert G. Ingersoll, the crown prince of skepticism; the center was occupied by Henry Potter, the Episcopal Bishop of New York; and on the right stood James Cardinal Gibbons, the best known Catholic prelate in America and a famous captain of moral orthodoxy

1. "Is Divorce Wrong?" *North American Review, 149* (1889), 513–38.

despite his political liberalism. The panelists replied to four questions on marriage and divorce posed by Samuel Dike. Ingersoll defended the free divorce position, Bishop Potter with some qualifications opposed divorce and remarriage in principle, and Cardinal Gibbons flatly condemned divorce for any reason. Cardinal Gibbons maintained that while judicial separation was sometimes necessary, Christ had explicitly forbidden remarriage and, accordingly, it was the plain duty of the states to repeal their divorce laws forthwith. Public response to the article pointed up the insoluble dilemma facing moral conservatives. While only the *New York World* endorsed Ingersoll's position, most papers favored Bishop Potter's middle-of-the-road approach.[2] What was to prove crucial here was not that Bishop Potter's strictures against divorce were less vehement than Gibbons', but that by following the old Anglican custom of permitting divorce in some cases (usually for adultery) Bishop Potter made substantial agreement among the enemies of divorce impossible. Those who, like the Roman Catholics, were unconditionally opposed to divorce could stand together; but once exceptions to the rule were allowed, agreement became virtually impossible, because the denominations entertained such widely divergent views as to what circumstances were legitimate grounds for divorce. This was the rock on which the conservative bark was repeatedly to founder.

2. "Marriage and Divorce," *Public Opinion* November 9, 1889, pp. 103–06. *The Omaha Bee* demanded that divorces be granted only for adultery. Nine other papers were divided on the need for national, uniform legislation to contain divorce.

If his stern views remained those of a minority, albeit an imposing one, the redoubtable Cardinal entertained no doubts as to the correctness of his church's stand. In later years he enlarged on his position, which had become, if anything, more pronounced with the passage of time. In 1909 the *Century* printed his last important statement on the subject, along with Professor Ross' endorsement of free divorce. Cardinal Gibbons cast a sour eye on the historical record and concluded that all divorce legislation ought to be repealed, for "the reckless facility" with which divorces were awarded everywhere in the country, with the happy exception of South Carolina, disgraced and besmirched the very name of the law.[3]

The Cardinal's great office and deservedly high reputation as an enlightened and progressive leader of his church gave substance to what might otherwise have seemed unimpressive, if pungent, observations. It remained for the Catholic press to give a more complete exposition of the Roman stand. The *Catholic World* was at this time the American Church's best known and most respected journal of opinion, and its commentaries were representative of Catholic thought. In a typical statement George Giglinger argued that there were compelling practical reasons for forbidding remarriage:

> When people understand that they must live together they learn to soften, by mutual accommodation, that yoke which they know they cannot shake

3. James Cardinal Gibbons, "Divorce," *Century, 78* (1909), 145–49.

off. They become good husbands and good wives, for necessity is a powerful master in teaching the duties it imposes.[4]

Giglinger and other Catholics believed, however, that the strength of the Church's position was its basis in the New Testament edicts against divorce. Remarriage was, to Giglinger, nothing less than "registered concubinage."

The *Catholic World* was contemptuous of other churches' efforts to resist divorce. Its editors were highly critical of Bishop Potter's contribution to the *North American Review's* symposium in 1889. They believed, with good reason, that the Protestant Episcopal Church had vitiated its position by allowing the innocent party in an adultery suit to remarry.[5] Giglinger asserted that if Christ had intended such an exception He would have mentioned it when He commissioned His apostles to teach all nations. Although Giglinger believed that public opinion in the United States was responsible for America's lax divorce laws, the *Catholic World's* approach was hardly designed to win friends for the Catholic position. In 1905 alone it published three articles attacking the Episcopalians for their stand on divorce. Two of these broadsides were written by the Reverend Bertrand L. Conway around a statement given to the press by Dr. McKim, then President of the

4. George Giglinger, "Divorce and its Effects on Society," *Catholic World, 78* (1903), 97.
5. Giglinger, "The Divorce Question," *Catholic World, 50* (1890), 555–56.

Episcopal House of Deputies and Dean of Virginia Theological School. Dr. McKim had been provoked by a public statement of Cardinal Gibbons criticizing the Episcopalian Triennial Convention for failing to outlaw remarriages. This led Dr. McKim to question the consistency of the Catholic Church, which, he alleged, substituted annulment for divorce. Conway devoted two articles to an extensive survey of the Church fathers' teaching on the subject.[6]

After establishing to his satisfaction the theological validity of Rome's position on divorce, Father Conway reproached Dr. McKim for justifying the remarriage of the innocent party in an adultery suit on the grounds that adultery alone destroyed a marriage. Father Conway pointed out that if one accepted this doctrine it would mean that a woman who continued to live with a man after he had committed adultery without her knowing it would be, in effect, living in sin, and any children born of the union would be illegitimate. Dr. McKim had touched on a more sensitive spot when he questioned the logic behind the provision allowing Catholics to secure annulments if their partners were unbaptized. Father Conway betrayed a certain uneasiness in coping with this criticism. He defended the canon by citing a hypothetical situation in which the wife is married to an unbaptized believer in birth control. Obviously she would have to resist his invitation to race suicide, and the annulment provision made it possible for her to frustrate his ambitions. This same il-

6. Bertrand L. Conway, "Dr. McKim and the Fathers on Divorce," *Catholic World, 80* (1905), 767–79, and "A Further Answer to Dr. McKim," *Catholic World, 81* (1905), 11–24.

lustration could, of course, have been used by a non-Catholic to justify divorce.

Father Conway's articles were restrained, scholarly critiques, unlike the blunt personal attack launched against William Croswell Doane, the Episcopal Bishop of Albany (N.Y.), by the Reverend John T. Creagh. Doane had criticized the Catholic position in a manner similar to that of Dr. McKim. Creagh retaliated by accusing Doane of "misrepresentation which is so gross and so reiterated, that it takes on the nature of a crime."[7] Doane's offense was so great that Creagh found himself unable to do more than suggest the Bishop's inaccuracies. He declared that in one paragraph alone Doane had made no less than 18 errors, a crime which Creagh's readers had to take on faith, as he did not trouble to list them.

This interchurch feud indicated the difficulties experienced by opponents of divorce in attempting to present a united front. Catholic literature sometimes gave the impression that the Episcopal Church was the greatest barrier to the abolition of divorce. In reality, Episcopalians were much closer to the Catholic position than other Protestants. Although Episcopal bishops did not excommunicate members for attending the remarriages of divorcees, as the Roman hierarchy sometimes did, a few at least would have liked to do so. The Episcopal Church had addressed itself to the problem as early as 1883, when a Pastoral Letter of the House of Bishops declared that "whatever may be accomplished by secular arms or policy in checking divorce,

7. John T. Creagh, "The Strange Reasoning of Bishop Doane," *Catholic World, 81* (1905), 288.

there must be a more searching remedy."[8] The bishops at that time were uncertain as to what this remedy should be, but by the 1890s some of them had reached certain conclusions as to what the Episcopal Church could do.

A small group of clergymen led by Bishop Doane began agitating for an amendment to the Canon on Divorce which would deny the sacraments to divorced persons. Bishop Doane was, at that time, a member of the High Church wing of the Episcopal Church. He was the son of a bishop and affected the dress and bearing of a mid-Victorian Anglican bishop, signing himself William of Albany in the English manner. He was an effective administrator, having constructed a Cathedral in Albany with an integrated religious center around it that was greatly admired by other bishops, and his interest in education won him seven honorary degrees for his services as Regent and Chancellor of the State University of New York.

Bishop Doane had difficulty in convincing his fellow prelates that drastic action was in order on the divorce question. In 1898 his amendment to the divorce canon was opposed by the powerful and progressive Bishop of New York, Henry Potter, and rejected by the House of Bishops. The lack of public support endorsed the bishops' decision. Bishop Potter had always supported the traditional Episcopalian policy of allowing the remarriage of the innocent party in an adultery suit. However, at his Diocesan convention in 1889 a few months after the triennial, Bishop Potter reversed himself and recom-

8. "Pastoral Letter to the House of Bishops" (unpublished), p. 10.

mended that Episcopal clergymen refuse to remarry divorcees.[9]

The following year a committee of the Episcopal General Conference published a report on divorce recommending that annulments be allowed for the usual reasons, and that the sacraments be denied to divorced Episcopalians who remarried, except for the innocent parties in adultery suits. It also suggested that such remarriages not be performed by a minister.[10] As the *Outlook* pointed out, this was almost certainly a compromise between the moderates and the Doane faction.

Bishop Doane's amendment was reintroduced at the next Triennial Conference in 1901 and was defeated by a narrower margin than in 1898. Reporting on the resolution, the *Outlook* observed that its proponents recognized that prohibiting remarriages "may and must do injustice in certain cases, yet that the general good of society and of the church requires the sacrifice of the isolated sufferer."[11] The dauntless Doane then organized an Inter-Church Conference on Divorce in New York City, consisting of representatives from many denominations. Despite his strong feelings, and presumably the similar inclinations of most other delegates, the Conference was unable to formulate a program and finally issued a pallid statement calling upon all min-

9. "Bishop Potter on Divorce," *Outlook,* October 7, 1899, p. 286.

10. "The Episcopal Church on Divorce," *Outlook,* November 24, 1900, pp. 729–31.

11. Florence E. Winslow, "The Episcopal Triennial Convention," *Outlook,* October 5, 1901, p. 268.

isters not to perform any marriages "forbidden by the laws of the Church in which either party seeking to be married holds membership."[12] The Conference also concluded that the proposed constitutional amendment giving power over marriage and divorce to Congress was undesirable, since the result would inevitably be a compromise that would lower standards in the best states.[13]

The failure of the Conference to agree on a concerted program did not dampen the *Outlook's* enthusiasm for interfaith cooperation on divorce. However, the first step toward this goal led to no second steps, and after a few years little was heard of the Conference. Similarly, the high-water mark in Doane's campaign within the Episcopal Church was reached at the Triennial Convention in 1904. At that time the Doane amendment was passed by the House of Bishops but failed in the Chamber of Deputies, because, according to the leader of the opposition, it was too far in advance of the spirit of the country.[14] Never again were the antidivorce elements in the Episcopal Church able to muster as many votes, and despite the introduction of similar proposals in later conventions, the Episcopal Church turned away from prohibition as a solution to the divorce problem.

The same evolution took place in other churches. The Unitarian Convention, which in 1891 had taken a fairly liberal position on the divorce question, retreated in

12. "Inter-Church Divorce Comity," *Public Opinion,* March 31, 1904, p. 408.

13. "The St. Bartholomew Conference," *Outlook,* April 2, 1904, p. 768.

14. "Remarriage after Divorce," *Outlook,* October 22, 1904, p. 455.

1905, issuing a mild statement criticizing divorce and urging adherence to a higher ideal of married life.[15] In 1904 the Presbyterian General Assembly narrowly defeated a move to forbid ministers to remarry divorced persons. The Presbyterians, like the Episcopalians, decided to leave the question of remarriage up to each minister.[16]

The Methodist Episcopal and Reformed Churches entertained similar proposals and endorsed the work of the Inter-Church Conference, while allowing the remarriage of the innocent party in an adultery suit. The Evangelical Lutheran Church, after extended discussion in the early years of the century, reaffirmed its traditional stand allowing divorce for adultery and desertion.[17]

As this brief look at the great denominations suggests, American Protestantism was keenly aware of the divorce problem. From about 1898 to 1907 the churches lavished attention on the question, but their labors were productive of more discourse than action. Almost every denomination discovered that no significant changes in any direction could be effected. Liberals, conservatives, and the merely confused pulled in so many directions that they cancelled each other out, and a policy of inaction was literally forced upon the churches. Thus conservatives, far from being able to form a united Christian front against divorce, could not move even a

15. "The Unitarians' Reticence on Divorce," *Outlook,* October 7, 1905, p. 291.

16. "Marriage and Divorce," *Outlook,* June 4, 1904, p. 246.

17. Lichtenberger, Chapter 7.

single denomination. While individual churchmen spoke out strongly against divorce, the institutionalized power of religion was neutralized as effectively as if by design, a circumstance which heightened the natural conservative tendency to look for conspiratorial hands behind the untoward movement of events.

The opposition to divorce was by no means confined to the leaders of Christian orthodoxy; it extended to many important figures in the rising Social Gospel movement. One such man was Shailer Mathews, a professor of New Testament history, leader in the Social Gospel movement, and an early president of the Federal (later National) Council of Churches. In *The Social Teachings of Jesus,* Mathews insisted that Jesus had specifically forbidden divorce except when a marriage had already been destroyed as the result of adultery. Mathews argued that desertion and other admitted abuses did not destroy marriage, and that Jesus himself had fought in Palestine against those who wrongly espoused just such a corrupt doctrine.[18]

A far more impressive analysis from the same point of view was provided by Francis Peabody, Plummer Professor of Christian Morals at Harvard and author of *Jesus Christ and the Social Question.* Peabody was a Higher Critic, a close friend of Samuel Dike, and an informed student of the social sciences. He put his substantial weight behind the familiar argument that divorce was inspired by an individualism rooted in Prot-

18. Shailer Mathews, *The Social Teachings of Jesus* (New York, 1909), Chapter 4.

estantism and the English common law that treated
man as an individual and not as a member of a family.
He believed, however, that this destructive force was
being challenged by a sociology based on an appreciation of social order. Peabody differed with many moral
conservatives in arguing that the patriarchal family was
not an ancient institution but a relatively new and advanced product of social evolution.

The family's major enemies were, in Peabody's
opinion, scientific socialism and the "reactionary force
of self-interested individualism." This individualism
seemed to him to be heightened by America's excessive
concentration on commerce and money-making—a
form of enterprise which represented the "survival in
human life of the instincts of the beast of prey, the viper,
or the hog."[19] These instincts undermined the family,
which, however, worked against individualism by social-
izing the will and embedding the individual in a web of
"altruistic interest." Jesus had recognized this by forbidding divorce. Peabody took considerable pains to
show Jesus' modernity, asserting that like contemporary
reformers he was an enemy of the reactionary individualism of the Mosaic divorce laws. Moreover, Peabody
explained that the alleged severity of Jesus' prohibition
of divorce melted away on closer scrutiny. Jesus had
realized that while some hardships might be caused by
refusing to allow exceptions, "social wreckage must not
obstruct social navigation. The view from above gives
significance and justification to much in the teaching of

19. Francis Peabody, *Jesus Christ and the Social Question*
(New York, 1903), p. 174.

Jesus which when seen from below may seem unreasonably severe."[20]

Peabody felt that the objective causes of divorce, such as industrialization and urbanization, were exaggerated by critics, but he admitted that they had some importance. Therefore, he was encouraged by the movement for social justice, which sought public housing and other reforms. But he maintained that the divorce movement could not be halted by social reforms and must await a spiritual regeneration of the nation. On a more sophisticated level, therefore, Peabody combined the same elements of moral conservatism and political progressivism which were characteristic of many Christian divorce reformers.

Much the same kind of message was preached by Dr. Charles Henderson, of the University of Chicago's theological faculty. Henderson argued in his *Social Elements* (1898) that the social importance of marriage was so great that divorces could not be allowed. He was enthusiastic about the possibilities of reform, believing that, by the elimination of sweatshops and other abuses, not only marriage but the whole basis of national life was being strengthened. By 1909, however, when his *Social Duties* was published, Henderson had receded from his earlier stand. Discouraged by the steady progress of the divorce rate, he reluctantly concluded that the state probably had to grant some divorces in order to prevent worse evils. This did not mean that the churches ought to condone such action, which was only necessary because of the sinfulness of man. "The law

20. Ibid., p. 161.

permits and countenances many acts which a person of high honor will not permit himself, nor countenance in his familiar associates."[21] Henderson's dour admission reflected the sagging morale of more than one Christian reformer. By 1909 it was clear not only that the divorce rate could not be arrested but, even more importantly, that a national consensus on the divorce question had become impossible, thanks especially to the new social sciences, of whose findings Henderson was keenly aware.

The thoughts on divorce of these three men were especially revealing of the strain imposed on progressive theology by the divorce movement. Each of them were important in the struggle to make Protestantism an effective instrument of social justice. Peabody in particular was a key figure in that band of preachers, teachers, and reformers whose work in the 1880s and 90s made Progressivism possible. All three were ardent supporters of social work and good friends of the settlement movement—especially Henderson, who once served as a settlement headworker. Their intelligence and dedication were outstanding, even at a time when such qualities were in good supply. Yet none of them were noticeably effective in dealing with an issue that involved an apparent conflict between the public welfare and individual rights. Their liberal and humane instincts pushed them toward an acceptance of divorce, but their common distrust of an individualism that had been used to justify so many social and economic crimes, their adherence to traditional moral norms, and their

21. Charles Henderson, *Social Duties* (Chicago, 1909), p. 47.

shared faith in the overriding importance of the people as opposed to separate persons, pulled them in the opposite direction. Thus, Mathews' arguments were feeble, Henderson's confused, and Peabody's vaguely brutal. Peabody's dictum that divorce should be forbidden because "social wreckage must not obstruct social navigation" was morally on a level with the broken-eggs-make-omelets school of ethics. Given this state of affairs it is easy to see why so few of their famous contemporaries became involved in the divorce question.

An even more telling example of what the divorce issue could do to a moral conservative with liberal social views was the sad case of Samuel W. Dike. Dike was the foremost authority on divorce outside the social sciences. He had begun his career as a Congregational minister and spent the first eleven years of his professional life in the decent obscurity of a small village in Vermont. The first indication that pastoral duties were not to remain his life work came in 1877, when he refused to officiate at the second marriage of a divorced man who belonged to the most influential family in his congregation. The fine moral sense behind his action, unfortunately, did not impress itself upon the two outraged families. Dike soon found himself a pastor without a parish. The enforced leisure that followed his resignation gave Dike an opportunity to study the problem and within a few years, thanks to the absence of competition, he knew more about divorce than any man in New England. As public alarm over divorce mounted, Dike's special qualifications thrust him into prominence. In 1881 he was invited to give a lecture on "Facts as to Divorce in New England" in Cook's popular lecture

series, and after his talk he participated in the formation of the New England Divorce Reform League. The
following year he became its corresponding secretary,
a position which he rapidly converted into a full-time
occupation.[22]

When the League was formed the actual number of
divorces per year was still relatively small, but the
20,000 divorces awarded in 1880 seemed a vast number
to most Americans, and the steady rise of the divorce
rate more alarming still. No one was ready to panic,
since the real dimensions of the problem were not yet
apparent. However, the solid moral leadership of New
England believed that the time had come for remedial
action, and the formation of a reform society followed
inevitably from that conclusion. Dike's correspondence
makes it clear that the eminent men who lent their
names to the Divorce Reform League felt that strength-
ening what were thought to be the deplorably lax divorce laws would solve the problem. Dike himself was
less sure. It was his principal charm that what was
luminously self-evident to his fellow toilers in the vine-
yards of reform was not always quite so clear to him.
While this habit of mind was valuable in its own way, it
was of little use to a moral reformer, who could not
reach the summit simply by asking questions or by reflecting on the need for additional data.

Dike began his career as a reformer in an entirely
orthodox way. In his Boston lecture he dutifully viewed
the moral climate of New England with alarm and described the family's ills as luridly as his fundamentally

22. Library of Congress, Dike Papers. An incomplete, un-
titled, typewritten autobiography.

conservative disposition allowed. Civilization itself trembled in the balance, he managed to cry at one point. Never one to minimize the importance of his subject, Dike observed the conventions of reform by solemnly declaring that the struggle to preserve the home was of the same order of magnitude as the recent battle to abolish slavery. Besides divorce, immorality of every kind menaced the American family. Fornication and lewdness were rising and he could prove it. Not only were more and more arrests being made on those grounds, but of the one hundred prominent men of Massachusetts he had polled, in what must have been the first survey of its kind, seventy-five agreed with him that licentiousness was on the march. No bigot, Dike paid tribute to the growing importance of Roman Catholicism by observing that, unlike their coreligionists in Europe, American Catholics were morally sound and would join with Protestants to save the home. In a final appeal to the lower instincts, he warned his audience that the time to fight was now, because "Mormonism, for one thing, challenges modern civilization and is preparing to stand battle."[23]

But this stirring address, Dike's greatest effort to rouse the conscience of his listeners in the customary way, had one fault—it was too reasonable. His guns were loaded not with moral cannonballs but with statis-

23. Dike's address was published in Joseph Cook, ed., *Christ and Modern Thought: The Boston Monday Lectures, 1880–81* (Boston, 1882). The connection between Mormonism and divorce, which will seem obscure to modern readers, reflected the common belief that divorce was really nothing more than consecutive polygamy.

tics. In the end, rather than challenging his listeners to stand at Armageddon and battle for the Lord or something equally dramatic, he made a rousing appeal for better education and a closer study of the problem. This approach, however admirable in principle, was hardly the way to launch a moral counter-offensive. Dike was obviously not of the stuff of which great captains of reform were made. He was modest, charitable, reasonably open-minded, and studious. None of these qualities was of the slightest use to a champion of uplift and regeneration.

It soon became apparent that Dike was the last man in the world to lead a crusade, even if it were the only way to maintain support for his society. As he went deeper into the problem he came to feel that divorce was caused more by the industrial revolution than by individual depravity. His drift toward liberalism was checked, however, by the sobering knowledge that a public revelation of his new vision would end with his being cast into the outer darkness. His standing in New England religious, educational, and philanthropic circles depended entirely on his status as a Christian reformer. His reputation would not long survive if he assumed a new and unprotected role as a free-lance social scientist.

Dike tried to escape this quandary in several ways. He devoted his own efforts largely to research and education, and did almost no lobbying, except for noncontroversial projects like government reports on marriage and divorce. He attempted to diminish his identification with reform, at least to the extent of making clear that he was not the kind of reformer who went around casting out petty devils wherever they appeared. Finally, like most men in similar positions, he employed to the full that marvelous human capacity for seeing what one wants to see. He managed to convince himself, despite every evidence to the contrary, that the conservative, religious men and women who supported his League could be induced to finance reasonably objective research on family problems and that it was possible to establish a dialogue between them and the social scientists.

By the end of the nineteenth century he was in undisputed possession of a self-made no-man's-land between two hostile camps. On one side were the traditional moralists, calling for war to the knife against divorce. Opposite them were most social scientists, some feminists and liberal clergymen, and others who believed with them that divorce was a necessary if not always attractive institution. Dike was bound to the moralists by background and association, but his sympathies were with the opposition, especially with the social scientists with whom he identified himself and from whom he got a certain recognition. He was one of the first members of the American Economics Association, having been invited to join when it was still a club made up of men "interested in economic studies and of liberal views."[24] He corresponded with Richard T. Ely, Franklin Giddings, Walter Willcox, and Albion Small among others, and helped Charles F. Thwing and George E. Howard find material for their books on the family.

24. Dike Papers, J. B. Clark to Dike, July 22, 1885.

Dike could not get too close to the social sciences without arousing the suspicions of his conservative supporters, nor could he violate his own convictions by simply endorsing the conservative position. Since he made great efforts to conciliate both sides and interpret each to the other, his own views were difficult to pin down. About all one can say is that he was equally opposed to divorce and to the efforts to suppress it. This commendably original position was nicely calculated to offend both groups without eliciting support from either. Despite his anomalous situation, Dike did manage to perform some useful functions. He was largely responsible for the congressional authorizations which made the two great government reports on marriage and divorce possible, and he resisted the efforts of major church groups to prohibit divorce. In 1898 he warned the National Council of Congregational Churches against endorsing the Caverno report, which urged ministers not to remarry divorced persons, and in 1908 he blasted the Federal Council of Churches for a similar proposal. He asked for recognition of the principle that "the divorce question cannot be made in these days to turn on the mere authority of ecclesiastical bodies or to the quotation of texts of scriptures as the final word," and urged that "we must go with the scientists to nature, where Jesus himself went, and carefully listen to what comes to us from her."[25]

Dike's last years were marked by disappointment and frustration. His position as The Expert on divorce had been pre-empted by the social scientists, while support

25. *Annual Report of the NLPF for 1908* (Boston, 1909), p. 15.

for his organization declined rapidly as old backers died and others became disenchanted. Many conservatives probably agreed with Walter George Smith, who in 1910 refused to contribute any longer to the League. Smith had been associated with Dike for many years in the movement for uniform divorce legislation, but he had come to feel that Dike was getting soft. After quoting from the League's previous annual report, where Dike had said that the divorce problem was essentially scientific in nature, Smith went on to write:

> That language, my dear Dr. Dike, is similar to the language of those gentlemen of the American Sociological Society whose teaching now in American colleges both for men and women is producing results that no Christian, no matter to what denomination he may belong, can look upon without alarm.[26]

On the other hand, at least a few liberals withdrew support because of Dike's conservatism. G. Stanley Hall, the great psychologist, wrote from Clark University: "I do not feel that my circumstances justify my further contribution. More and more I believe in divorce under certain conditions."[27]

His diminished prospects made Dike all the more erratic and distracted. For several years he spent much of his time advocating church efficiency, as if scientific management could accomplish what all his years of speaking and writing had not. Since his mind had been

26. Dike Papers, Smith to Dike, March 22, 1910.
27. Hall to Dike, January 9, 1911.

formed in the age of Darwin, he naturally looked to biology for comfort, and biology did not fail him. The discovery of animal mutations led him to hope wistfully that some day scientists might be able to produce social mutations which would retard the divorce rate. So forlorn a yearning exposed the meagerness of his resources, for Dike was neither a great scholar nor a leader of men, but only a country pastor who had stumbled accidentally into a new field where he lacked the equipment to succeed. He had neither the shrewdness and constancy that made an authentic reformer like George Washington Gladden so attractive nor the stubborn wrong-headedness that enabled simple moralizers to build careers by the relentless prosecution of petty vices. Perhaps his greatest fault was bad timing. He was too old when he became interested in divorce to shake off the habits of his generation. He sensed dimly that these standards were increasingly irrelevant in the urban, industrial society coming to maturity, but it was not until the Social Gospel became the orthodoxy of a later generation that people like Dike could find productive employment. In his own small way he was a casualty of the Victorian convention which forbade neutrality on moral questions and forced a man either to crusade or to keep silent.

The collapse of Dike's League for the Protection of the Family two years after his death in 1913 did not signal the end of agitation against divorce, but it was a blow to the cause nonetheless. Together with the failure to align the Protestant churches solidly against divorce, it meant that subsequent efforts of conservatives would be even more fragmentary and ineffectual. Lacking a durable, institutionalized base outside the Catholic Church, conservatives found it difficult to maintain the organization and momentum required to gain more than local victories. The weakness of the organized opposition to divorce, let me emphasize again, did not reflect the frailty of public sentiment so much as it did the divisions among conservatives. Massive alarm was not translated into mass action because the forms of conservative discontent were so varied and contradictory, both inside and among the great denominations. In the long run, such stability and continuity as the movement against divorce enjoyed was provided by the modes of thought that animated conservatives. As these ideas remained fairly constant throughout most of this period, they warrant closer attention than I have given the activities of conservative organizations.

THE CONSERVATIVE MIND

Neither the transient and insubstantial opposition to divorce nor the formal thought of theologians reveals as much about the moral conservatives as does their polemical literature. The thinking of middle-class America on the divorce question is always affected much more by newspapers, magazines, and popular books than by learned studies and reports, and perhaps the most legitimate function of the press is its way of articulating the deep anxieties of the literate masses. The press may not mold opinion, but there is little doubt that it gives expression to very genuine fears. In our own time popular concern over juvenile delinquency, drug addiction, and racial violence is reflected in a flood of printed matter, much of it of dubious value, to be sure. Only one article in ten may say something of intrinsic value, yet all of them mirror aspects of our national thought and character, about which we cannot be too self-conscious.

This caveat may seem unnecessary, but it must be remembered if we are to appreciate the significance of what is to follow. If most of these statements seem shallow, clumsy, repetitious, poorly thought out, and ill-informed, that is the nature of popular journalism, particularly when sensational or controversial matters are under discussion. Our contemporary magazines are not better edited or more enlightened than those of the turn of the century; indeed, the reverse is probably closer to the truth. But we are more sensitive to the absurdities of the past than of the present, and inclined to accept the hoariest clichés if they are reworded to give a modern ring. A measure of charity is called for, then, in appraising the often tendentious material now under consideration.

The fundamental conviction that informed almost every attack on divorce was the belief that the family was the foundation of society (or the state, the race, and civilization, depending upon the speaker), and that divorce destroyed the family as an institution and consequently threatened the existence of that larger entity of which it was the basic unit. For the most part, when moral conservatives spoke about the family, they meant the patriarchal family that they understood to be responsible for all that was valuable in the Western world. This assumption easily survived the news that divorce was most common in the highly developed states. Upon reading this disclosure in the Bureau of Labor's 1889 report, a conservative writer in the *Forum's* December issue insisted that, despite the frequency of divorce in the most moral states, good government and social order could not coexist with divorce. The modern awareness that divorce, far from menacing society, does not even threaten the family as an institution would have astonished conservatives. Even today many find it difficult to understand how we can have the highest divorce rate in the world and still marry earlier, have more children, and devote more of our energies to the family than almost any other industrial society. Both divorce and the family are more popular than ever—something few men could have foreseen a half century ago.

The universality of the family-as-foundation argument can be easily shown. Theodore Schmauk, editor of the *Lutheran Church Review,* President of the Lutheran General Council, and a prominent theologian, characterized the family as the "great and fundamental institution in social life." The *Catholic World,* in an attack on H. G. Wells, felt that it had proved that Wells failed to see that the family was "the cradle of civil society." The same point was often made by Lyman Abbott, who once accused a prosperous citizen of being "the worst kind of Anarchist" for obtaining a divorce.[1] Divorce, he declared, was worse than simple anarchy, because if the state were overthrown it could be reconstructed, but if the family went down, all would be lost.

The *Nation* gave a topical twist to the argument in 1899 by associating it with imperialism. After noting that civilization builders were produced only by pure homes, the *Nation* urged aspiring imperialists to clean

1. Theodore Schmauk, "The Right to be Divorced," *Lutheran Church Review, 28* (1909), 661. W. E. Campbell, "Wells, the Family, and the Church," *Catholic World, 91* (July 1910), 483. "The Worst Anarchism," *Outlook,* August 11, 1906, p. 826.

up the family mess at home before going off to shoulder the white man's burden. "It is homes which legislation makes permanent," the *Nation* said, "that qualify people to spread civilization."[2]

The most surprising advocate of the family-as-foundation thesis in this context was Felix Adler. Dr. Adler earned a Ph.D. in Semitics abroad, but on his return to the United States he broke with the rabbinical tradition and founded the Ethical Culture Society. By "culture" Adler meant growth, and throughout his long and useful life he struggled for popular recognition of a theology based on love and free of dogma. Adler used his stature as a religious and educational leader (he taught ethics at Columbia and founded several schools for working-class children) to promote a wide variety of social reforms. A tireless campaigner for better housing, labor unions, public health, religious tolerance, and other causes, he became one of the most respected liberal spokesmen in New York.

Given Adler's unorthodox beliefs, he might have been expected to speak for the right to divorce, and for a time he did. In an 1889 address reprinted in his society's journal he defended divorces obtained on the grounds of "adultery, desertion, cruelty, depravity, intemperance, criminality, and insanity."[3] By 1915, however, Adler had come to quite different conclusions, and in a series of lectures he outlined a new basis for judging divorce. He had decided that marriage existed solely to "perpetuate the physical and spiritual existence of the human

2. *Nation,* May 18, 1899, p. 370.
3. Felix Adler, "The Ethics of Divorce," *Ethical Record, 29* (1890), 200–09.

race, and to enhance and improve it."[4] He criticized what he called the modern view of marriage—as illustrated by Ibsen's *A Doll's House*—as anarchical and mad. At the same time he endorsed the "old time family ideal" and declared that its preservation was indispensable to the future of the race. Therefore Adler denied the legitimacy of divorce in any case and for any reason.

Something very powerful must be at work when so tolerant and humane a man can come out sounding like the crustiest Tory. In Adler's case it would seem to have been the family-as-foundation argument that induced such a complete about-face. While Adler's conversion demonstrates the ubiquity and persuasiveness of this argument, it also suggests why so much emotional steam was generated by the divorce controversy. If divorce threatened civilization itself, then it called for the most stringent penalties. That this conviction was widely entertained is beyond dispute, but at the same time it is hard to believe that most Americans took it quite literally. Societies which believe their existence to be at stake react with more fury than divorce ever attracted. One has only to think of the host of laws directed against Anarchists, Wobblies, and Communists in the past fifty years to appreciate the difference. Still, divorce was not lightly regarded, and the weight attached to it by conservatives owed something to their belief that more was at issue than mere principle.

The unanimity of conservatives on the consequences of divorce did not extend to their understanding of its

4. Felix Adler, *Marriage and Divorce* (New York, 1915), p. 15.

causes. Here there was as much diversity as the greatest democrat could want, ranging from the obvious to the absurd. Nothing was fraught with more confusion or invested with greater importance than the role—actual and ideal—of woman in this process. Since about twice as many women as men obtained divorces, most conservatives recognized that divorce stemmed, at least in part, from the altered temper of American womanhood. Even those who were not disposed to put their faith in statistics believed that as women were uniquely responsible for the family, they bore a special responsibility for its failure. But conservatives were not accustomed to viewing moral actions in historical perspective, nor relating them to deep-seated social movements. Thus the massive absorption of women into the urban, industrial work force was normally disregarded in favor of erratic, subjective, highly personalized explanations.

Women writers were much given to such unproductive analyses. Most of them found it difficult to understand divorce as anything but the result of character defects. An early symposium in the *North American Review,* appropriately entitled "Are Women to Blame?" typified this approach.[5] The *Review's* female panelists believed that women were responsible for the divorce rate because they developed romantic expectations that could not withstand the realities of married life. Women were, moreover, impatient, inconsiderate, jealous, and usurpers of the male's traditional functions. The solution to woman's sorry state, one writer suggested, lay in cul-

5. Rebecca Harding Davis, Rose Terry Cooke, Marion Harland, Catherine Owen, Amelia E. Barr, "Are Women to Blame?" *North American Review, 148* (1889), 622–42.

tivating the womanly virtues and a love of God. The same spirit was reflected almost two decades later by Anna B. Rogers, a popular essayist, in her book *Why American Marriages Fail* (1909). Profound reflection had persuaded Mrs. Rogers that marriages failed because American women were too individualistic, acquisitive, and irresponsible. Despite's men's manifest superiority as the world's doers and thinkers, men encouraged women in a narcissism which obscured their primary function as wives and mothers.

The strong note of self-hatred apparent in the writings of these professional women, who so eagerly demolished their own sex, was the price they paid for success in what was still a man's world. This line of reasoning sometimes produced very strange results. One woman journalist who tried to find a higher ground for justifying woman's inferior status than the usual references to duty and the nest-building instinct was Harriet Anderson. She had come under the influence of a German savant, Dr. George Groddeck, and the conjunction of her needs and his ideas was not a happy one. Like most conservatives, Miss Anderson believed that men were the movers and shakers of the world, and that the rising tide of feminism threatened to choke off the sources of male creativity which were rooted in a man's personality. Personality, as she understood it, was a mystic something that only man possessed, which accounted for his greatness.

Miss Anderson did not carry her speculations to the point of denying woman an honorable position in the scheme of things. If woman lacked personality (it was never clear whether Miss Anderson believed personality to be an attribute or a state of being), she was at least a symbol. And not just any sort of symbol, but a "symbol of divine nature, a power working through man to accomplish what she will." Woman could accomplish what she would because "the man loves his wife as the symbol of the All, this divine impersonality which compels his allegiance."[6] Miss Anderson went on to explain how all this related to the dreary problems at hand. Women ought not to marry for love, although love was their forte, nor once married should they practice birth control, but they should instead manage to have fewer and better children. She urged women to be creative, but since creativity was presumably an attribute of personality which only men possessed, it is not altogether clear how this was to be accomplished. As an anonymous critic put it in a letter to the *Atlantic Monthly,* "Miss Anderson's paper does summon confusedly for us a vision of woman, half prophetess, half bond-slave, sitting reverent and meek, at the hearth of bewildered man."[7]

Fortunately, American women were not without more vigorous counsel, conventionally phrased and addressed to the Victorian stereotype of a frail, spiritualized womanhood. Mrs. Katrina Trask, poet, essayist, and wife of the New York banker Spencer Trask, attacked divorce from the shelter of her wealth and social position, announcing that woman's place was in the home and not in the market place or voting booth. She understood woman to be that "brilliant creature" and "careful

6. Harriet Anderson, "Woman," *Atlantic Monthly, 110* (1912), 179–80.

7. "Woman—One Word More," *Atlantic Monthly, 110* (1912), 284.

mother . . . who brings her faculties of delicate discernment and swift-winged intuition to share and lift the load of him she loves."[8] Robert Lawton, professor of English and author of *The Making of a Home* (1914), characterized women in much the same way. They were more spiritual, more religious, more idealistic, more compassionate, endowed with greater love, finer beauty, a larger capacity for suffering, greater gentleness, and more kindness than men. All of these virtues were contingent, however, on women remaining at home, for once outside its blessed confines they became coarse and unattractive.

Some conservatives took a grimmer view: one writer argued that women had barely succeeded in subjecting brute man to monogamy. Feminists who questioned traditional marriage threatened to undo this achievement and reduce marriage from a highly spiritual to a crudely sensual institution.[9]

In one way or another these writers were all appealing to women's self-interest. They urged that the patriarchal family system worked to the advantage of women because they were so weak, or dull, that they could not survive outside it. The tender-minded stressed the fine quality of women's disabilities, while others, like Lyman Abbott in *Christianity and Social Problems* (1896), harshly reminded them of their Christian duty and inescapable biological obligation to breed and nurture.

8. Katrina Trask, "Motherhood and Citizenship," *Forum* *18* (1895), 614.

9. Elizabeth Bisland, "The Modern Woman and Marriage," *North American Review, 160* (1895), 753–55.

The moral decay which conservatives believed responsible for the increase in divorce was often explained as a decline in idealism. Idealism had not yet acquired the vaguely negative connotations associated with it today, and to be an idealist was generally accounted a good thing. Nor had the modern polarity between realism and idealism become established. High ideals were thought to be useful as well as ennobling. This concept, which Henry F. May calls "practical idealism," informed American thinking on a great many subjects besides marriage. There were, of course, all sorts of ideals, high and low as well as true and false, so it was important that the degree and intensity of ideals be appropriate to their object. Many believed that young girls habitually approached marriage with overinflated ideals, which were inevitably punctured by the imperfections of their mates. What they must do when this happened was not to get a divorce but instead to rebuild their ideals "on a foundation of common sense."[10]

In striking the right balance it was crucial, however, to avoid aiming too low. Bishop Doane declared that the function of religion was to "lift man up to the ideal and not to let the ideal down to man" by permitting divorce. Theodore Schmauk cried out against "the low ideals" of divorce advocates, and Felix Adler insisted that the ideal side "turns out in every case to be the social side."

Of course it was impossible to discuss marital ideals without reference to history's greatest idealist. Hugh Northcote, a New Zealand moralist recommended by no less an authority than Havelock Ellis, believed that

10. Lavinia Hart, "When Woman's Ideals Fall," *Cosmopolitan, 33* (1902), 695–99.

Jesus' lofty edicts on marriage had been formed despite his having been surrounded by people advocating "infinitely lower and less worthy ideals."[11] The influence of the Higher Criticism was manifest in Northcote's explication, for he made a sharp distinction between marital ideals, which were unattainable, and Christian charity, which allowed for human frailties. He praised the Church of England for following Christ's personal example by refusing to sanction divorce, thereby upholding the ideal, while allowing civil authorities to grant divorces in cases of great hardship.

In the same way Shailer Mathews believed that Jesus probably accepted the need to grant divorces for other reasons than adultery, but that Jesus felt it vital to maintain the principle of permanent marriage in order to protect the sacredness of the marriage bond. Katrina Trask also regarded ideals as targets and not standards and charged the Episcopal Church with failing to appreciate that Christ saw marriage as an ideal state rather than an institution to be defended at all costs. She was disturbed by the negative approach to divorce demonstrated at the Episcopal Church's 1904 convention and called for a "vital, not a verbal," interpretation of marriage law.[12]

This distinction between goal and norm was not usual among exponents of practical idealism, such as America's foremost lay moralist, Theodore Roosevelt. The substance of his Earl Lectures, given under the auspices of Pacific Theological Seminary in 1911, was that peo-

11. Hugh Northcote, *Christianity and Sex Problems* (Philadelphia, 1907), p. 212.
12. "Lights vs. Legislation," *Arena, 33* (1905), 16–26.

ple were continually told to live up to moral standards which were practically unattainable. He pointed out that such admonitions as the one frequently given to youth to eschew the things of this world would, if taken seriously, create a generation of public charges. With characteristic directness, Roosevelt observed that to "tell them such things in the name of morality is to invite them to despise morality."[13] Indissoluble marriage was, he continued, an eminently realizable ideal if certain conditions were observed. The double standard should be eliminated, he said, for we could not uphold one rule of conduct for ourselves and another for our wives without risking divorce.

What distinguished Roosevelt's Earl Lectures was not their substance, for his ideas were the common coin of moral conservatism, but their tone. While he could be shrill to the point of hysteria on some topics—war, for example—he confronted other controversial matters with poise and sanity. He could be sensible about divorce because his thinking on moral questions was primarily of a piece. This was not true of most traditionalists, who often came to the study of marriage and divorce with divided minds. The case of Margaret Deland illustrates not only the conflicts which a conservative position on divorce sometimes engendered but the special emphasis placed by conservatives on the relationship between marriage and happiness.

Few critics of divorce, whatever their religious background, doubted that duty came before happiness, or that the stern imperatives of Pauline morality were ap-

13. Theodore Roosevelt, *Realizable Ideals* (San Francisco, 1912), pp. 6–7.

propriate to modern marriage. But this was a view far more compatible with Victorian orthodoxy than with the liberal ideas beginning to emerge at the end of the nineteenth century. It was hard to argue that women should be freer, moral judgments more humane, and happiness a goal to be pursued, while at the same time denying relief to the maritally oppressed. As we have already seen, men like Felix Adler and Shailer Mathews in effect did just that, but only by skirting the implications of their posture. Margaret Deland, who spoke from the same general position, faced the problem squarely.

One of the things that prevents us from probing more deeply into the reasons why these people took the positions they did is that we know so little about them. Most of them were not important enough to merit biographies, and few of them wrote memoirs, so we must take their explanations largely at face value. Mrs. Deland is an exception to this rule, but her autobiography rather obscures than clarifies the sources of her inconsistency. She was raised in what she called "the barbarous orthodoxy of the Eighteenth Century."[14] Her early indoctrination was supplemented by the program of a girls' boarding school in New York which concentrated on deportment, study, and conservative religion. Despite this unpromising beginning, the civilizing influence of the metropolis and the effects of an art education at Cooper Union worked their customary magic. In 1880 she broke with her Calvinist foster parents, married a Unitarian despite their warning that Unitarians were little better than atheists, and moved to Boston—the capital city of

14. Margaret Deland, *Golden Yesterdays* (New York, 1940), p. 6.

Victorian reform. There she acquired a moderate feminism, upheld the rights of unwed mothers at a time when it was not acknowledged that such moral lepers had any rights, and began an extraordinarily successful career as a novelist.

In 1910, when her reputation was at its height, Mrs. Deland delivered a mighty blast against divorce. In making her attack she used every weapon in the moral conservative's arsenal, beginning with a critique of feminism, which, she said, was now so well established that its good features could be taken for granted. One wonders how many Americans in 1910 conceded her point, or how many followed her argument that feminists were overly sentimental because they campaigned against houses of prostitution. If successful, she declared, feminists would simply be dumping prostitutes into the street, to the detriment of social order and good law enforcement.

Feminists, to Mrs. Deland, were wrong on prostitution, wrong on the expanded suffrage, and wrong on divorce. They sentimentalized over divorce instead of appreciating the biblical injunction that "it is expedient that one man should die for the people." The victims of unhappy marriages could not be allowed divorces, because permanent marriage was not only the one institution which distinguished man from the beasts but the very foundation of civilization. "If we let the flame of idealism be quenched in the darkness of the senses," she cried, "our civilization must go upon the rocks."[15] If marriage was to be saved, young women must under-

15. Margaret Deland, "The Change in the Feminine Ideal," *Atlantic Monthly, 105* (1910), 296.

stand that men were instinctively promiscuous and their lapses from grace were no excuse for divorce. Indeed, male weakness offered women splendid opportunities for spiritual growth through suffering.

Obviously Mrs. Deland's hardheaded (one is tempted to say wrongheaded) approach to divorce represented the surfacing of her Calvinist background. She could be kind to pregnant girls but not to oppressed wives, for the former were only victims of man's fallen estate, while the latter would selfishly bring down the temple to gratify their lusts. However inconsistent or inexplicable her position on divorce may seem as compared with her views on other moral questions, there is no questioning her candor or her unblinking recognition of the facts of life. In this she was far from typical of moral conservatives. Most of them condemned the unhealthy modern emphasis on married happiness, which was believed to be a major cause of divorce, but few appreciated what they were asking women to bear. Mrs. Deland assumed that spiritual growth through marital suffering would be unpleasant, but Lavinia Hart was able to work up a certain enthusiasm for it. She knew that "all roads lead to good as all rivers run eventually to the sea." In the case of a bad marriage, good could be realized through the "purging, purifying influence of suffering."[16]

Miss Hart, Mrs. Trask, the *Outlook,* and other conservative spokesmen were inclined to feel that to be really beneficial suffering must be voluntary, but Felix Adler abhorred sentimental temporizing. Compulsory

16. Lavinia Hart, "The Divorce Germ," *Cosmopolitan, 37* (1904), 206.

suffering, he thundered, had just as much spiritual worth as voluntary anguish. Therefore, both individual and social interests were served by prohibiting divorce. It was not even necessary to grant divorces to innocent victims, who could not be allowed to dissolve their marriages in any case, lest misery "be imported into thousands of households, from which it might be averted." Why anyone should worry about importing misery when it had such a happy spiritual effect remained unclear.

The pursuit of happiness and other undesirable modern tendencies led many conservatives to join with Hugh Northcote in thinking that the prohibition of divorce was necessary to prevent "the general conception of marriage from degenerating into one which enervates character and moral strength." A writer in the popular *American Magazine* sounded an equally depressed note when he observed that "it is a reflection on our character as a nation that men and women should not stand up more solidly against the decrees of fate or chance."[17] To combat this moral deterioration, conservatives agreed there was only one real remedy—"patience, endless patience, fortitude, and unselfishness."[18]

The last major cause which conservatives believed responsible for the spread of divorce might be called The Rise of the Isms. Individualism, socialism, and feminism were all thought to be working in concert to promote divorces. Conservatives were inclined to use these

17. Anonymous, "Marriage and Divorce," *American Magazine, 66* (1908), 311.

18. Anonymous, "The Views of a Wife and Mother on Divorce and Remarriage," *Critic, 46* (1905), 211.

terms almost interchangeably, because they saw individualism and socialism as complementary, if not identical, impulses. This association seems strange today because we regard them as antagonistic movements. Socialism and individualism are not inherently more antithetical today than they were at the turn of the century, but our ways of looking at them have been profoundly affected by subsequent events. Fifty or sixty years ago, when liberal democracy seemed everywhere to be advancing, moral conservatives saw themselves as the guardians of communal values threatened by the new emphasis on the individual as against the family, the community, and the collective traditions of society. But in our totalitarian age when fascists and communists have committed every sort of crime in the name of the state, the race, or society, many American conservatives have reversed their historic position and now see themselves as champions of individual freedom against the onrushing socialist commonwealth. This shift has nothing to do with the internal dynamics of socialism, nor does it make much sense to have people calling themselves conservatives while insisting that the individual's claims take precedence over those of society, but it is at least historically explicable.

Divorce conservatives, then, were in perfect agreement that a dangerous individualism was responsible for many divorces. Margaret Deland expressed what was probably a majority view when she accused emancipated women of having an imperfect sense of social responsibility. They selfishly obtained divorces without regard for the common welfare and demonstrated again that "the pursuit of personal salvation and team-play are rarely found together." Professor Lawton called frankly for the "suppression of the individual in favor of the community," while Felix Adler attacked individualism in terms already familiar to readers of Irving Babbitt and Paul Elmer Moore. For Adler, as for Babbitt, Rousseau was the individualistic villain who had propagated "false democratic ideals" at the expense of social order.

It is important to remember that these anti-individualist moral conservatives were of many persuasions. Political and religious conservatives were no less adamant in opposing divorce than some progressive sociologists, or religious modernists like Adler and Deland. What made a moral conservative was not a particular political or religious philosophy, but a belief in the unity of the human community. The depth and breadth of this vision, underlying as it did so many of the churches, sects, parties, and classes that divided Americans, was apparent to moral conservatives and made it hard for them to understand why they were doing so badly in the struggle to contain divorce. If most people opposed divorce, then how did one account for its steady growth? The frustration produced by this situation, and the peculiarly abstract and impersonal character of the divorce movement led, inevitably, to a search for human agents. Some conservatives needed more tangible opponents than remote social forces, and found them on the left.

The existence of a substantial literature defending divorce enabled conservative scapegoaters to uncover a feminist-socialist-anarchist plot to subvert the family. The sinister machinations of this combine were a constant source of interest, and, while it was more of a twisted tribute to the conservative imagination than anything else, it was taken seriously by people who ought to have known better. Given the indisputable fact that radicals were, in some instances, actually antifamily, it was easy to believe that the destruction of the home was an essential ingredient of radicalism, and that all who criticized traditional marriage or favored divorce were therefore radicals. The mechanism involved will not seem unfamiliar to those of us cognizant of the infinitely more serious political witch-hunting of later years.

By 1897 the conspiracy theory was so taken for granted that a writer in the *Century* could simply mention in passing that socialists endorsed divorce "as a means of ultimately destroying marriage altogether."[19] Professor Peabody believed that domestic instability was not an integral part of the socialist program, but he was disturbed by the tendency of German socialists to talk as if it were, and he concluded that they were correct in asserting that the family could not survive the destruction of private property.

The *Catholic World* paid close attention to the popular socialist writers, with emphasis on their anti-familialism. W. E. Campbell attacked socialism with exceptional vigor, announcing that it could do nothing to discipline the materialistic lusts of men because it was "the most exaggerated and universal expression of those lusts yet known to history."[20] Beyond its lustfulness,

19. Marion Crawford, "The Increase of Divorce," *Current Literature, 21* (1897), 262–63.

20. W. E. Campbell, "H. G. Wells, Part 4," *Catholic World, 91* (August 1910), 625.

socialism offended Campbell because it was attempting to destroy the family as a "private place." Another feature of socialist thought that annoyed *Catholic World* writers was its disregard of traditional Catholic teaching. Thus Thomas J. Gerrard informed his readers with a perfectly straight face that G. B. Shaw took no account of divine grace in his analysis of marriage. G. K. Chesterton had shrewdly described Shaw as an inverted Puritan, and Gerrard tried clumsily to show how this was reflected in Shaw's antisacramentalism:

> Once again the affinity between Shavianism and Puritanism is evident. Depart from the Catholic ideal at the start . . . and then the way is straight and easy to the anarchy involved in easy and cheap divorce.[21]

The casual reader will find it difficult to identify the affinity in question; the serious reader will find it even harder. The main thing, of course, was to slam G.B.S., and this Gerrard did, to the entire satisfaction of his audience.

A less muddled attack on the critics of marriage appeared in the *Unpopular Review,* an excellent conservative quarterly sponsored by Henry Holt. Margaret C. Robinson attacked feminism as a regression to barbarism and anarchy and noted that "the Feminist program . . . is identical with the ideal of the Socialists."[22] Her major objection to feminism was that it encouraged

21. G. K. Chesterton, "Marriage and George Bernard Shaw," *Catholic World, 94* (1912), 471.

22. Margaret C. Robinson, "The Feminist Program," *Unpopular Review, 5* (1916), 326.

women to compete economically with men although women lacked the equipment to succeed in such a struggle. She was cheered to find Ellen Key agreeing with her on this point and suggested, accurately no doubt, that this was why so many German feminists disliked Miss Key.

Since Theodore Roosevelt believed that there was no baseness of which socialists were incapable, his charge that socialists were promoting free love (in the March 20, 1909, *Outlook*) occasioned little surprise. Oddly enough, in contrast with the usual custom *Current Literature* did not let Roosevelt go unchallenged. After summarizing the former President's remarks, the editors printed a rebuttal from the *Christian Socialist* denying all of T. R.'s numerous charges, except his indisputable contention that not all socialists were as chaste as one might wish.[23]

Although radicals were helping to change the climate of moral opinion, it is doubtful that their writings were a proximate cause of the rising divorce rate. But the fact that conservatives believed them to be so powerful tells us a good deal about the conservative mentality. It had already become conventional to blame radicals for the social problems they commented upon, and most conservatives were nothing if not conventional. Moreover, the socialists' devil theory was comforting because it reduced the magnitude of divorce. If divorce were a product of urban, industrial society, little could be done about it; if it were caused by agitators, suppression could

23. "Socialism and Domestic Morality," *Current Literature*, *46* (1909), 476–77.

be made to appear a valid response. But here, as with so many other aspects of divorce, conservatives seem to have done themselves a world of good simply by ventilating their hostilities. Speaking out against the critics of marriage was sufficiently cathartic to make action unnecessary—the word proved an adequate substitute for the deed.

In discussing conservative feelings about women, idealism, and happiness, we have been dealing with well defined ideas to which most conservatives subscribed. Of course these notions did not exhaust the fund of invention moral conservatives brought to bear on the problem. They advanced literally dozens of explanations for divorce and offered a variety of proposals for its limitation. On the whole, explanations outside the consensus were inclined to be highly idiosyncratic, unrepresentative, and sometimes merely foolish. Again, let me remind the reader that divorce is one of those things about which every man thinks himself an expert. Great problems like those of war and peace or depression and inflation inspire a degree of humility in politicians and journalists that is altogether absent when juvenile delinquency, education, and similar topics come under discussion. So it was, and still is, with divorce.

Moral conservatives were typically American in that they instinctively looked for legal solutions to their problems. Stiffer divorce laws were considered most appropriate, but occasionally someone brought forth a different idea. One of the more respectable efforts to cut the divorce rate was the "divorce proctor" system used in a few cities. The divorce proctor was an agent of the court empowered to cross-examine witnesses in divorce proceedings, conduct background investigations, and make recommendations. In his first year in office W. W. Wright, Kansas City's divorce proctor, reduced the divorce rate by 40 per cent. Wright believed that only one divorce in ten was justifiable, and he boasted that he could reduce the divorce rate by that much given an adequate staff. However sensible this approach in principle, Wright's aggressive mode of attack, as interpreted by the *Ladies Home Journal,* left something to be desired. In a typical case we are informed that he tongue-lashed the wife, found the husband a better job, told them to buy a house on time to focus their energies on a common goal, and urged them to have children, as they "bind married folks together."[24]

If the divorce proctor system was at least a serious effort to do something positive to limit divorce, other suggestions ranged from the trivial to the absurd. Some bespoke simple ignorance, as when Anna Steese Richardson, a professional journalist, announced that the alimony laws were responsible for two-thirds of all divorces. Not only was her statement patently false, since the 1909 Bureau of the Census report pointed out that alimony was awarded in only two out of every twenty-two divorces, but her solution was even more beside the point. She wanted a sliding scale of alimony payments which would force divorcees to work or remarry. Since this was exactly what most of them did

24. Courtney Ryley Cooper, "Man who is Casting our Divorce," in Julia E. Johnsen, ed., *Selected Articles on Marriage and Divorce* (New York, 1925).

79

do, it is not easy to see what Mrs. Richardson thought to accomplish.[25]

Mrs. Dwight Hillis, writing in the *Outlook* for May 16, 1916, reflected an equally deep understanding when she disclosed that the main cause of divorce was the hypersensitivity of young wives spoiled by luxury. Her solution was to upgrade the status of housework. How the idle rich were to be persuaded of the social utility of doing their own domestic chores was a problem to which she did not address herself. In the same spirit the *Catholic World's* George Giglinger placed the blame for divorce on coeducation and middle-class social climbers, while Lyman Abbot gave the impression that most divorces were obtained by men whose wives refused to sew on their vest buttons.

Happily not all conservative solutions were so light-minded or irrelevant. The most ingenious attempt to find an extralegal solution to divorce was made by J. McKeen Cattell. Cattell was a remarkable man who had studied psychology in Europe, earning a Ph.D. at the University of Leipzig. He held the first American chair in psychology (at the University of Pennsylvania) and later founded the Department of Psychology at Columbia University, and headed it until 1917.[26] He edited many scientific magazines, including *Popular Science,* and served at various times as president of the

25. "Easy Alimony," *McClure's Magazine, 46* (1916), 16–18.
26. Cattell's discharge in 1917 touched off one of the most celebrated academic freedom controversies of the day. He had strong pacifist sympathies which led him to write Congress in support of a bill to exempt draftees from serving overseas against their will. His letter came to the attention of Nicholas

American Psychological Association, the American Association of University Professors, and the American Association for the Advancement of Science.

Cattell believed that the schools and the cities were the major forces operating against the family. While he did not think that the problem of the city was susceptible of immediate solution, he felt much could be done to minimize the destructive influence of universal education. Children, he felt, ought not to be subjected to all the education they could stand, for much of what passed for education consisted largely of "the scholastic trivialities inherited from the idle classes."[27] Moreover, much of the school routine was actually damaging to the child. The long hours of confinement weakened his health, while the extension of education imposed a heavy burden on families of modest means. In school the children were exposed to the ministrations of a "vast horde of female teachers" who tended to "subvert both the school and the family" because of their spinsterish attitudes. Insofar as higher education was concerned, Cattell dismissed the whole curriculum as a waste of time for the gifted, who could discover what they needed to know themselves, and a waste of money for the slow learners, who could not be educated anyway.

The solution to both the educational and family

Murray Butler, Columbia's bellicose, nationalistic President, who demanded Cattell's resignation. This move was followed by the sympathetic resignation of Charles Beard. *National Cyclopedia of American Biography, 34,* 337–38.

27. J. McKeen Cattell, "The School and the Family," *Popular Science Monthly, 74* (1909), 85.

crises, Cattell thought, was to employ teaching couples who would instruct on a half-time basis in well equipped home-schools. Formal instruction would be supplemented by local experts in an integrated work-study program. Cattell was certain that this would improve the health of the students, maintain a home-like atmosphere in the school, encourage early careers and early marriage, and put education on a useful basis. Actually his plan, although revolutionary by the standards of his day, had much to commend it. The home-school taught by a married couple as an extension of their family life would have been difficult to arrange, but many other features of his plan were later adopted in more piecemeal fashion by progressive educators. The plan's major weakness was that it barely touched the family problem. It was an imaginative approach to education, but it had very little to do with divorce.

A less ambitious approach based on the same line of thought was advanced, a few months after the Cattell article, by Joseph Lee. Lee was an amateur social worker and philanthropist from a socially impeccable Boston family. From his experience in the playground movement, Lee argued that the family was the child's natural environment, and that work in the home was correspondingly more valuable than work outside it.[28] Fearing that the welfare services increasingly available to needy families had the effect of weakening family unity, he asked that some way be found to curb this tendency. Looking at the range of child welfare services,

28. Joseph Lee, "The Integrity of the Family a Vital Issue," *Survey,* December 4, 1909, pp. 305–13.

he concluded regretfully that most of them had to be continued, except for the school lunch program. There was no need to take the child away from the family dinner table and deprive him of its ceremonial and unifying influences.

Of course social workers knew that to deny a poor child lunch at school was, in many cases, to deny him lunch altogether; the Lees may have enjoyed a ceremonial mid-day repast, but the families of working men did not. Even if this were not so, Lee's solution seems a curiously simple one. Torn between his lifelong devotion to welfare work and his equally strong attachment to the family as an organic unit that was to some extent weakened by these services, he was reduced to grasping at straws.

Another suggestion that had more to commend it was Jebro Tunio's proposal to encourage early marriages. Given the fact that men were marrying later, it seemed clear to Tunio that they expected more of their wives because they had more experience with women. The only way to combat this unwholesome sophistication was to establish eighteen as the correct age for a man to marry, since "what he don't know of, he can't miss."[29]

Other proposals of indifferent merit were made from time to time. Some conservatives thought a subsidy for deserted or widowed mothers might strengthen them against the blandishments of divorce and/or remarriage; more felt that the guilty party in a divorce suit should be subject to criminal prosecution. None of these recommendations inspired much in the way of excite-

29. Jebro Tunio, "Marriage and Morality," *Forum, 53* (1915), 282.

ment, and most conservatives struck to the tried and true approach of legal restriction, or gave way to apathy and indecision.

Aside from the inherent difficulties involved in changing legislation or initiating new approaches, conservatives were prevented from sustained, concerted action by their inability to reach agreement on several basic matters. In the first place, they could not decide whether the prohibition against divorce should be absolute or qualified. The absolute prohibitionists, as we have already seen, believed that allowing divorce for one reason would lead to the granting of divorces for any reason. The moderates argued that the New Testament recognized adultery as a legitimate cause, and that this was a logical position, since adultery effectively destroyed marriage. Catholics and other absolutists replied to this by citing passages in the New Testament supporting their views, and by pointing out that desertion and other offenses were as destructive to marriage as adultery.

Equally perplexing was the question of the remarriage of divorced persons. The Catholic Church forbade it, and high-church Episcopalians attempted to secure a similar canon. Most of the Protestant churches allowed remarriage—sometimes only to the innocent party in an adultery suit. The question of remarriage was central to the divorce problem, because everyone recognized the legitimacy of judicial separations in extreme cases. The difference between a separation and a divorce was essentially that under civil law the divorced were allowed to remarry. Hence the extreme conservatives maintained that remarriage could not be allowed, and proposed, in effect, to abolish divorce.

Mrs. Deland advocated prohibition because civilization and the common good demanded it. She added that divorcées were poor marital risks anyway, and not entitled to a second chance. The Reverend Charles Caverno compared divorcees to single people. "There are a great many people who are not married at all, who live honorable lives, and their cases do not trouble us."[30] Why, then, he inquired, were divorced people the objects of so much concern? Others advocated prohibition because they thought most divorces were secured in order to legitimize illicit loves. E. J. Phelps argued that prohibition would eliminate "perhaps ninety-nine hundredths of the divorce cases."[31] The publication of the Bureau of Labor's *Marriage and Divorce,* which showed that remarriages rarely occurred in the first year after divorce, did little to squelch the assumption that divorces were secured for the purpose of immediate remarriage. This remained one of the most persistent themes in conservative literature.

Some divorce conservatives defended prohibition on the grounds that remarriages were harmful to children. Thus the *Outlook's* "Laica" wrote that "high ideals of home life are an impossibility under even the most decent circumstances of any divorced remarriage."[32] Laica repeated another familiar demand when she urged the Episcopal Church to refuse to remarry all divorced

30. Charles Caverno, "Uniform Divorce Law," *Bibliotheca Sacra* (April 1912), in Johnsen, *Selected Articles,* p. 291.

31. E. J. Phelps, "Divorce in the United States," *Forum, 8* (December 1889), 352.

32. "Laica," "The Children's Side of Divorce," *Outlook,* February 22, 1902, p. 479.

persons as a way of encouraging the social ostracism of remarried divorcees. Most prohibitionists agreed with the author who asserted that the elimination of divorce would lead to greater caution in the selection of mates.[33]

Given these divisions, it is easy to see why moral conservatives were marked by a dour, defensive pessimism. Their doctrines and their assessment of marriage's chances were hardly calculated to inspire jubilation. Many of their statements reflected conventional, even stylized, patterns of response. One had to say that the family was the foundation of society, that modern men and women put too much stress on happiness, that ideals were decaying, and that individual rights were being exalted at the expense of the common welfare. The dire warnings which accompanied these prophecies were also conventional, and to some extent were probably not meant to be taken literally. But however tired and lifeless many of these tracts may have been, there is no mistaking the passionate sincerity of a Margaret Deland or a Felix Adler. People do not take stands that clash with the principles of a lifetime except for good reason.

The Old Guard naturally understood divorce to be part, as William Graham Sumner once put it, "of the decay of doctrines once thought most sound and the abandonment of standards once thought the definition of good order and stability."[34] But the surprising thing

33. Andrew E. Eichmann, "The Divorce Evil: Some of Its Recent Aspects," *Arena, 23* (1900), 88–92.

34. William Graham Sumner, "The Family and Social Change," in *Papers and Proceedings of the American Sociological Society, 3* (Chicago 1909), 15.

about the conservative argument against divorce is that it was articulated largely by men and women who were in most other respects liberal. Laymen Deland, Cattell, and Lee were progressive on other public questions, as were their clergymen counterparts. Cardinal Gibbons was one of the great liberal prelates, Bishop Potter was in the forefront of municipal reform in New York, and Felix Adler was, of course, a notably effective civil libertarian and reformer. Samuel Dike was very much in sympathy with the liberal theologians and social scientists of his day, and the three Higher Critics—Peabody, Mathews, and Henderson—occupied strategic positions in the movement to reform Protestant theology. Indeed, among the moral conservatives we have discussed, only Bishop Doane and Margaret Robinson could be said to have fundamentally conservative inclinations, and even Doane is an arguable case.

This is not to say that most moral conservatives were liberal on other questions, but rather that the public debate over divorce was carried on almost entirely within what might broadly be called the liberal community. This should come as no surprise, for true conservatives were so much of a mind that there was no reason for them to discuss such questions—periodic denunciations sufficed. In the same manner today, serious debate on the Communist challenge takes place largely among liberals. Conservatives merely vie with one another in proclaiming their anti-Communist beliefs—they are all hard-liners. But liberals are both hard and soft—hawks and doves, if you will—and their urgent need to speak with one another gives the debate an unwanted stridency at times. This is always the case with what are essentially fratricidal struggles, and the quarrel over divorce was just this kind of a fight.

The bitter tone of so many conservative polemics against divorce and its advocates owed something, therefore, to the sense of betrayal felt by the Felix Adlers and Margaret Delands. Their progressive friends and colleagues were letting them down, and this conviction could not help but demoralize them further. This suggests, then, that the progressive consensus was less complete than we often think.

The turn of the century is quite rightly called the Age of Confidence, for it was a time when there was a general disposition to see the movement of history as progressive. However, men and women who could speak with equal assurance of the rise of social justice and the decline of private morality were obviously not in complete harmony with the spirit of their epoch.

If moral conservatives meant only a fraction of what they said about the consequences of divorce in the years before Wilson became president, then the flood of divorces in the late teens and early twenties were reason enough for their alienation. This is not to say that divorce was as important as the presumed perfidy of our allies or the excesses of labor unions in stimulating the postwar reaction—only that it foreshadowed what was to come. Many of the figures we have examined in this chapter had clearly lost some of their faith in the promise of American life years before disenchantment became fashionable.

Chapter

4

THE ORIGINS OF THE NEW MORALITY
Part 1

By the middle of the nineteenth century, Anglo-American society had formulated a moral code based on three related principles—the permanency of marriage, the sacredness of the home, and the dependence of civilized life upon the family. None of these ideas was new, but they did not become universally accepted until the Victorian era, when they quickly received such general support that men found it impossible to believe that customs had ever been otherwise. But with human beings, as with physical objects, actions bring reactions, if not necessarily opposite and equal ones. The cult of domesticity encouraged prostitution, made easy divorce a virtual necessity, and inspired attacks that grew into a competitive ideology. The argument for easy or free divorce was distinct from the attack on marriage itself (indeed, those who argued for divorce often felt it was the only way to save marriage as an institution), but the two were related in sometimes strange and curious ways.

The radical critics of marriage usually believed in divorce as a stepping-stone to the free union of the future. The public generally failed to distinguish between divorce advocates and the New Moralists, who represented very different approaches to the marriage problem.

If divorce advocates were usually moderate on most moral questions, the New Moralists, who were radical by definition, sometimes cherished conservative sympathies. Some of the most extreme critics of orthodox marriage believed in a free union that differed from the old slavery only in the forms surrounding it.[1] But despite individual variation, the attack on marriage, which began almost as soon as the family became the center of Victorian life, constituted a full-fledged assault on the orthodox moral code of the nineteenth century. It preceded most of the changes in family life that we associate with the twentieth century; it conditioned the public for the alterations in sexual standards that became manifest after the First World War; and, of course, it influenced the struggle over divorce. If in one way the New Moralists handicapped the proponents of divorce by making it possible for the orthodox to charge them with secretly plotting the destruction of marriage, in another way they

---

1. When Annie Besant decided that she and George Bernard Shaw ought to live together she drew up a formal contract stipulating the terms of their relationship in such detail that Shaw on reading it was moved to exclaim, as he recalled many years later: "Good God! This is worse than all the vows of all the churches on earth. I had rather be legally married to you ten times over." Arthur H. Nethercot, *The First Five Lives of Annie Besant* (Chicago, 1960), p. 230.

advanced the cause of divorce by making it seem a comparatively moderate response to the marriage question—as indeed it was.

The case for a new code of behavior between the sexes, which I have elected to call the New Morality, had its roots in the secular, skeptical climate of opinion that developed in the nineteenth century. Free love was, of course, hardly a new idea. Socialists and communists had long flirted with the notion, and John Humphrey Noyes had succeeded in abolishing marriage in his Oneida community. But the advances of science and the growth of libertarianism to some extent altered the traditional arguments against marriage. The early communists disliked marriage because it was antisocial and broke up the community into separate units. Perfectionists objected to marriage because it was selfishly un-Christian: it encouraged jealousy, suspicion, and exclusiveness at the expense of brotherly love and fellowship. As Noyes, in whose thought both these traditions appeared, put it, at the Marriage Feast every dish should be free to every guest.[2]

In the nineteenth century, however, libertarian and individualistic arguments were added to the old critique. Freethinkers objected to marriage because it inhibited individual growth, deprived married persons of some liberties, and imposed a kind of serfdom upon women. This was the position of Victoria Woodhull, who seriously embarrassed the cause of woman suffrage by publicly advocating free love in the 1870s.[3] It also

2. Robert Allerton Parker, *Yankee Saint: John Humphrey Noyes and the Oneida Community* (New York, 1935).

3. Blake, *Road to Reno,* p. 113.

seems to have informed the doctrines of the Boston-based Free Love Association, whose president, Ezra Heywood, published a newspaper called *The Word* at about the same time.[4] However far apart they may have been on other issues, certain socialists and individualists had come to similar conclusions about marriage by the last quarter of the century. Even though they had reached the same end by different routes, their arguments tended to reinforce each other, and so it was not unusual to find socialists attacking marriage by invoking the rights of the individual, and individualists advocating a new relationship between the sexes on behalf of the common good.

Another thing which helped end the furtive, underground existence that free love had hitherto enjoyed was the solid support it gained from the new social sciences. The Victorian age was notable not only for its scientific revolution but also for the emergence of the social sciences into a position of prominence. Indeed, until the nineteenth century there was really no social science to speak of. There had been historians and philosophers of genius before then, of course, but the attempt to study human behavior with the rigorous methods of science is of fairly recent origin.[5] Once begun, however, the study of man in history and man in society could not be halted,

4. Carol Flora Brooks, "The Early History of Anti-Contraceptive Laws in Massachusetts and Connecticut," *American Quarterly, 18* (1966), 3–23.

5. The term social science was apparently first used in 1791, but it did not come in to general use for some time. See K. M. Baker, "The Early History of the Term 'Social Sciences,' " *Annals of Science, 20* (1964), 211–26.

nor the consequences of empirical, open-minded inquiry controlled. The Victorians wanted desperately to believe that there was a single, universal code of morals firmly based on divine revelation and common sense. But once the pioneering social scientists had done their work, cultivated men and women would never again be able to express their moral convictions with the old certitude.

W. E. H. Lecky was one of the great figures who effected this transformation, by shaking the established pieties and intruding doubt where only certainty had reigned. The method he used was historical relativism. His brilliant *History of European Morals* (1869) had a deep and lasting effect, for he demonstrated that in other times other morals had prevailed, and strongly suggested that they had much to commend them. Lecky's mastery of the sources was impressive, and his elegant prose a joy to read, but what gave his work its greatest force was the deeply compassionate spirit which pervaded it. He was powerfully vexed with his countrymen for the cruelties they perpetrated in the name of religion and morality, and he was determined to show them that what they believed to be absolute norms were merely the product of habit and custom. "The morals of men," he declared, "are more governed by their pursuits than by their opinions. A type of virtue is first formed by circumstances, and men afterwards make it the model upon which their theories are framed."[6]

Lecky was willing to concede that there was some

6. William Edward Hartpole Lecky, *History of European Morals: From Augustus to Charlemagne* (New York, 1955), p. 150.

kind of basic moral core that remained constant, but he argued that the standards demanded of individuals and the relative value attached to different virtues did change, and it was in this area that Englishmen most needed to be enlightened. Lecky set out deliberately to challenge the prejudices of his fellows. He wrote his *History* not for its own sake but for the effect it would have on "that moral intolerance which endeavors to reduce all characters to a single type." "No one can have failed to observe," he went on, "how common it is for men to make their own tastes or excellences the measure of all goodness, pronouncing all that is broadly different from them to be imperfect, or low, or of a secondary value."[7]

Those readers whose sensibilities survived the early chapter from which these remarks are drawn (delightfully entitled "The Natural History of Morals") discovered that the shift from a pagan to Christian standard of morality had not been an unmixed blessing for Western man. Christian dogmatism virtually ended the custom of mixed marriages, which in the ancient world had been a civilizing custom that inspired tolerance. Moreover, the church, by insisting that all sexual unions outside of marriage were criminal, encouraged prostitution and other antisocial practices. "By teaching men to regard this doctrine as axiomatic, and therefore inflicting severe social penalties and deep degradation on transient connections, it has profoundly modified even their utilitarian aspect and has rendered them in most countries furtive and disguised."[8] Nowhere had the

7. Ibid., p. 156.
8. Ibid., p. 351.

effects of this principle been more injurious than in Lecky's own country, where acts "which naturally neither imply nor produce a total subversion of the moral feelings, and which, in other countries, are often followed by happy, virtuous, and affectionate lives, in England almost invariably lead to absolute ruin."[9]

As damaging, perhaps, to Christian women as prostitution was the way in which they were educated:

> Their minds are usually by nature less capable than those of men of impartiality and suspense, and the almost complete omission from female education of those studies which most discipline and strengthen the intellect increases the difference, while at the same time it has been usually made a main object to imbue them with a passionate faith in traditional opinions, and to preserve them from all contact with opposing views. But contracted knowledge and imperfect sympathy are not the sole fruits of this education. It has always been the peculiarity of a certain kind of theological teaching that it inverts all the normal principles of judgment, and absolutely destroys intellectual diffidence. On other subjects we find, if not a respect for honest conviction, at least some sense of the amount of knowledge that is requisite to entitle men to express an opinion on grave controversies. But on theological questions this has never been so.[10]

9. Ibid., p. 285.
10. Ibid., pp. 354–55.

In his quiet way Lecky did much to encourage a rational, tolerant, pragmatic approach to the problem of regulating sexual activity. To an area where unreason, prejudice, hypocrisy, and dogmatism had held unchallenged sway he brought an inquiring spirit and an outraged conscience. He believed that his study demonstrated that monogamy was the best domestic institution and the one most conducive to happiness:

> But beyond this point it would, I conceive, be impossible to advance, except by the assistance of a special revelation. It by no means follows that because this should be the dominant type it should be the only one, or that the interests of society demand that all connections should be forced into the same die. Connections, which were confessedly only for a few years, have always subsisted side by side with permanent marriages; and in periods when public opinion, acquiescing in their propriety, inflicts no excommunication on one or both of the partners, when those partners are not living the demoralising and degrading life which accompanies the consciousness of guilt, it would be, I believe, impossible to prove, by the light of simple and unassisted reason, that such connections should be invariably condemned. It is extremely important, both for the happiness and for the moral well-being of men, that life-long unions should not be effected simply under the imperious prompting of a blind appetite.[11]

11. Ibid., p. 349.

Thus, for almost the first time, free love was sanctioned by a respectable, authoritative voice from outside the circle of true believers.

Before long Lecky's conclusions were reinforced by one of the greatest intellectual figures of the age, Herbert Spencer. In his *Principles of Sociology,* first published in 1876, Spencer came out firmly on the side of free divorce. With his customary infelicity he declared that

> It may be that the maintenance of the legal bond will come to be held improper if the natural bond ceases. Already increased facilities for divorce point to the probability [that] . . . there will come a time when the union by affection will be held of primary moment and the union by law as of secondary moment: whence reprobation of marital relations in which the union by affection has dissolved.[12]

For Spencer to say that social evolution was moving in this direction was the same as his saying that he approved of it. Recognizing that this position put him substantially in advance of public opinion he observed, "That this conclusion will be at present unacceptable is likely—I may say certain."

Endorsing free divorce was not, obviously, the same thing as advocating free love. Spencer did not go as far as Lecky, and the impact of his position was somewhat diluted by the multiplicity of his interests. But Spencer's method was perhaps even more subversive of the prevailing dogmatisms than his formal conclusions. Al-

12. Herbert Spencer, *The Principles of Sociology* (3d ed. 2 vols. New York, 1892), *1,* 753.

ready there existed a substantial body of knowledge about the customs of primitive peoples, and Spencer was even more interested in man's cultural diversity than in his historical transformations. Therefore he pulled together a mass of evidence on the institutions of primitive societies and forced his less sophisticated readers to concede that the habits of Victorian England (and America) were so far from being universal as to appear almost eccentric. The comparative method thus used is a mighty instrument for breaking down prejudices, and Spencer's wide following was hard put to reconcile his material with their beliefs.[13]

Lester Ward was a brilliant, self-trained sociologist and freethinker whose position on marriage and morals was very close to that of Lecky and Spencer.[14] With Lecky he viewed the advent of Christianity as nothing less than a "calamity," particularly as it led to the degradation of women into a species of property. He too

13. Of course the task was not entirely beyond them. Spencer's corpus was so immense that his readers customarily took from it only those bits and pieces which were compatible with their own convictions. A typical example of the confusion this led to was Elizabeth Rachel Chapman's "Marriage Rejection and Marriage Reform," *Westminster Review, 130* (1888), 358–77. Mrs. Chapman was an ardent Spencerian who wrote many articles attacking divorce. In this piece she attempted to show that even though Spencer favored divorce, his analysis itself demonstrated that monogamy was the peak of evolution and therefore led to the conclusion that divorce should be abolished.

14. He edited a free-thought journal, *The Iconoclast,* in 1870 and 1871. J. M. Robertson, *A History of Freethought in the Nineteenth Century* (London, 1929), pp. 449–50. Robertson considered Ward the most antireligious of the great sociologists.

regarded monogamy as the highest form of marriage, even though "the natural tendency of the race is toward polygamy, as a result of the grasping character of men, just as it is toward monopoly of goods."[15] What Ward protested against was society's mad drive to impose monogamy on every single person in rank defiance of "the irrepealable laws of nature, one of the most persistent of which is that by which the sexes demand and seek each other."[16] The root of the problem was that: "Modern society assumes, firstly, that all can marry if they will; secondly, that where they do not, it is because they have no attachments for the opposite sex; and thirdly, that all can abstain."[17]

Each of these propositions seemed to him wholly or partially false, as some men were compelled by circumstance to find sex outside of the marriage relation. "It is not enough to assert that it is only the bad and depraved who do this, because it is not true."[18] Ward, like Lecky, had a deep sympathy for the prostitute, who existed to meet the excess of demand over supply in the economy of sex. Prostitutes sold themselves in order to live, "for life is dearer than virtue, and there is often more true virtue in this surrender of virtue than there would be in preserving it."[19] Neither Ward, Lecky, nor Spencer were attempting to overthrow the family system. All three believed in monogamy as the normal

15. Lester F. Ward, *Dynamic Sociology* (2 vols. New York, 1883), *1*, 630.
16. Ibid., p. 624.
17. Ibid., p. 625.
18. Ibid., p. 628.
19. Ibid., p. 629.

marital relationship, but each of them thought that Victorian morals were destructively rigid, and all of them tried to show that Victorian norms had no special historical or scientific sanction. Ward, Lecky, and Spencer were, I suspect, the most influential proponents of this point of view, but they were supported by a good many other figures (Maurice Westermarck, Fredrick Engels, Henry Maine, etc.), whose work pointed in the same direction.

The existence of this body of thought, therefore, encouraged the growth of a more outspokenly radical approach to the regulation of sexual behavior. This was particularly true of the extreme followers of Herbert Spencer, who went a good deal further than the Master himself. A conspicuous example of this group, who sometimes called themselves Individualists because they hoped to apply the principles of laissez-faire to virtually every area of life, was the Honorable Auberon Herbert. Herbert, although he was the son of a peer, was a noted freethinker, a Liberal M.P., and anti-Sabbatarian, and an eager faddist. In a letter to the *Pall Mall Gazette* on the Parnell affair in 1890, he said of the Divorce Court, "No fouler institution was ever invented; and its existence drags on, to our deep shame, just because we have not the courage frankly to say that the sexual relations of husband and wife, or those who live together, concern their own selves, and do not concern the prying, gloating, self-righteous, and intensely untruthful world outside them."[20]

20. Beswicke Ancrum, "The Sexual Problem," *Westminster Review, 141* (1894), 527.

The Individualists typically assumed that monogamy was the wave of the future, but that its strength had no relation to the law, which here, as in most other relations, was capable only of mischief. One Individualist put this in terms that must sound familiar to anyone who has been exposed to contemporary right-wing propaganda, even though he reflected a rather different point of view:

> The State can more or less control regular marriage relations that need no control, but it cannot provide against irregular sexual relations which can alone be dealt with by the morality social influence fosters, when it knows that it has to look after its own affairs, and is not blinded into inaction by fancying that they [sic] are being seen to by its miracle-worker Government.[21]

To some Individualists even Auberon Herbert, who conceded the right of the state to enforce alimony and child support payments, went too far in accommodating himself to the popular mania for legislation. In a stern essay for the *Fortnightly Review* (which under the editorship of Frank Harris was then one of the most interesting and provocative journals in the English language), Wordsworth Donisthorpe charged Herbert with weakly evading the issue—which was whether the state had any right at all to regulate marriage. Many Individualists assumed that the law of contract applied to marriage, and that on these grounds the state had an obligation to enforce the marriage contract. But Don-

21. William Schooling, "Marriage Institutions," *Westminster Review, 135* (1891), 395.

isthorpe argued that if it was conceded that the state had a right to intervene in these matters, then the whole vexed question of what should be regulated and what should not be regulated could never be settled. Since selective enforcement presently obtained, Individualists who applied the law of contract to marriage were being untrue to their principles.

Nor had Donisthorpe any patience with those who contended that monogamy could not be preserved without laws to enforce it. If this was the case, he snorted, then law was warring against nature, and the observable tendency of civilized man toward monogamy was wholly artificial. One could not claim that monogamy needed the force of law behind it without abandoning belief in social evolution. The true state of affairs could be demonstrated by asking what would happen if all marital legislation were swept away. To Donisthorpe it was obvious that most people would behave very much as they always had. However, he thought it likely that adultery, prostitution, breach of promise suits, and long engagements would disappear. Moreover, a kind of natural balance would be struck by which those marriages that ought to dissolve would give way, and those that were socially successful would endure.

Donisthorpe was not himself entirely unequivocal. He admitted that fathers would continue to be responsible for the support of their offspring under the new dispensation. But with this one exception he believed that everyone would be better off if the whole apparatus of sexual regulation were simply discarded. The final, and to him clinching, argument was that whatever its social consequences, freedom was an absolute good, and that freedom never claimed the power to solve all social problems—at best it could only ease some of them. His major premise was not functional but ideological. Marital legislation was repressive, for coercion was always wrong, and the burden of proof was on its proponents who had to offer compelling evidence that the social order could not survive without this tyranny. He believed such proof could not be obtained, and concluded by reminding his readers of the overriding principle "that every citizen should be allowed the fullest and widest possible freedom in all things, so long as he or she does not infringe on the equal freedom of fellow citizens."[22]

So radical a proposition could not expect to attract many followers, and it is probable that most freethinkers preferred to strike a balance between individual rights and social responsibility. Thus Beswicke Ancrum condemned the notion that impurity consisted of sexual intercourse between all but married persons and argued that the sexual relation was no concern of the public. But it seemed to him that the products of such unions should be protected by the state, which had the duty of seeing to it that no child was left uncared for as a result of the new freedom.

The link between free thought and socialism was best demonstrated by Karl Pearson's *Ethic of Freethought*.[23] Pearson was about as close to being a socialist as a freethinker could be. He made the usual case for free union (including the customary argument that it would ensure

22. Wordsworth Donisthorpe, "The Future of Marriage," *Fortnightly Review, 57* (1892), 271.
23. Karl Pearson, *The Ethic of Freethought* (London, 1888).

a purer monogamy), but he believed that to make the new system really work it would be necessary for the state to subsidize all mothers as a matter of right. In this fashion not only would children be well provided for but women would be truly emancipated, as unmarried and divorced mothers would be given the same opportunities for self-fulfillment and advancement as single women. Like many freethinkers Pearson was a confirmed feminist, but he was unusually concerned with the disadvantages motherhood imposed on women. His subsidy scheme, therefore, was intended at one stroke to solve both the marriage problem and the woman problem.

This mixture of socialism, feminism, and free thought gained a wide circulation through the articles of Mona Caird, which began to appear about the same time as Pearson's *Ethic*. Miss Caird was a woman of very modest intellectual attainments. Her ideas were commonplace and undistinguished, and no one took her very seriously except the public. Her slight essays on the failure of marriage caused a literal sensation in England and were widely reprinted in the United States.[24] Her notoriety seems to have been mainly a result of the fact that she was the first woman to articulate in the public press ideas that had been circulating in radical quarters

24. Her collected work appears in Mona Caird, *The Morality of Marriage and Other Essays on the Status and Destiny of Women* (London, 1897). One of her articles in the *Westminster Review* provoked so much comment that when the *London Daily Telegraph* asked for reactions to it, the paper received 27,000 letters in two months. For samples of this largely hostile flood see Harry Quilter, ed., *Is Marriage A Failure?* (London, n.d.).

for some years. It was not only what she said but what she was that made her remarks shocking. Because of their novelty some of her articles were reprinted in the United States, and consequently Americans who knew very little about the English Individualists learned of their attack on marriage from Miss Caird.[25]

Miss Caird was not quite so radical as she seemed. One of her critics sensibly pointed out that what she was really asking for was easier divorce laws, the right of mothers to control their children, and contract marriage. These ideas were, for the most part, not very startling by the standards of 1890.[26] Perhaps not, but Miss Caird's extreme rhetoric was. It was her custom to nail down her points with this kind of statement: "If the woman's claim were granted, if she could secure a liberty as great as that of man, in all the relations of life, marriage, as we now understand it, would cease to exist; its groundwork would be undermined."[27] It is easy to see why conventional moralists were bound to react strongly to such a declaration. Nor was Miss Caird's advocacy of contract marriage calculated to put the orthodox mind at ease. The idea that marriage contracts should be written for a specific length of time, after which the marriage would simply cease to exist

25. For example see "The Millennium of Marriage—Mona Caird's Views," *Current Literature, 16* (1894), 40–41, reprinted from the *Boston Herald,* and "The Practice of Marriage," *Current Literature, 18* (1895), 316–17, reprinted from the *Saturday Review.*

26. Clemintina Black, "On Marriage: A Criticism," *Fortnightly Review, 47* (1890), 586–94.

27. Mona Caird, "The Morality of Marriage," *Fortnightly Review, 53* (1890), 318.

unless the contract were renegotiated, was brought up frequently enough. Edith Ellis called it "A Novitiate for Marriage," and Judge Lindsey "Companionate Marriage" a few years later. But regardless of the terms in which it was couched, the notion that marriages ought deliberately to be made provisional was more disturbing than divorce itself to most Victorians.

Mona Caird's feminist orientation was most apparent on two questions. She wanted the state to make it possible for mothers to work by guaranteeing them maternity leaves and similar benefits, and she wanted to emancipate women from sex. Feminists who called for free divorce or free love were frequently accused of promoting sensuality. In truth, it was more often the other way around: they objected to marriage because it bound wives to serve the sexual appetites of their masters. A Victoria Woodhull who wanted to expand women's sexual opportunities was very much the exception. Most radical feminists saw marriage not as an agency for inhibiting sexuality but as a mechanism for promoting lust and license. Miss Caird went so far as to attack marriage not simply for its overt sexuality, but for its excessive intimacy, which destroyed romance and coarsened the moral fiber. "So long as wives permit their husbands to come and go in their apartments without let or hindrance," she remarked, "just so long will marriage prove a failure, except where natural absence of refinement prevents the inevitable friction."[28] Free love in this sense really meant, therefore, freedom from love rather than freedom to love.

28. Mona Caird, "The Practice of Marriage," p. 317.

It was on precisely this point that Grant Allen, who shared with Miss Caird a considerable American notoriety, took issue with the radical feminists. Allen was a biologist who wrote novels, poetry, and a great number of essays on contemporary problems. He was a Fabian socialist, a close disciple of Darwin and Spencer, and perhaps the most thoroughgoing proponent of the New Morality in England. Richard Le Gallienne, a good friend and his best and most sympathetic critic, thought him, his bad press notwithstanding, the "most variously gifted man of letters of his time."[29]

As Allen's ideas were strongly flavored both with socialist and free-thought elements, a word of explanation may be in order. Freethinkers were a very mixed lot, and there were so many freethought societies, and so many variations within them, that generalizations are hard to make. Most freethinkers probably did not take as radical a stand on the marriage question as those discussed here, but the antimarriage position was entirely consistent with the philosophic basis of free thought. To some, free thought was only a stage in their personal development. Of those who did evolve, some moved toward the extreme individualism of an Auberon Herbert. Their position was so far removed from socialism that some critics believed they actually promoted it by making the alternatives to socialism seem ridiculous or impossible. Herbert, for example, was opposed in principle to all taxation.[30]

29. Richard Le Gallienne, "Grant Allen," *Fortnightly Review, 72* (1899), 1022.

30. See Arthur Withy, "Pseudo-Individualism or the Present Slavery," *Westminster Review, 142* (1894), 485–96.

Others found it equally easy to move in the opposite direction; Annie Besant during her pilgrimage from Anglicanism to Theosophy was for many years a leading figure in Charles Bradlaugh's National Secular Society, the leading English free-thought association, before becoming a Fabian. But those who moved on from free thought usually retained fragments of it. Allen, therefore, found it possible to be both a socialist and a Spencerian—however incompatible they may seem to us.

Allen's first objection to the feminist ethic represented by Mona Caird was mainly biological—as befitted one who had been trained as a natural scientist. It seemed to him that feminists simply refused to face up to the biological imperatives which bound the entire human race. Women had to have an average of four children apiece to guarantee the species' perpetuation, but every time this was pointed out to them they invariably replied that you were "casting their sex in their teeth."[31] From where Allen stood, the feminists who idealized "the unsexed woman," or who argued that all women should be self-supporting, were "traitors to their sex." This kind of feminism was going against nature and taking a dangerously short-sighted view:

> What is essential and eternal it neglects in favor of what is accidental and temporary. What is feminine in women it neglects in favor of what is masculine. It attempts to override the natural dis-

31. Grant Allen, "Plain Words on the Woman Question," *Fortnightly Review, 52* (1889), 452.

tinction of the sexes, and to make women men—
in all but virility.[32]

The proper goal of the woman movement was not
general celibacy "but general marriage and the ample
support of women by the men of the community."[33]
Although conceding that this was "rank Toryism,"
Allen denied the right of women to free themselves
from motherhood. "Whether we have wives or not—
and that is a minor point about which I, for one, am
supremely unprejudiced—we must at least have
mothers."[34]

Allen made clear what he wanted of women a few
years later in an essay called "The New Hedonism."
Here he compared what I have called the New Morality
with the older more ascetic creed. "The old asceticism
said, 'Be virtuous, and you will be happy.' The new
hedonism says, 'Be happy, and you will be virtuous.' "[35]
A good motto for the new hedonist, he suggested, might
be "Self-development is greater than self-sacrifice."
Asceticism was primarily religious in nature, he argued,
but "religion is the shadow of which culture is the substance. The one pretends to be what the other is in
reality."[36] It was the duty, therefore, of the hedonist to
substitute culture for religion.

Among its many crimes, the old ethic had been notable for its suppression of the sex instinct. "But I main-

32. Ibid., p. 456.
33. Ibid., p. 458.
34. Ibid., p. 458.
35. Grant Allen, "The New Hedonism," *Fortnightly Review*,
61 (1894), 377.
36. Ibid., p. 382.

tain, on the contrary, that everything high and ennobling in our nature springs directly out of the sexual instinct." This was true not only of human beings, but of the whole natural universe.

> Thus, even below the human level, we see that the instinct of sex has been instrumental in developing all the finest feelings which the lower creation share with us or foreshadow for us. The sense of beauty, the sense of duty; parental responsibility, paternal and maternal love, domestic affection; song, dance, and decoration; the entire higher life in its primitive manifestations; pathos and fidelity; in one word, the soul, the soul itself in embryo—all rise direct from the despised "lower" pleasures.[37]

Among men the greatest works of art and the finest emotions were products of human love. "The hedonist, therefore, recognizes in the sex-instinct the origin and basis of all that is best and highest within us."[38]

Hedonism was not the right word for the moral code Allen advocated. He did not believe that pleasure should be the only motive of human conduct, and he expected that women would continue to feel obligated to bear children and men to support them. But to declare that pleasure, and especially sexual pleasure, was a good thing in and of itself was a marked departure from the established ways of ordering the affairs of men. Where women were concerned, he proposed to strike a new bargain. They were to continue with the tiresome business of child-bearing as in the past, but they were to be

37. Ibid., p. 387.
38. Ibid., p. 391.

compensated by being assured of an adequate level of support whether they were married or not. They were also to be given the maximum amount of freedom that did not conflict with their maternal duties, and they were to be encouraged to develop their sexual natures to the fullest. This conflicted with the prevailing feminist thought, which Allen quite rightly understood to be antisex. At their most extreme, feminists seemed to regard the facts of life as a male plot to keep them from an equal share of the world's work. But even the more moderate did not regard an enhanced sexual life as adequate payment for the denial of professional opportunities.[39]

The trouble with Allen's moral code, as Le Gallienne pointed out, was that, like so many of his kind, he took a very simple view of life. By love he really meant a sexual comradeship, which he described in words like "frank, hearty, and honest." But love is much more terrible and complex than he was prepared to see. His failings as a moralist were most apparent in his novel *The Woman Who Did*.[40] As an essayist Allen was fairly

39. In this respect Allen anticipated the line of argument that Betty Friedan has branded *The Feminine Mystique* in her useful polemic (New York, 1963). In later years many people sympathetic to the woman movement were to speak against women competing in the job market with men. Havelock Ellis was already echoing Allen's remarks (or vice versa) and soon Freud would give a whole arsenal of phrases like "penis envy" and "castration complex" to those who believed that femininity was a purely domestic commodity which withered in the marketplace.

40. Grant Allen, *The Woman Who Did* (Boston, 1895).

successful. What he meant to say came through easily, although his notion of the ideal marital relationship remained confused and obscure. But as a novelist he was simply hopeless. He regarded *The Woman Who Did* as his most important book, and even Le Gallienne, who thought it his worst novel, could do no more than charitably concede that it was an effective tract. Le Gallienne contended that it was possible for a bad novel to be a good book if the ideas it pressed were valuable enough. But even by this standard the novel was a failure. Unfortunately, *The Woman Who Did* was the most popular of Allen's books, and in America it was the primary effort for which he was known.

The book's melodramatic plot won it a wide audience despite its numerous defects. It concerned an emancipated Englishwoman named Herminia, whose high principles prevented her from enduring the slavery and degradation of marriage. When her lover ignobly tried to persuade her to marry him, she rejected his blandishments, only to find herself with an illegitimate child after his untimely death. Despite the life of poverty and shame which this unhappy series of events condemned her to, Herminia succeeded in raising the little girl so well that upon becoming a young woman she attracted the eye of a worthy gentleman. Fearing that this union would not be consummated in marriage if the gentleman's family discovered her scarlet past, Herminia thoughtfully committed suicide, making it possible for the young people to live happily ever after.

The novel was widely understood to be an advertisement for free love. That Allen intended it to be seems most unlikely, for Herminia ruined her life by refusing to marry. He probably meant it to demonstrate the hypocrisy of contemporary attitudes toward sex, but the clearest moral to be drawn from the work was the desirability of orthodox marriage. If Herminia had not been such a fool as to turn down her lover's offer, she could have lived a normally happy life. Herminia was entirely faithful to her principles. She refused to enslave herself by living with the man she loved. Ten years later when she had a chance to gain respectability by marrying another good man, she turned him down so that her child could become the first 100 per cent free woman in England. But having made all these sacrifices and lived up to the highest standards of advanced feminism, she was rewarded with a daughter of perfectly conventional beliefs. Despite the lurid subject matter, by Victorian norms, it is impossible to escape the conclusion that *The Woman Who Did* was a profoundly moral book.

This did not entirely escape reviewers. The *Bookman,* a pedestrian American journal, commented that "it is a perfectly straightforward, serious book, written in a more obviously instructive tone than we have been accustomed to since our perusal of the religious fiction put into our hands in youth." But the *Bookman* typically concluded that

> his glorification of the mere brute instinct of mating, and his denial of the worth of those in whom it is repressed till it is tempered and ennobled by a sense of the responsibilities of life, is a senseless and shallow slander of human nature. In this one point, *The Woman Who Did,* an entirely uncon-

vincing but honest book is calculated to do not a little harm.[41]

Its critical reception and Allen's clumsy handling of a delicate theme obscured most of the book's message, but those who read it could not avoid learning that Allen considered sex to be a good, if dangerous, thing. To this extent *The Woman Who Did* helped diffuse the new gospel of sex and, perhaps, justified the trepidation of his critics.[42]

Another English advocate of free love, whose in-

41. "The Woman Who Did," *Bookman, 1* (1895), 119.

42. If in retrospect the calibre of Allen's thought seems unimpressive it is worth observing that there was more to him than I have had room to indicate. Anyone who could elicit such a beautiful memorial as Richard Le Gallienne's essay was obviously a man of substance. Le Gallienne concluded his obituary with these words. (In explanation of the first line, Le Gallienne had previously mentioned that Allen wrote on such a range of subjects that his friends used to say when a disputed point arose that they would "look it up in Grant.") "Well, we shall 'look it up in Grant' no more. The swallows he loved to see flying in and out from the eaves of his beautiful house at Hindhead will come back, but he will come back no more. The nightjar, his favourite bird, will perch near the windows at twilight with its hoarse, sad, churring cry, but Grant Allen will hear it no more. All the goodness, the humour, the tenderness, the imagination, the intellect, the brilliance, the love and laughter that were Grant Allen are now a little dust.

"At his funeral I had in my pocket his little volume of poems, as we turned away from the sad place where we had left him, two of his beautiful lines were murmuring in my mind:
'Perchance a little light will come with morning,
Perchance I shall but sleep.'
"Perchance!" Le Gallienne, "Grant Allen," 1025.

fluence in America was probably greater than Allen's, was Edward Carpenter. Carpenter was more radical than Allen in the sense that his definition of love included homosexual as well as more normal relationships, but his message was easier to take because it was softly put by comparison with Allen's bald declarations. Although Carpenter too was a Fabian, the sources of his inspiration were literary rather than scientific. The greatest single influence on his thought was Walt Whitman, whom he first encountered as an undergraduate at Cambridge University in the 1860s, and he was moved also by *Walden,* which impelled him toward the simple life. His intellectual and artistic obligations were so apparent that he was sometimes called the "Walt Whitman of England," although his friends more commonly referred to him as the Noble Savage.[43]

Carpenter's image as a rustic natural philosopher owed a good deal to his popularizers, chief among whom was Edith Ellis. In a typical essay she attempted to summarize his philosophy of "democratic mysticism," which stressed that "the rich and the poor alike can begin to live beautifully and simply."[44] But she was especially interested in his approach to sex:

> Edward Carpenter is a prophet of the soul and of the body. He proclaims the emancipation of the

43. Carpenter's autobiography, *My Days and Dreams* (London, 1921), is illuminating. The *Forum* called him "The Walt Whitman of England," *32* (1902), 394. See also the sketch of him in D. L. Hobman, *Olive Schreiner: Her Friends and Times* (London, 1955).

44. Edith Ellis, "Edward Carpenter's Message to His Age," *Forum, 44* (1910), 174.

soul through the completion of its relation to the body. In his gospel paganism and Christianity are not at war, but are allies. All our faculties, all our instincts, and even all our weaknesses, are so much raw material to aid the life of the soul. To over-emphasize the body is to hide the soul.[45]

Carpenter's prophetic character was best demonstrated by his *Love's Coming of Age,* which was by far the most popular of his many books in America. Its publication history is itself interesting for what it says of changing public standards in this area. When Carpenter completed it in 1895, the trial of Oscar Wilde had so alarmed publishers that he was forced to bring it out himself. In 1902 a commercial publisher finally agreed to handle it, while by 1915, as he remarked in his autobiography, "the tide of such literature has flowed so full and fast that my book has already become quite a little old-fashioned and demure."[46] This was true largely of its form, not its content, which was still radical despite his emphasis on spiritual values and his criticism of sexual excess.

How intoxicating, indeed, how penetrating—like a most precious wine—is that love which is the sexual transformed by a magic of the will into the emotional and spiritual. And what a loss on the merest grounds of prudence and the economy of

45. Ibid., p. 177.
46. Carpenter, *Days and Dreams,* p. 177.

pleasure is its unbridled waste along physical channels.[47]

Although Carpenter was equally critical of asceticism and libertinism, his readers must have felt that he favored the latter. Like most feminist sympathizers, he believed that women would gain the most from a new birth of freedom. "Even more than man should woman be 'free' to work out the problem of her sex-relations as may commend itself best to her—hampered as little as possible by legal, conventional, or economic considerations."[48] He did not agree with Allen that maternity was central to the feminine role; on the contrary he argued that women could be productive in other ways and should be encouraged to express themselves however they chose.

Carpenter was critical of marriage because it cut people off from life. Married persons were expected to sink into rapturous domesticity, and its effect was to heighten their selfish instincts, blunt their human interests, and induce boredom. The ideal marriage he described thusly:

> A Marriage, so free, so spontaneous, that it would allow of wide excursions of the pair from each other, in common or even in separate objects of work and interest, and yet would hold them all the time in the bond of absolute sympathy, would

47. Edward Carpenter, *Love's Coming of Age* (London, 1903), p. 11.
48. Ibid., p. 62.

by its very freedom be all the more poignantly attractive, and by its very scope and breadth all the richer and more vital—would be in a sense indestructible.[49]

Like virtually all the New Moralists, Carpenter assumed that monogamy was so firmly rooted, so historically correct, that society could afford to modify it.

The most genuinely radical aspect of Carpenter's sexual philosophy was developed in his chapter on the free society. Here he went beyond his earlier remarks, which were by the standards of the New Morality fairly commonplace. In the free society, he predicted, the underground sexual customs of the past and present would surface and transform themselves into useful, healthy, alternatives to monogamy.

> Polygamy, for instance, or some related form of union, supposing it really did spontaneously and naturally arise in a society which gave perfect freedom and independence to women in their relation to men, would be completely different in character from the old-world polygamy, and would cease to act as a degrading influence on women.[50]

The life of the courtesan "might not be without dignity, honor, and sincere attachment." Most startlingly of all, Carpenter suggested that the ancient bacchanalian festivals contained a valuable element of "nature-sex-mysticism" which had unhappily been lost, "yet we cannot but see that this element is a vital and deep-lying one

49. Ibid., p. 103.
50. Ibid., p. 117.

118

in humanity, and in some form or other will probably reassert itself."[51]

Carpenter's tolerance of—even enthusiasm for—deviant sexual practices set him apart from other New Moralists, whose concept of the sexually good life was on the whole quite prim and proper. This was almost certainly because Carpenter was the only identifiable homosexual in the group. In his memoirs he confessed that he had never been drawn to women, although he had female friends, but the most convincing piece of evidence in this regard was his book on homosexuality. *The Intermediate Sex* was a guarded but thoroughgoing propaganda effort on behalf of the people he called Urnings or Uranians.[52] Urnings lived on the dividing line between the sexes. Apart from their sexual habits they were perfectly healthy and normal, except that they possessed finer feelings, greater aesthetic sensibilities, and more fidelity to one another than the promiscuous mass of men. The annals of art and history were distinguished by an abundance of great Urnings, although the Urning way of life reached its peak during the Golden Age of Greece.

All this sounds familiar today when the homosexual polemic has become common currency, but it might have been expected to cause something of a sensation at the time. That it did not seems to have been due to its potential explosiveness. The reviewers talked all around the point, and so it was never made. Similarly, while Carpenter's inclinations were well known to his friends,

51. Ibid., p. 118.
52. Edward Carpenter, *The Intermediate Sex* (New York, 1921).

they did not broadcast the information. Apparently his sexual drive was not especially robust—more of an affinity than a drive—and so there was never any particular need to expose him. Thus a pertinent bit of information about him was never widely known, and he attracted readers who otherwise might have had second thoughts about the philosophy of a man whose own sexual life was in many ways such a poor advertisement for his ideas.[53]

Far more conventional were the views of H. G. Wells, whose great popularity in the United States spread the orthodox socialist position far and wide. The basic Marxist answer to the marriage question had been outlined by the German Social-Democrat, August Bebel, at the beginning of our period. The burden of Bebel's

---

53. There was in England at the time a kind of homosexual underworld made up of literary, public school, and university figures. Carpenter does not appear to have mingled socially with other literary homosexuals, but he shared their cultish tastes, which included a boundless admiration for Walt Whitman, an idealization of Greek pederasty, and a highly romantic view of relations between men. Except for an occasional messy scandal like Oscar Wilde's, few of them were ever exposed although their proclivities were an open secret in literary circles. The Victorians did not want to know about such things, or have them known. Thus, when John Addington Symonds' father learned that the Headmaster of Harrow was a practicing homosexual, he forced the luckless educator to resign but did not expose him, and the secret was well kept during both their lifetimes. Ironically, Symonds later became an active homosexual himself. For a fascinating account of this milieu see Phyllis Grosskurth, *The Woeful Victorian: A Biography of John Addington Symonds* (New York, 1965).

argument was that in primitive times free marriage had been the norm. By emancipating women and ending the legal regulation of sexual relations socialism was not attempting a novel innovation, but proposing rather to reconstruct a state of affairs that "generally prevailed before private property dominated society."[54] Wells' contribution to this fundamental position was mainly rhetorical. He demanded a functional, no-nonsense approach. It was simply that "upon the consistent presentation of sexual morality as existing entirely for the sake of offspring and of the general stock of energy, the continuation of the present progress of our civilization most assuredly stands."[55]

In a characteristically exuberant preview of the future just after the turn of the century, Wells announced that by the year 2000 moral standards would be shifting and uncertain. Monogamy would dissolve and sexual standards would alter greatly. The present moral code would "remain nominally operative in sentiment and practice, while being practically disregarded," and each group would set its own real standards, making for a variety of sexual subcultures within the community.[56] Wells thought that most socialists were too timid about the future of the family. They knew it would have to give way to higher forms, but the fear of socialized families

54. August Bebel, *Woman and Socialism* (New York, 1912), p. 467. It was first translated into English as *Woman in the Past, Present, and Future* in 1885.

55. H. G. Wells, "Morals and Civilization," *Fortnightly Review, 67* (1897), 267.

56. H. G. Wells, "Anticipations: An Experiment in Prophecy —II," *North American Review, 173* (1901), 73–74.

was greater and more potent at the turn of the century than the fear of socialized industries. In keeping with his own injunction he wrote in the *Independent,* a liberal, Christian magazine, that "Socialism, in fact, is the state family. The old family of the private individual must vanish before it just as the old waterworks of private enterprise, or the old gas company."[57] "The Socialist," he continued,

> does not propose to destroy something that conceivably would otherwise last forever when he proposes a new set of institutions and a new system of conduct to replace the old proprietary family. He no more regards the institution of marriage as a permanent thing than he regards a state of competitive industrialism as a permanent thing.[58]

Foremost among the remarkable English socialists who wrote on the marriage question was Havelock Ellis. As a pioneer sexologist Ellis enjoyed a well-deserved reputation for scientific accuracy in his own time, and while much of his work was rendered obsolete by the discovery of the unconscious, his monumental *Studies in the Psychology of Sex* still commands respect. The *Studies* was such a huge and expensive work that it never made the best-seller lists, and Ellis had difficulty in getting it published, owing to its detailed and explicit scrutiny of sexual behavior. But those interested enough to make the effort could gain access to it, and it was an

57. H. G. Wells, "Socialism and the Family," *Independent,* November 1, 1906, p. 1026.
58. Ibid., p. 1028.

important influence on the advanced opinion of his day. Although scientific, or at least scholarly, in his approach to sex, Ellis entertained views much like Carpenter's. "The Orgy," he observed,

> is an institution which by no means has its significance only for the past. On the contrary, the high tension, the rigid routine, the gray monotony of modern life insistently call for moments of organic relief, though the precise form that that orgiastic relief takes must necessarily change with other social changes.[59]

Like the majority of New Moralists, Ellis favored divorce as a first step toward the day when sexual acts would be regarded as entirely private and free from any form of state regulation. It seemed lamentable to him that "sexual morality is the last field of morality to be brought within the sphere of personal responsibility."[60] But by far the most striking aspect of Ellis' work was his championing of sexual variety and expertise. Those primitive societies that trained their young in the erotic arts offered, he believed, a useful model for the Western world. His chapter on the "Art of Life" was buttressed with extensive quotations from the erotic classics of the East, and he dealt in great detail with the importance of the female orgasm and the various positions and techniques which were most likely to elicit it. Thus, almost singlehandedly, he made available detailed sexual in-

59. Havelock Ellis, *Studies in the Psychology of Sex* (6 vols. Philadelphia, 1925), *6*, 222. This volume was copyrighted in 1910.

60. Ibid., p. 406.

formation that the young in particular desperately needed to know.

For all the healthy-minded objectivity that distinguished his books, Ellis himself was a strange and devious man. One of his friends described him as "unusually timid, excessively cautious, secretive, preoccupied with private fantasies of sex and religion, faintly exotic even in his appearance."[61] Far from being a sexual athlete, he confessed to not having had a satisfactory sexual experience until he was in his sixties.[62] But his inability to profit from his own teachings did not prevent Ellis from encouraging the young to practice the very things which afforded him so little gratification. While his most graphic passages were not readily available, he gained a wide audience for his philosophy of sex through his essays calling for greater sexual freedom and a fuller appreciation of erotic play.[63]

The gap between the public image and the private reality was even greater for Ellis' wife Edith. Their marriage was far from happy, despite their real affection for each other. They lived apart much of the time, in a relationship which Mrs. Ellis elevated into a new prin-

---

61. Hobman, *Olive Schreiner,* p. 65.

62. Arthur Calder-Marshall, *The Sage of Sex: A Life of Havelock Ellis* (New York, 1959).

63. A fair sample of his message can be found in *Little Essays of Love and Virtue* (New York, 1921). As an indication of his popularity the *Readers' Guide to Periodical Literature* lists 33 articles by or about Ellis during the years 1900–09. This compares favorably with the 55 items the enormously popular Wells merited, and the handful relating to Carpenter.

ciple by calling it "Semi-Detached Marriage," and Ellis' biographer believes that he encouraged his wife to contract homosexual liaisons, about which she was not particularly enthusiastic. But all this remained below the surface, and Mrs. Ellis was generally featured as a stirring example of what the new freedom could do for women. During her successful tour of the United States shortly before her death, she was interviewed by the *Independent,* which reported that "the continuing buoyancy and widening hopes of their life, she says, are the outcome of an experiment in perfect equality of the sexes." Her happy experience had taught her that "love gains most of all from the opportunity to flourish in freedom when, separated from material ties, it suffers scrutiny and grows in sunlight."[64]

But at the very moment when Mrs. Ellis delivered herself of these misleading observations (misleading even though she may have believed them to be true), she was dying, not growing. Later her essays were to be gathered together and published posthumously as *The New Horizon in Love and Life.*[65] Here one finds the whole range of devices which the New Moralists thought would revolutionize the human condition. Divorce, she maintained, was the only escape from unsuccessful marriages, but in the future free marriage would make divorce unnecessary. One essay, written in the 1890s, called for trial marriages ("A Novitiate for Marriage") and sex education to diminish the number of divorces.

64. Ernestine Evans, "A Woman who has found Freedom," *Independent,* May 25, 1914, p. 135.
65. Edith Ellis, *The New Horizon in Love and Life* (London, 1921).

In another article she argued—somewhat ingenuously, one is bound to think—that her life with Havelock proved the advantages of separate residences for husband and wife. As she put it, "if monogamy is to be the relationship of the future it will have to widen its doors, subjugate its jealousies, and accept many modern devices for spiritualizing physical passion."[66]

In her sad way Mrs. Ellis represented most of what was dubious in the New Morality, but she did not speak for anything like a majority of feminists. Most emancipated women were listening to very different voices and hoping for quite another solution to the marriage problem, as we shall see.

66. Ibid., p. 27.

Chapter

5

THE ORIGINS OF THE NEW MORALITY
Part 2

It should be apparent by this point that while the New Moralists were all feminists, they differed profoundly as to what women should do with their enlarged opportunities. Some, such as Grant Allen and the Ellises, visualized the new freedom largely in sexual terms. Others, such as Mona Caird, saw the emancipation of women in essentially vocational and professional terms. Although Miss Caird was the first woman in the late Victorian era to push this contention to the point of notoriety, she lacked the intellectual force and distinction of her peers. It remained for figures like Olive Schreiner and Mrs. C. P. Gilman to articulate effectively the classical feminist demand for more work and less sex.

Charlotte Perkins Gilman was the most original, and in America the most influential, feminist theoretician. In this respect she inherited the mantle of Elizabeth Cady Stanton. But whereas Mrs. Stanton was primarily a freethinker and suffragist, C. P. Gilman was a socialist intellectual who saw women's suffrage as only one of the things relating to the condition of women. Mrs. Gilman was not a great leader like Mrs. Stanton, but was a fluent and enormously productive writer. Her two most important books, *Women and Economics* (1898) and *The Home* (1903), were the most seminal attacks on domesticity and the most stalwart defenses of working women offered in this period.

Mrs. Gilman's views were directly related to her personal history—something not always true of other feminist intellectuals, whose ideas were often abstract or the products of sympathetic understanding rather than experience. Mrs. Gilman's mother was an intensely domestic woman, who never adjusted to being deserted by her husband. The family moved 19 times in 18 years and lived very close to poverty. The young Charlotte had been deeply attached to her father, and the loss of parental affection caused by his desertion and her mother's withdrawal led her to vow that she would never love her own children to the point where they would be unable to live without her. She attended an art school and at the age of 24 married the painter Charles Walter Stetson. But all his fine personal qualities were not enough to prevent her from having a nervous breakdown shortly afterwards. She later recalled the situation in these words: "Here was a charming home, a loving and devoted husband; a highly competent mother to run things; a wholly satisfactory servant—and I lay all day on the lounge and cried."[1]

1. C. P. Gilman, *The Living of Charlotte Perkins Gilman* (New York, 1935), p. 89.

After six years of this, Mrs. Gilman felt compelled to divorce her husband for the sake of her sanity. Thereafter she improved, but she never entirely recovered from her breakdown or regained her former powers of concentration. In the next forty years she wrote twenty-five books and gave thousands of lectures, but she estimated that she could have done twice as much work if she had been able to write more than three hours a day —her usual limit. During the next few years she traveled widely, became a socialist, and established herself precariously as a professional writer and lecturer. In 1896 she went to England for the International Socialist and Labor Conference and met many of the Fabians, including Grant Allen. She recalled telling Allen that she admired his popular science writings, but not the potboilers he wrote for money. Allen informed her that a man's first duty was to support his family—a point she was hardly willing to concede, as she had already sent her own daughter to live with her ex-husband, now remarried, because she could not support the child on her income as a free-lance writer.

Mrs. Gilman's reputation was secured with the publication of *Women and Economics,* which she wrote in 58 days. Although, as one might expect, the book was sloppily done, it contained a number of arresting thoughts vigorously expressed, and rapidly gained a wide audience. In it Mrs. Gilman argued that marriage was essentially an economic relationship, in which women were consistently shortchanged. Attacking the notion that marriage was economically productive, she asserted that women were valued primarily as cheap domestic labor. However useful their services, such women did not produce social wealth; married women consumed but they did not produce. Just as they were not paid for their domestic work, they were not rewarded for bearing children, since barren women received essentially the same treatment as fruitful ones.

Marriage also overemphasized sexuality, because the most desirable women had the best marital opportunities. This natural selection on the basis of sexual attractiveness (the "sexuo-economic relationship," she called it) tended to create a race of small, delicate females, although this type did not obtain among the other animals. Sexual overspecialization was enfeebling the upper classes, Mrs. Gilman thought, at the same time as it encouraged fortune-hunting among many women. Society condemned marriage for wealth, but it placed a premium on such arrangements by preventing women from earning their own livings.

Fortunately, women were beginning to recognize the importance of economic independence. The self-supporting woman would end the exaggerated importance of sex caused by economic dependence. She would create a marriage based on the free choice of equals, which would be more stable and more productive than the old form, and it was the duty of forward-looking Anglo-Saxons to encourage this movement toward finer women and less brutalized males.

Mrs. Gilman was highly critical of the argument that work for women was destructive of home and family values. In the first place, she reasoned, marriage and the family were not identical. Marriage was a socially sanctioned sexual union, while the family was created by the addition of offspring. The family was a primitive, au-

130

thoritarian institution, whose functions were being destroyed by modern society. Finally, the home differed from both marriage and the family in that it was simply a place to live. If Mrs. Gilman was critical of the family, she was absolutely contemptuous of the home:

> Science, art, government, education, industry—the home is the cradle of them all, and the grave if they stay in it. Only as we live, think, feel, and work outside the home, do we become humanely developed, civilized, socialized.[2]

Mrs. Gilman concluded her attack by describing the ideal human dwelling. She envisioned the home of the future as a complex of individual dwelling units served by central kitchens, nurseries, and recreation areas, and staffed by specialists in cooking, cleaning, and child care. It would liberate women from the drudgery of housekeeping and child-raising, and leave them with time and energy enough to hold down a job while devoting more time to their children than under present conditions.

Her assault on the home, the very center of orthodox piety, might have been expected to earn her a vast notoriety. That it did not seems to have been because the climate of opinion had already mellowed since the early 90s, when Mona Caird's less trenchant writings caused such a sensation. The more radical feminists were prepared to accept Mrs. Gilman's arguments, and even many of those who did not saw a certain value in them.

2. *Women and Economics* (Boston, 1898), p. 222.

One suffrage leader told her, "After all, I think you will do our cause more good than harm, because what you ask is so much worse than what we ask that they will grant our demands in order to escape yours."[3] The tranquility that Mrs. Gilman's book failed to shake convinced her that another was required to destroy the false ideas supporting the home and to pave the way for a new domestic order.

The Home, which resulted from this decision, was a brilliant exposé of what she termed the "Domestic Mythology." Most impressive was Mrs. Gilman's systematic disposition of the arguments used to maintain the home in its present form. The most ridiculous of these, she thought, was the concept of "the privacy of the home." Who, she asked, has any privacy in the home? The home represses individuality, and the effort of any member to keep apart from the whole is resisted because "the family, used to herding, finds it hard to respect anybody's privacy, and resents it."[4] The father may earn a little privacy if he has a study or a den, but the mother and, especially, the children have none.

> Under the close, hot focus of loving eyes, every act magnified out of all natural proportion by the close range, the child soul begins to grow. Noticed, studied, commented on, and incessantly interfered with; forced into miserable self-consciousness by this unremitting glare; our little ones grow

3. Gilman, *Living,* p. 198.

4. C. P. Gilman, *The Home: Its Work and Influence* (New York, 1903), p. 40.

permanently injured in character by this lack of one of humanity's most precious rights—privacy.[5]

One result of this "is that bickering which is so distinctive a feature of family life." Another is the affectionate dominance of the strongest member of the family which enforces peace. If most families have little privacy, those with servants (a more numerous group then than now) have even less. Beset by tradesmen, callers, and the telephone, the harassed family instructs its servants to say that no one is home. Thus "to be in private, you must claim to be out of it." The more affluent construct parlors and drawing rooms to keep callers out of the inner chambers as part of "our whole system of defence and attack; by which we strive, and strive ever in vain, to maintain our filmy fiction of the privacy of the home."[6]

The "sancity of the home" received even shorter shrift from Mrs. Gilman. Noting that the home was especially concerned with the most elemental processes of eating, sleeping, resting, and so forth, she pointed out that these are necessary functions, but asked if they are more hallowed than the others. The idea of the home's sanctity was originally related to ancestor worship and the harem —when each home had an altar it was literally sacred, and the harem was, of course, the essence of mystery and taboo. But a real, healthy modern home was no more sacred, and possibly less so, than a schoolhouse.

Another myth for Mrs. Gilman was the idea that a maternal instinct demands a home for its fulfillment.

5. Ibid., pp. 40–41.
6. Ibid., p. 45.

The care of children was a matter of reason, not instinct, Mrs. Gilman declared. Why do half the nation's children fail to grow to maturity?

> Who, in the name of all common sense, raises our huge and growing crop of idiots, imbeciles, cripples, defectives, and degenerates, the vicious and the criminal; as well as all the vast mass of slow-minded, prejudiced, ordinary people who clog the wheels of progress? Are the mothers to be credited with all that is good and the fathers with all that is bad?[7]

In truth, mother instincts had made no contribution at all to the progress of the race, which owed its advances to teachers, doctors, scientists, and the like rather than to mothers. "Matriolatry" was a drag on the human race, Mrs. Gilman insisted, for the processes of nature were to be studied rather than worshipped. There would be time enough to honor motherhood, she felt, when mothers began to turn out better children.

The home, then, was an inefficient mess characterized by waste, ugliness, and confusion. The father exhausted himself to support it and the mother exhausted herself operating it. The father escaped from the home through his work, the child dreamed of escaping it, but the mother had no choice except to suffer its exactions. Mrs. Gilman was contemptuous of those who sentimentalized the home. The home, she contended, was an authoritarian structure that militated against a sense of justice. Women became timid and weak because the home demanded it of them, while the children got love and

7. Ibid., p. 59.

indulgence, but not justice. Home life, because it was selfish and introverted, prevented the growth of a large social ethic. Honor could not develop there, nor could compassion, or any of the great emotions required for a better society. In summation, "the home is the cradle of all the virtues, but we are in a stage of social development where we need virtues beyond the cradle size."[8]

Although Mrs. Gilman condemned the home for its effect upon the present generation, she was especially concerned with its influence on children. It is for the child's sake that the home exists, we are told, but the facts are otherwise. Houses were not built with children in mind; the dwellings of fertile and childless couples look exactly alike. Boys reacted to the home, therefore, by fleeing from it as soon as they could. In this respect they imitated their fathers, and rightly so, for "the world is the real field of action for humanity." But society confined girls in the home; they were not free to compensate for its defects through new experiences as boys were. Even educated girls usually returned to the home, their training was therefore largely wasted, for "it is use, large free, sufficient use that the mind requires, not mere information." Women's intellects reflected the poverty of their experience, and so "the woman is narrowed by the home and the man is narrowed by the woman."

In all these ways, Mrs. Gilman concluded, the home was demonstrably a failure:

> It hinders, by keeping woman a social idiot, by keeping the modern child under the tutelage of

8. Ibid., p. 183.

the primeval mother, by keeping the social conscience of the man crippled and stultified in the
clinging grip of the domestic conscience of the
woman.[9]

I have dealt with Mrs. Gilman's ideas at such length
because they remain pertinent today. Many people will
(and did) find her special solutions to the problem of
domesticity unpalatable. Communal housing, catered
meals, cooperative nurseries, and the like are not to
everyone's taste. But at a time when women marry
earlier and live longer than ever before, and yet are in no
way prepared to live that part of their life—and it is now
the largest part—which begins when all their children
are in school, it is clear that something must be done.
In no other industrial country is the problem so acute,
because nowhere else has the need to provide women
with a real alternative to domesticity been so ignored.

The other most important minister of the feminist
gospel of work was Olive Schreiner, a strange, unhappy
English colonist in South Africa. While working as a
school teacher among the Boers, Miss Schreiner wrote
three novels and experienced a shattering love affair,
followed by a severe illness, during which she became
addicted to narcotics. After this she went to England,
arriving there in 1881, and two years later her best
novel, *The Story of an African Farm,* was published and
created an immediate sensation. For a variety of reasons
—its exotic setting in the little-known African Veldt, the
heroine's free union, elements of sadism, a tense, melodramatic style—the book was a great success and gave

9. Ibid., p. 315.

its young author an enduring reputation as an artist and feminist. Although she wrote comparatively little during the next twenty-five years, the impact of her book continued to be felt, and its many translations spread her influence to other countries. Almost fifteen years after its publication, in an essay on "Feminism in France" an English journalist observed that "it would appear that *The Story of an African Farm* is accepted by the 'hommes-feministes' school with all the veneration due a new gospel."[10]

In England Miss Schreiner stayed for a time with Beatrice Potter (later to become Mrs. Sidney Webb), met Havelock Ellis, and through them came to know many of the leading radical intellectuals and New Moralists. Havelock Ellis in particular exercised a great influence on her. She was very close to him for a time, and later to Edward Carpenter, whose ideas on the intermediate sex appealed to the strongly masculine component of her personality. She eventually returned to South Africa, married, and devoted herself to feminist causes. It was not until 1911 that her fullest statement on the feminine condition, *Woman and Labor,* appeared in America. For reasons that are not altogether clear from a reading of the book, it gained a wide audience and converted many women, including her biographer, to feminism.

In theory at least, Miss Schreiner was not quite as hostile to sex as many of the advanced feminists. But her ideas on the question were much like Carpenter's: she maintained that the new woman's concept of love

10. Virginia Crawford, "Feminism in France," *Fortnightly Review, 67* (1897), 533.

was "one more largely psychic and intellectual than crudely and purely physical."[11] In keeping with her own nature, she looked to the emergence of a "laboring and virile womanhood, free, strong, fearless and," almost as an afterthought, "tender."[12] Her main concern, however, was to see greater vocational opportunities for women. Her often-repeated motto was "we claim today, all labor for our province." With Mrs. Gilman she feared that if women were not allowed to adjust themselves to the imperatives of the industrial age, and continued to be confined in the home, they would degenerate into mere parasites. Much of Miss Schreiner's best writing was designed to expose the hypocrisy of male resistance to the entry of women into the world of work. It was not that men objected to women working, she pointed out, for they were not seriously opposed to the army of underpaid women in industry, it was only when women attempted to gain well-paid, interesting jobs that the male sex perceived a threat to civilization.

Ellen Key, on the other hand, was a prominent exception to the rule that feminists were more concerned with the freedom to labor than the freedom to love. To the New Moralists' uneasy mingling of erotic mysticism and libertarian ideals, Miss Key proposed to add a more traditional ingredient—the cult of motherhood. Thus she was much closer to male feminists like Ellis and Grant Allen than to the militant feminists, who had mixed feelings about her. Miss Key was a Swedish teacher, lecturer, and critic, who received international

11. Olive Schreiner, *Woman and Labor* (New York, 1911), p. 271.
12. Ibid., p. 271.

acclaim at the turn of the century for her writings on love, marriage, children, beauty, freedom, and kindred subjects. Her sentimentality, her worship of motherhood, and her unending paeans on behalf of love and freedom seem trite and lifeless today. But during her lifetime she was a controversial figure, and her biographer took great pains to answer the charges leveled at her by Swedish critics.[13] A more complex person than this brief sketch suggests, Miss Key defended socialism and free divorce before either was a safe cause. Ironically, this champion of marriage and motherhood died single and childless.

A large part of Miss Key's output was translated into English, and in the second decade of the twentieth century she received more attention from the American press than most New Moralists. She had something for almost everyone. Radicals claimed her as one of their own because of such statements as: "The ideal form of marriage is considered to be the perfectly free union of a man and a woman."[14] At the same time *Current Literature* applauded her for refusing to join the feminists. If the obdurate *Nation* accused her of attempting to reverse the course of civilization, so sensitive an interpreter of the public mood as the editor of the *Ladies Home Journal* praised her *Education of the Child* as a "perfect classic."[15]

13. Louise Nystrom-Hamilton, *Ellen Key: Her Life and Her Work* (New York, 1913).

14. Ellen Key, *Love and Marriage* (New York, 1913), p. 358.

15. "Ellen Key's Masterly Interpretation of Ibsen's Women," *Current Literature, 50* (1911), 411–13; *Nation,* March 14, 1912, p. 261. Bok's remarks were in a G. P. Putnam advertise-

A 1911 article in *Forum* underscored the conservative tendencies in Miss Key's work. It pointed out that Miss Key approved of divorce as a last resort, but only if "the individual is sure that he has extracted every possibility of happiness and growth that it [marriage] holds."[16] Even more encouragingly, Miss Key saw the New Woman as a Priestess of Life, who would express her femininity by minding her own business. For if women "descend from the peaks of enthusiasm to plod with men in the marketplace of compromise they will be only lesser men instead of full-statured women."[17] With Ellen Key one could have the best of both worlds. Although she favored subsidies for mothers she also encouraged women to stay at home, and when she endorsed free divorce she did so within a conservative context. "To the serious," she once said, "divorce will always be serious."[18] Despite her quasi-radicalism American journalists chose to interpret her as a "sound innovator," and so she became a bridge between the New Moralists and the American public. To the extent that she was actually read, however, she did help break down the idealized portrait of Victorian marriage—an institution she condemned for exhibiting "the coarsest sexual habits, the most shameless traffic, the most agonizing soul murders, the most inhuman cruelties;

---

ment at the back of Hamilton's biography. He also wrote an introduction for her *Education*.

16. Hanna Astrup Larsen, "Ellen Key: An Apostle of Life," *Forum*, 46 (1911), 389–90.

17. Ibid., p. 395.

18. Key, *Love and Marriage*, p. 328.

and the grossest infringements of liberty that any department of modern life can show."[19]

On balance, however, Miss Key probably contributed more to the conservative adjustment to the Revolution in Morals than to the radical attack on marriage. Floyd Dell considered her essentially a conservative on these matters and described *Love and Marriage* as the "Talmud of sexual morality."[20]

By the 1920s it was becoming clear that, like divorce, the new demand for sexual freedom was essentially compatible with the institutional status quo. Conservatives had feared that marriage would cease to be viable if sex became generally available to women outside of it. But we now know that the one does not necessarily follow the other. The erotic revolutionaries succeeded in making people aware of their sexual partner's need for variety and satisfaction, and sexual contacts outside of marriage may actually have become more frequent among the middle classes—especially middle-class women. Yet marriage as an institution is hardly less secure, or the cult of domesticity less pervasive, than in the nineteenth century. Conservatives continue to be unhappy about the rise of promiscuity and, of course, they resist it when they can. But it proved to be something they could live with. Thus the old-line feminists who were dubious about the emphasis on eroticism by the New Moralists in time had their suspicions confirmed.

19. Ibid., p. 290.
20. Floyd Dell, *Women as World Builders* (Chicago, 1913), p. 83.

The cause of the New Moralists was greatly advanced in the 1890s by the breakdown of Victorian literary prohibitions. Throughout the nineteenth century non-fiction writers were substantially free to say what they pleased as long as they said it nicely. Descriptions of the techniques of lovemaking and contraception, for example, were not allowed, but within these broad limits a substantial freedom obtained. Where art was involved, however, the standards were much more severe. Works of fiction, poetry, or drama were carefully scrutinized for their moral effects, and very mild deviations from the norm were vigorously censored. The publication of Swinburne's *Poems and Ballads* in the 1860s, for example, had caused a great scandal, and his first publisher was forced to withdraw it. As late as 1883 it was possible for a critic to observe smugly that

> Sensuous love is no longer in good form in the modern novel—the hero no longer loves her because her eyes are bright and her lips rosy—but because she feeds his soul. . . . Not so was it in the days of Tom Jones or Tristam Shandy. The age is refining and we are of and in the age. Let us be truly thankful![21]

But such gratitude was to be short-lived, for within a few years a body of literature came into being that defied the Victorian canons of propriety on virtually every count. Books like *The Woman Who Did* and *Trilby* were read in the 1890s by thousands who would have found them repellent a decade earlier. The de-

21. F. H. Stoddard, "The Modern Novel," *New Englander,* 42 (1883), 629.

cadents, the *Yellow Book,* and the translations of Sir Richard Burton were all parts of a literature which, as V. F. Calverton observed over forty years ago, emphasized passion and license. The shift from delicacy and evasion to realism and candor in the treatment of sexual themes took place with remarkable speed, and the shock that this new frankness produced can hardly be appreciated in a time when sexual explicitness has become a literary convention. For seventy-five years the distance between literature and pornography has been narrowing, so that now we are more likely to be surprised by the imprisonment of a publisher on obscenity charges than by the content of his publications. We can, therefore, have but little sense of what it was like when art crossed the threshold and entered again into the underworld of human emotions.

The first severe shock to Anglo-American sensibilities was administered by a writer who was neither English nor American. The London production of Ibsen's *A Doll's House* in 1889 marked the real beginnings of the literary assault on Victorian taboos. Although Ibsen said nothing in the play that advanced feminists had not said before, the message was somehow much more frightening and distasteful on the stage than in the pages of a distinguished journal. It was, of course, the special ability of art to move the emotions and give burning life to abstract principles that led to its being so heavily guarded in the first place.

But *A Doll's House* was not banned, and within a short time there was an Ibsen boom under way in England. In 1890 George Bernard Shaw published his *Quintessence of Ibsenism,* the first book in English on

143

Ibsen, and the following year saw no less than three of his plays produced in London. At that time William Archer, Ibsen's most sympathetic and best-informed English critic, observed that "I can call to mind no other case in literary history of a dramatist attaining such sudden and widespread notoriety in a foreign country."[22] It seemed to Archer that Ibsen had become so great in England because, unlike the French writers and dramatists who were equally outspoken and vigorous, he wrote about a society that was recognizable to Englishmen. And his subjects were so timely and relevant that they had a greater effect than any English play in the previous half century.

By far the most unsettling of Ibsen's plays was *Ghosts,* which when it was performed in 1891 created an immediate demand for its suppression. "With almost incredible cowardice, the reactionary critics rushed whining to the Lord Chamberlain, and implored him to protect them from another such strain on their intelligence and shock to their prejudices."[23] Archer believed that this critical fiasco was the result of the lamentable ignorance of English drama critics compared with their much better-educated French contemporaries, who gave Ibsen the intelligent handling he deserved. But there was more to it than that. In his survey of Victorian England, G. M. Young concluded that there were only two things on which all Victorians really agreed—representative institutions and the family. These constituted a fixed pivot around which every-

22. William Archer, "The Free Stage and the New Drama," *Fortnightly Review,* 56 (1891), 664.
23. Ibid., p. 667.

thing else revolved. All other questions might be disputed, but not these two. In consequence,

> Sexual ethic had attracted to itself so great a body of romantic sentiment: it was so closely associated, and even identified, with virtue in general, with the elevated, the praiseworthy, the respectable life, that the faintest note of dissidence might attract a disproportionate volume of suspicion and censure.[24]

Young underestimated the amount of criticism that did obtain at the end of the age, but he caught the anxious, almost hysterical protectiveness that discussions of the family aroused in England. The French valued family life but not to the point of being frightened by Ibsen; the English were easily horrified, and Ibsen nearly drove them to the wall. The exaggerated anxiety such attacks uncovered suggests, however, that the Victorians had a good deal less confidence in the family than might have been supposed. Was it really such a fragile institution that it had to be defended so ferociously? Or was the strain of confining the sexual impulse within a domestic cage beginning to tell? The French had discovered that promiscuity and the family were not incompatible, given the right conditions. But the Victorians believed otherwise and, despite their failure to attain universal chastity, continued to press for a single standard of morality that was as noble as it was unattainable. Perhaps criticisms of marriage and the family, apart from their impiety, were fiercely re-

24. G. M. Young, *Victorian England: Portrait of an Age* (Garden City, 1954), p. 227.

sented because they touched a sensitive nerve already rubbed raw by the endless struggle against carnality.

The violence of the press's response to *Ghosts* suggests that it released some of the unconscious hostilities generated by the Victorian war on sex. It was true that *Ghosts* was a tough, almost savage thrust at the conventional wisdom on marriage, and it dealt with venereal disease. But it was very far from being:

> An open drain, a loathsome sore unbandaged; a dirty act done publicly; a lazar house with all its doors and windows open. *The Daily Telegraph*
>
> Garbage and Offal. *Truth*
>
> As foul and filthy a concoction as have ever been allowed to disgrace the boards of an English theatre. *The Era*[25]

In his working notes for the play Ibsen described the type of women Mrs. Alving, its leading character, was meant to represent:

> These women of the modern age, mistreated as daughters, as sisters, and wives, not educated in accordance with their talents, debarred from following their mission, deprived of their inheritance, embittered in mind—these are the one who supply the mothers for the new generation. What will be the result?[26]

25. Victor F. Calverton, *Sex Expression in Literature* (New York, 1926), p. 261.

26. *The Oxford Ibsen* (6 vols. London, 1961), *5,* 468. From his notes on the play.

The result in Mrs. Alving's case was brutal. Raised conventionally, she married conventionally only to learn that her husband was a debauched beast. Her first, and best, instinct was to leave him. But convention forced her back, and after his death convention dictated that she shield her son from the truth about his father. In the end, after extorting a promise from her to kill him should he lose his reason, her son went mad from the effects of a venereal disease inherited from his father. Thus, ruin and destruction were the consequences of her propriety.

Ibsen meant to shake the established verities, and wherever Victorian standards prevailed—in Scandinavia, Germany, England, America—he succeeded. Although few of his plays were staged in this country before the twentieth century, his work was known and feared by the literate public, who learned of it from the English press and the translations of his plays which appeared in the 1890s. But in the English-speaking world Ibsen, who was always considered rather too avant-garde, probably had less to do with the breakdown of Victorian literary gentility than Thomas Hardy.

Unlike the Grant Allens, who could be dismissed as low-principled hacks, Hardy was an acknowledged master and an artistic force to be reckoned with. He had for years been moving closer to realism, and with the publication of his *Jude the Obscure* in 1895 the question of how much candor was to be allowed in fiction was squarely posed. Hardy was not an ideologist and, although he had unorthodox views on marriage and divorce, he regarded *Jude* as a very moral book. The critics insisted on bringing up the dread name of

Zola in connection with it, but what was crude and earthy about the novel, Hardy thought, reflected his debt to Fielding. This element was represented mainly by Jude's wife Arabella, a woman of strong appetites, whose comparatively unadorned approach to the business of living scandalized critics. Arabella was, however, almost marginal to the book's main theme, which concerned Jude's relationship with his mistress Sue, an almost New Woman of delicacy, refinement, and high if confused principles, by whom he had several illegitimate children. The novel ended tragically. After their children were killed, Sue, stricken with remorse and piety, returned to her husband's bed and board despite her love for Jude. He then sank into a fit of despond from which he soon died.

In one sense the novel conformed to the established moral code and, like American movies of the 1930s and 40s, demonstrated that the wages of sin is death.[27] But Hardy made it clear that Jude's tragedy owed much to the weakness of Sue's character. They were both victims of social and religious hypocrisy, but it was Sue's failure to resist orthodoxy that brought them down. Jude was dogged by capricious fate and blind, bad luck, but he could endure what Sue could not and died before surrendering to the judgment of society. Like Hardy himself, Jude moved from Christianity to fatalism. When their children died, his response was to

27. In this connection see Arthur Knight and Hollis Alpert, "The History of Sex in the Cinema," notably part 6, *Playboy, 12* (1965), which describes the means by which the movie industry evaded the strictures of its own production code against sex, crime, and violence.

quote from *Agamemnon:* "Things are as they are, and will be brought to their destined issue."[28] And when Sue cried out that they were being punished for fighting God, Jude answered that they had only been struggling "against man and senseless circumstances."[29]

To many critics Jude's death was not enough to redeem Hardy's vivid characterizations and un-Christian philosophy. The Bishop of Wakefield announced that he had burned his copy, and the American *Bookman* condemned it as a "moral monstrosity." Jeannette Gilder in the *New York World* had this to say: "When I finished the story I opened the windows and let in the fresh air, and turned to my bookshelves and I said: 'Thank God for Kipling and Stevenson, Barrie and Mrs. Humphrey Ward. Here are four writers who have never trailed their talents in the dirt.' "[30] Not all reviewers were hostile to the book. The *Saturday Review* thought *Jude* a masterpiece, a judgment which inspired one critic to attack the *SR* for condoning a work "steeped in sex."[31]

But the essay that best summed up the Victorian response was written by Margaret Oliphant, pre-eminent among the genteel novelists of the old order. She addressed herself to the novels of recent years, the authors of which belonged to an alleged "Anti-Marriage

28. Thomas Hardy, *Jude the Obscure* (London, 1929), p. 409.

29. Ibid., p. 413.

30. Reprinted in Florence Emily Hardy, *The Later Years of Thomas Hardy* (New York, 1930), p. 50.

31. Robert Yelverton Tyrrell, "Jude the Obscure," *Fortnightly Review, 65* (1896), 858.

League." Except for actual pornography, she cried, "nothing so coarsely indecent as the whole history of Jude in his relations with his wife Arabella has ever been put in English print." The novel as a whole was remarkable for its "grossness, indecency, and horror."[32] Mrs. Oliphant was hard put to decide whether Jude's relations with his lawful but lusty wife were more disgusting than his common law marriage with the less inelegant Sue. Arabella was "a human pig," but Sue's "pretended reserve" was almost more indecent. All in all it seemed to her that Hardy was out to destroy marriage and degrade womanhood.

With *The Woman Who Did* Mrs. Oliphant was on surer ground. Herminia, she shrewdly noted, was nothing more than the sum of all school-girl vices. She was self-willed, foolish, unteachable, wrong-headed, autocratic in her ignorance and presumptuous. A very strange figure indeed, Mrs. Oliphant thought, to set up "as a pioneer of progress and as the leader of a great revolution."[33] But the vastness of her indignation was caused by the moral and not the literary failings of Allen and Hardy. Mrs. Oliphant did not appear to think that passions would now be unbridled on every hand in consequence of the new novel, but something as bad had happened. "The conversation of the drawing-room is already most sensibly affected. Things are discussed freely and easily which it would a few years ago have been a shame to mention or to think of."[34] By mention-

32. M. O. W. Oliphant, "The Anti-Marriage League," *Blackwood's Edinburgh Magazine, 159* (1896), 138.
33. Ibid., p. 144.
34. Ibid., p. 149.

ing the unmentionable, men had reduced themselves to the level of beasts, and so the Anti-Marriage League was succeeding in its foul designs.

Mrs. Oliphant's ingenuous fear of The Word was, of course, eminently Victorian. In her eyes it was almost more reprehensible to talk publicly about illicit sex than to practice it, more terrible to expose the evils of prostitution than silently to condone it. In 1885 when W. T. Stead exposed the traffic in girls by buying nine of them within a ten-day period for less than £30, there were those who thought his *Maiden Tribute of Modern Babylon* a greater threat to public morals than the White Slave trade itself.[35] It was not the way in which sexual themes were handled that was disturbing to people like Mrs. Oliphant—Grant Allen's allusions to sex were as delicate as anyone could possibly wish—it was their being brought up at all that offended.

Shaw's experiences with *Mrs. Warren's Profession* further underlined this truth. The play was Shaw's third, and while he wrote it in 1893, it was not until 1898 that he attempted to have it performed. The Lord Chamberlain refused to pass it, but Shaw was able to publish it in 1898 among his *Plays Pleasant and Plays Unpleasant*. It was first publicly performed in America seven years later, but the English ban was not removed until 1925. It concerned a Mrs. Warren, the successful head of an international brothel syndicate. She had been driven to prostitution in her youth by poverty, but through sound management had raised

35. See H. L. Beales, "Victorian Ideas of Sex," in *Ideas and Beliefs of the Victorians* (London, 1950), pp. 351–58.

herself into the executive class. She was able, however, to keep her profession a secret from her daughter for many years. Eventually, of course, her daughter discovered the truth, renounced her mother's support, and found a job in London. At the end of the play Mrs. Warren, having failed to achieve a reconciliation, vows to devote the rest of her life to wrong-doing.

Like most of Shaw's plays, *Mrs. Warren* was full of long speeches designed to press home moral points, especially his belief that "rich men without conviction are more dangerous in a modern society than poor women without chastity."[36] It was essentially a socialist tract and about as titillating as a Tom Swift adventure. Indeed, it seemed to Frank Harris that this was why the Lord Chamberlain banned it. Summing up the English reaction, Harris concluded: "So about all the quarrel amounted to was that Mrs. Warren's Profession was not up to a sufficient standard of immorality. It was true to life and not spicy enough to pass the censor."[37]

The play's American reception was much more various, in keeping with the dispersed, pluralistic, and regional character of American life. It was first staged by a successful producer, Arnold Daly, and the well-known actress Mary Shaw was featured in the title role. It opened in New Haven, where a rowdy student audience was stunned into appreciative silence by Mary Shaw, who gave up any attempt to act the part and delivered most of her lines from center stage as if she was preaching a sermon—as of course she was. This

36. Preface to play in George Bernard Shaw, *Complete Plays with Prefaces* (6 vols. New York, 1962), *3,* xxvii.
37. Frank Harris, *Bernard Shaw* (New York, 1931), p. 180.

awed the students, who gave the play ten curtain calls. Nonetheless it was banned after one performance by the mayor of New Haven, who had not seen the play or, in fact, ever heard of George Bernard Shaw. One day was also the extent of its New York run in the famed Garrity Theater, even though the play had been censored in advance by the Police Commissioner. Miss Shaw was less surprised at this than by the response of her friends, who did not send her a single telegram or letter of encouragement on opening night. Moreover she received a three-page letter of condemnation from the critic who had been most responsible for her successful tour with *Ghosts*.

But subsequently Miss Shaw learned that the play had been closed primarily because William R. Hearst was running for mayor and had used the fact that the theater was currently leased by a Tammany official to charge that Tammany was engaged in corrupting the public's morals. Tammany banned the play to undercut Hearst and not because the city fathers had found it immoral. Subsequently Miss Shaw went on the road with *Mrs. Warren* and enjoyed a successful tour. The play was never banned anywhere else, and even in New York the State Supreme Court eventually ruled that it contained nothing injurious to morals. On the road the play was often attacked by clergymen and newspapers, but Miss Shaw was just as often invited to address student and professional groups, and she got an excellent reception from the women's clubs. G. B. S. insisted that *Mrs. Warren* was essentially a play for women, and so did Mary Shaw, although for different reasons. She believed its theme was the "pathos of a motherhood

153

that is not legitimate, but is as loving and protective as a legitimate one."[38]

The difference between the English and American receptions of the play points up a few of the many distinctions, subtle and overt, that I have had to gloss over for the sake of economy and order. There was, it seems to me, essentially one fundamental Victorian moral code that obtained in both countries, but this is not to argue that American morality was made entirely in the image of England's. America still looked to England for guidance in matters of thought and taste, but English culture often suffered a sea change while crossing the Atlantic. Moreover, America lacked a cultural capital like London. In these matters London was England, but New York was not America. A book or a play could be banned in New York and flourish in Chicago. The new was likely to find recognition in England before America discovered it, but in many ways American society was more responsive—more susceptible perhaps —to change. The literary breakthrough which began with Hardy and Ibsen was, after all, brought to completion by American writers in the 1920s. Indeed, the whole revolution of morals went further and faster in America in large part because there was no network of powerful institutions to retard it, in other words, no Establishment. Divorce itself was one of the most obvious features of this phenomenon. The demand for free divorce began in England at about the same time, if not earlier, that it did in America. But progress toward this

38. Mary Shaw, "My 'Immoral' Play: The Story of the First American Production of 'Mrs. Warren's Profession,'" *McClure's, 38* (1912), 684–94.

goal was much slower there than in the United States because the Church of England's great authority barred the way. With no established church to halt its progress, the resistance to divorce was always localized, diffuse, and generally unsuccessful.

We should not find it surprising, therefore, that the New Morality, which came to this country largely by way of England, was much more influential in the United States. It was not that the American soul was more easily inspired, rather that the American body, in its social context, was less inhibited. The New Morality owed its strength to the cumulative effect of a great many propagandists rather than to the writings of any particular one. But Floyd Dell, whose assessments of the younger pre-World War I artists and intellectuals are unusually reliable, and who was himself a representative member of that generation, offered about the best judgment we are ever likely to get on the question. With the notable exception of Walt Whitman, who "freed us— from whatever chains most irked," he believed the major literary influences on his generation were predominantly European.[39] Of those considered here, Dell thought that Wells, Ibsen, and Carpenter had the greatest impact.

For the most part, therefore, it was the sexual ideologists who exercised the most immediate influence. The literary assault on Victorian conventions soon made possible the publication of once-forbidden works like *Maggie, A Girl of the Streets* and *Sister Carrie*, and together they created a sexually charged atmosphere of

39. Dell, *Intellectual Vagabondage*, p. 117.

great importance. The message, however, was carried by self-conscious partisans dedicated to overthrowing the old orthodoxy. To understand the consequences of their philosophy we need to know something about its inadequacies. Almost half a century of experience with the new sexual canons suggests that the pioneers' most crucial error was their exaggerated sense of the ease with which sexual gratification could be obtained. They assumed that if the old taboos were repealed and a modicum of technical information made generally available, almost anyone could have a sane and satisfying sex life. Not only inveterate simplifiers like Wells and Allen shared this essentially mechanical view of the sexual act, but even more sensitive and poetic figures like Carpenter and Ellis failed to appreciate the complexities of a process that further study has only rendered more baffling and obscure.

Their own experiences ought to have made them a little less oracular and didactic. It is possible to appreciate the humanity of their vision and understand that the noble freedom they hoped to see established was born of their own frustrations and failures, but it is hard to condone the easy confidence with which they assured the world that a little knowledge and a little poetry were all that was needed to throw off the weight of history. Their own lives suggested very strongly, in fact, that the reverse was true. Few of them succeeded in emancipating themselves, and those who accomplished this feat did so at the expense of their fellows. Carpenter, as we have seen, was probably a homosexual, yet his propaganda was understood to advocate heterosexual love. The consequences of this deception cannot

156

be traced, but his aberration did manifest itself in curious ways. For example, their friends believed that Kate Salt, for many years secretary to Bernard Shaw, never consummated her marriage with Henry Salt because Carpenter had convinced her that she was an Urning.[40]

The unhappy sex life of the Ellises is another case in point. They lived apart much of the time because Havelock was not interested in having conjugal relations, and separate residences were convenient for him. But their separation was elevated into a matter of high principle, and the young were urged to follow their enlightened example. Havelock's famous account of his wedding night, which he spent outside of the bed covers, is a further illustration of the reverse effect by which certain intellectuals converted their liabilities into assets. Supposedly his restraint demonstrated an uncommon tact and sensibility in an age of rude deflorations. But when we know that his gentlemanly continence owed as much to his sexual inadequacies as anything else, the gesture looks quite different.

Ellis knew a great deal about sex from study and observation, and no one would contend that the scientist must directly participate in the phenomenon he observes. But he was accustomed to using his own experience to illustrate his points and, given his sexual failures, this habit of his must be regarded as disingenuous at best. Moreover, sex and marriage are such universal experiences that those who fail in them personally and yet claim to be authorities are not in quite the same posi-

40. Fremantle, *Band of Prophets,* p. 62.

tion as other scholars and scientists. The marriage coun-
selor with three divorces to his credit or the child
psychologist whose children become delinquent must
expect to have their credentials questioned. But Ellis
became an authority on sexual techniques despite his
failures, and Ellen Key made a great reputation for
herself in the field of motherhood without ever having
a child.

As a dedicated and experienced philanderer H. G.
Wells belonged to a different category. But his ardent
pursuit of sexual pleasure had its unhappy aspects, for
he could not resist seducing the daughters of his friends.
In at least one instance poetic justice was served. He
seduced the daughter of Hubert Bland, a brother
Fabian, who was himself notorious for exactly the same
thing, having filled his wife's house with the offspring of
his illicit unions. All this was productive of much discord
in the Fabian fellowship. Mrs. Pember Reeves was believed to have defected from the Society because of
Wells' affairs. Thus, while in one sense Wells' consistency was admirable, in another way it raised a
question as to the broad utility of the principles he
sustained.[41]

Since the pain and confusion of the sexual ideologists'
private lives was never allowed to mar the smooth confidence of their publications, they promoted an ethic
that had little to do with current realities, and gambled
everything on sex being a relatively simple process that
had been rendered complex by superstition and ignorance. Their arguments had the immediate effect, as we

41. Ibid.

shall see later, of persuading young radicals that the case for free love had been successfully made. The anarchists and bohemians could rise above marriage secure in the knowledge that it was obsolete and irrelevant to the new era they were helping to create. But more significant for the future was the dilution and diffusion of the New Morality, aided by the literary breakthrough in the popular press. The public discussion of divorce was perhaps the first important means by which this process was effected. Divorce was increasingly justified in the same terms and with the same arguments used by the New Moralists to defend the varieties of free love. One could not insist, as yet, that people had an intrinsic right to sexual gratification, but it became possible during the Progressive era to argue that married persons had a right to expect their union to be pleasurable, and that the failure of marriage in this respect was a legitimate ground for divorce.

In this respect, the modest arguments of Lecky, Spencer, and Ward were probably most important to the future of divorce. Because they were the first men of authority to think about the sexually unthinkable, they made the later debate possible and, because they confined their observations rather strictly to the Victorian preoccupation with permanent marriage, they created a fund of scholarship on which the later advocates of easy divorce drew heavily. Their contribution remains impressive even today because, for the most part, their work was in the best tradition of the nineteenth-century social sciences—serious, responsible, well documented, and solidly persuasive. By comparison, the next generation of social scientists concerned with these questions seemed a little thin and pallid. With such lightweights as Grant Allen and Ellen Key there is, of course, no grounds for comparison at all.

The artists—Ibsen, Hardy, Shaw—were almost as valuable, though it is hard to compare the effectiveness of such disparate idioms. The effect of Lecky and company was gradual and cumulative, while Ibsen and his fellows caused immediate sensations. The sustained trickle and the flash flood may, in the end, have had equal consequences. Ibsen's plays were implied recommendations for divorce. Obviously Nora would divorce her husband, and Mrs. Alving sinned by failing to divorce hers. Hardy, although he was not in the advocacy business at all, was more sophisticated in his treatment of divorce than Ibsen, because he began where Ibsen left off. Jude attempted divorce, clearly the appropriate response to his situation, but was defeated finally because of bad luck, circumstance, and the complexities of human nature, which defied mechanical solutions. Hardy, in his genius, realized that divorce was not central but almost irrelevant to relations between men and women, and that only convention made it seem so important. It would take more than one literary generation before this basic truth became widely appreciated. *Jude* was brilliant, therefore, because it cut through the prevailing modes of treating marital questions to touch the heart of the matter. Hardy's boldness came from his instinct for the essential, but, ironically, his readers could not get beyond the candor of his language, which so startled them that they missed what was most daring and original in *Jude the Obscure*.

160

Ibsen and Hardy deserved to be widely read, and while they were probably read for the wrong reasons, they made themselves felt all the same. Shaw, too, had a large audience, but as usual he relied so much on rhetorical virtuosity that what he had to say was obscured by the manner in which he said it. The remainder of the New Moralists seem to have attracted attention only to the extent that they were trivial, light-minded, or sensational. Mrs. Gilman's *The Home,* in many ways her most original and provocative book, added nothing to her reputation, while the rigorously consistent Individualists were almost unknown in this country. Havelock Ellis' masterwork, *Studies in the Psychology of Sex,* compelled respect, but his personal philosophy of sex got much more respect than it deserved, as did the views of such derivative and shallow figures as Carpenter, Key, Caird, et al. Their relative popularity, however, says something about the process of assimilation that was then under way.

The New Moralists believed that a major restructuring of society was in the offing and that this would be associated with entirely new value systems. But the absorption of their weakest positions by the advocates of divorce pointed the way to what actually happened. Instead of dispensing with marriage as an institution, the new sexual ethic, when it came, operated to strengthen many of the existing norms. Divorce and promiscuity did increase, but in ways that did not affect the popularity of marriage or the cohesion of families. In effect the long-awaited single standard of morality finally arrived, but it was based on an equality of opportunity. The male lost his sexual privileges as promiscuity came to be seen, in theory at least, as much the woman's right as the man's.

Of course this transformation is still far from complete, as witness the confused discussion about sex today, but it has gone far enough so that we can speak of a new hypocrisy having replaced the old. We pay lip service to chastity at the same time as we countenance a degree of sexual variety unheard of in the nineteenth century. Moreover, new anxieties have developed appropriate to our new concerns. The middle classes especially are now expected to achieve levels of dexterity and satisfaction that in the past were confined to sexual athletes—hence our frenzied search for the elusive feminine orgasm without which no marriage can be complete.[42] If women no longer anticipate the sexual act with fear and trembling, they now approach it with expectations that in the normal course of events must go unsatisfied and become guilt-producing. Marital anxieties have, perhaps, been elevated to higher, freerer levels, but tensions persist which are all the more difficult to resolve because of their sophistication. The primary requirement for a Victorian wife was fortitude in the face of male appetite. A modern wife must be ingenious, resolute, tirelessly inventive, and resilient. The advantages of her position are not quite so obvious, therefore, as we are supposed to think.

42. If we are to believe Masters and Johnson, this particular search is now ended. We must, however, await the coming of their second volume for an explanation of how the orgasm is to be regularly effected. William H. Masters and Virginia E. Johnson, *Human Sexual Response* (Boston, 1966).

Rather than talking about a revolution in morals, it might be more useful to consider how little change has actually taken place. The family continues to be the sun around which our social life revolves, and the taboos against homosexuality, orgiastic behavior, abortion, and so forth still have much of their old force—especially in law, which generally lags behind custom in these matters. The major difference is that ordinary, heterosexual behavior has become a kind of consumer good that can be freely advertised and exploited. One clue to the reasons behind this particular shift was offered during the very years with which we are concerned by the noted economist Simon Patten. He characterized his era as the time of transition from a "pain or deficit" economy to a "pleasure or surplus" economy.[43] Higher income levels and greater leisure permitted a large segment of the population to enjoy for the first time vices which had previously been restricted to the few. The emphasis on denial and austerity that had been necessary in an economy of scarcity was hardly appropriate to an economy where consumption was becoming more important than production. Although the Progressive years were not quite affluent by our standards, they were close enough to it so that Patten could discern the shape of the future. Widespread prosperity meant, therefore, a reduction of constraints and a heightened appetite for previously forbidden pleasures that harmonized with the demands of a consumer-oriented economy.

While this is far from the whole answer, it is easy to see that the family is more useful from an economic

43. Simon Patten, *The New Basis of Civilization* (New York, 1912).

163

standpoint than the individual is, because the family is more likely to use goods like tract homes, station wagons, and portable television sets than the single person. On the other hand, sex can be used to sell goods by endowing them with erotic content, and it can be directly sold, as in the entertainment industry, without disturbing many of the traditional norms and institutions. A sexual revolution in this limited sense did not threaten to rock the boat, therefore, in anything like the degree that the abolition or profound modification of marriage would have done.

At first the new ideas about sex had been confined to radical circles. Floyd Dell's generation of young bohemians had been freed by Walt Whitman, but it was people like Wells, Ibsen, and Carpenter who gave them a positive sense of the kind of sexual ethic that was most appropriate to the world just then on the verge of being born. For others, like Mabel Dodge, sex *was* the new world.[44] But the experience of the 1920s demonstrated that there was nothing inherently radical about sexual freedom. Instead of the cultural transformation its prophets had anticipated, the New Morality led merely to the establishment of divorce as a valid (and perhaps necessary) part of the family system, and the legitimization of certain kinds of promiscuity. Far from disrupting the old order, the new sexuality strengthened it, as the spread of Freudianism offered additional reasons for women to stay at home and accept their feminine

44. See the splendid essay on Mabel Dodge in Christopher Lasch, *The New Radicalism in America, 1889–1963* (New York, 1965).

destinies. Hence, the radicals of the 1930s paid very little attention to the sexual question, whose possibilities for revolutionary action seemed to have been largely exhausted.[45]

There is, consequently, a double irony in the revival of sex as an issue by the newest radicals of our own time. Not only does this tendency constitute a return to an historically bankrupt tradition of radical thought but it emphasizes an area of human experience which is peculiarly vulnerable to the existing social economy. Capitalist society has demonstrated its ability in the

---

45. Betty Friedan has demonstrated that Freudianism and the social sciences have worked in recent years to maintain the cult of domesticity and a fairly traditional concept of the social role of women. In fact, the accommodation of the new ideas on sex was well on its way to being accomplished by the end of the 20s. The effect upon feminism of this assimilation will be dealt with in my forthcoming book, which is tentatively entitled *Everyone Was Brave.*

In the 1930s the argument over the future of the family was largely dropped by radicals for the obvious reason that more pressing problems claimed their attention. It is, therefore, with a mixture of surprise and nostalgia that one discovers an occasional statement today reminiscent of the confident prophecies of half a century ago. Recently the *Times* reported a speech by a psychologist on "The Urban Man of the Future" which closed on this note: "There may be major changes in our concept of the family as the basic unit of civilization, Dr. Farson said. Such changes already have come about, he said, because the high divorce rate has created families with one adult, and fusion of families with children of different marriages." *New York Times* (April 16, 1966).

In view of this perhaps we ought to say that the debate is highly attenuated rather than entirely dead.

past to make sex pay in ways that do not menace the established verities, and there is little reason to think that it will not continue to do so. No doubt most of us could use more and better sex than we actually get, but the attempt to turn this craving into a program of radical action constitutes not only a serious misreading of our past but sadly underestimates the assimilative character of American civilization. Instead of building a new society, the newest sexual radicals are likely to find, as their predecessors did, that they have only succeeded in making the old one more attractive.

But the acceptance of divorce as an inescapable part of the family system—an evil part perhaps, but unavoidable for all that—preceded America's coming to terms with the sexual question. It constituted, therefore, the leading edge of what we still call the Revolution in Morals. The struggle over divorce in the Progressive period was one of the first confrontations between the old and new ways of looking at moral problems, and it is almost a classic example of how this sort of change is effected. There are a number of reasons why divorce seems more useful for understanding this process than, say, prostitution. For one thing, people were talking about divorce for almost a generation before the White Slave Panic made the free discussion of prostitution feasible. Divorce was, as it happened, almost the only "respectable" sexual problem that could be publicly debated. For another, there was a good deal of evidence, in the shape of census reports and such, bearing on divorce, and thus discussions about it were not quite so formless and amorphous as those on questions about which no one knew anything. There were, in fact, experts on divorce who had a substantial influence on public opinion and who constitute a fascinating case study of how in our time expertise has come to be a dominant force in many kinds of public issues. The most important of these experts, the social scientists, will be considered in the next chapter.

Chapter

6

DIVORCE AND THE SOCIAL SCIENCES

In the late nineteenth century, when the social sciences were coming into being, their professional requirements and their subject matter were only vaguely defined. Despite the pioneer work of such great and original intelligences as Lester Ward and John Stuart Mill, most people understood sociology to mean almost anything relating to social problems. Periodicals, for example, often had a sociological section for news items on such things as poverty, the labor question, and family matters. Most social scientists were self-anointed, and if they had any special training it was as often as not in theology. They were usually engaged in the business of solving social problems through the heavy-handed application of the conventional morality. In many instances whether these solutions worked was of less importance than the validation of Christian orthodoxy—piety, not progress, was their major concern. The arrival at the end of the century of the first generation of professionally trained social scientists effected, therefore, not so much a change as a revolution in the handling of social problems.

Historians are well aware of the significance of such figures as Richard T. Ely, John R. Commons, and Thorstein Veblen, who successfully challenged laissez-faire and social-Darwinist principles and laid the technical and intellectual foundations for the reforms of the Progressive era. But the influence of the new sciences went far beyond this and penetrated into the sacred precincts of personal morality and domestic life, which had not previously been the objects of expert investigation and instruction. The first professionally trained social scientists emerged at just about the time that divorce became a matter of public alarm and so, more through coincidence than design, they found themselves embroiled in a controversy charged with barely suppressed tensions and anxieties. While the divorce crisis had its origins in the rapidly growing divorce rate, most of the protagonists had at least a vague sense of the questions being raised by the New Moralists as to the future of marriage and the family. The struggle over divorce was, therefore, related to the whole complex of moral norms that conservatives felt to be threatened. It was both an immediate and specific problem and the leading edge of a moral transformation that was odious and alarming to a very high degree. As such the public discussion of divorce was fraught with the same passion that today is attached to adolescent sexuality and pornography—but with an intensity of feeling that we cannot easily imagine.

The first American scholar to study the family in a

serious way was Charles F. Thwing, and his master-work, *The Family* (1887), was the fullest expression of the conventional wisdom on divorce. Never again would it be necessary to explore at such tiresome length why orthodox Christianity was fully justified in condemning divorce. Thwing was suitably equipped for this task, as he had been a Congregational minister for eleven years before being called to the presidency of Western Reserve University. As a minister and educator Thwing had credentials that were more impressive to his audience than those of any secular Ph.D. Moreover, he was far from being an unlettered man. A self-trained scholar whose bibliography ran to over a thousand items, Thwing was well read in the appropriate literature.

Modeling his work on the institutional historians then much in vogue, Thwing began his study of the family in prehistory, and spent an inordinate amount of time on ancient Rome and Palestine before he discovered the origins of the modern family in the German forest. From there he moved quickly to an analysis of divorce, which he believed to be caused largely by the excessive in-dividualism and secularism of modern times. These points were central to the argument against a liberal policy on divorce. The growth of secularism menaced the home by encouraging immorality, while a selfish in-dividualism put personal happiness above the interests of society. Thwing, like his more liberal successors, be-lieved that the growth of industry had much to do with the problem, but the moral basis of divorce was a theme to which he continually returned. In this he faithfully re-flected the views advanced by the numerous critics of divorce in the periodical press.

Thwing resembled them also in his fears. While he was less hysterical than many, he was a little afraid of the women movement (which he supported in other ways), because it was more interested in woman's rights than in her duties. He was alarmed by the declining birth rate and insisted that procreation was the primary human obligation. Like so many other Americans in the turbulent 1880s and 90s, Thwing feared social instability and stressed the importance of the family as a conservative institution. The individual, on the other hand, was "a radical and a progressive," and his antisocial characteristics were encouraged by contemporary radicals who simply failed to appreciate "the depravity and selfishness of the individual."[1] Sex was another disturbing aspect of the problem. Facing up to its thorny implications, Thwing observed austerely that "while we cannot admit, therefore, that sexual gratification enters in the purpose of a true marriage, it is nevertheless true that it forms an element of marriage."[2]

Thwing's solution to the divorce problem flowed inevitably from his assumptions. If church and state alike were threatened with destruction by the license of a radical and unrestrained individualism, then it must be halted through the virtual abolition of divorce. This authoritarian solution was perfectly in keeping with the demands of public opinion, and Thwing's book was welcomed as another step forward in the nineteenth century's march toward moral perfection. For several generations the opposition to divorce would be based on

1. Charles F. and Carrie Thwing, *The Family: An Historical and Social Study,* 2nd ed. (Boston, 1913), p. 176.
2. Ibid., p. 139.

171

the arguments he had compiled. But if Thwing summed up the conservative case against divorce, he did so in a way that was almost obsolete at the time of its presentation. The introduction of graduate training on the German model and the growing respect for scientific objectivity made Thwing's work unacceptable by the new standards, and his conclusions ran contrary to the spirit accompanying the professionalization of sociology.

This was apparent as early as 1891 with the publication of Walter F. Willcox's *The Divorce Problem.*[3] Willcox was primarily a statistician, whose interest in divorce had been aroused by *Etude Demographique du Divorce,* by the French demographer Jacques Bertillon. Bertillon convinced him that the prohibition of divorce was an ineffective response to the problem and that divorced persons should be allowed to remarry. Willcox's study was to have an equally persuasive effect on many American students of divorce. He accomplished this by a close analysis of the bulky Bureau of Labor report on marriage and divorce, and by drawing certain conclusions of his own from it.[4] By basing his case largely on the hard evidence available, rather than on moral principles or generally accepted theories of social behavior, Willcox effected a minor breakthrough in the study of delicate social questions.

For the first time in America statistical evidence was

3. Walter F. Willcox, *The Divorce Problem* (New York, 1891).

4. The first government report was later republished as the first volume of U.S. Bureau of the Census, *Marriage and Divorce 1867–1906* (Washington, 1909).

used to demonstrate that the divorce rate could not be effectively reduced by legal maneuvers, and that to really suppress the evil would require drastic restrictions on marriage and divorce. By carefully working through a mass of European and American data, Willcox showed that none of the alternatives were feasible. Restricting marriage only increased the number of common-law marriages. Forbidding the remarriage of divorced persons was pointless, because most people did not obtain a divorce with the immediate intention of remarrying. Restricting divorces could be done only by making them prohibitively expensive, a device that was alien to American ways of thinking, because it discriminated against the poor.

But Willcox's presentation had little initial effect. In the first place, it ran against the grain of public opinion. Secondly, the expert audience to which it was addressed hardly existed. It would require another fifteen years to develop a body of social scientists, liberal clergymen, and social workers capable of appreciating what Willcox had done. Technical monographs rarely enjoy a wide currency in any case, but even if thousands of people had read Willcox in the early nineties, it is hard to believe that it would have made any real difference. His clear, cogent arguments based solidly on statistical evidence represented almost an affront to those engaged in the public debate over divorce, for everyone knew that the duty of the social sciences was to shore up the sagging walls of orthodox morality and social convention.

Even if Willcox's work was discordant and untimely, it did enjoy a kind of underground reputation. While most of those opposed to divorce honored his arguments by ignoring them, at least a few—notably Samuel Dike—were deterred from political action by his array of evidence. While Willcox was deprived of immediate acclaim, in time he was to enjoy both professional esteem and the satisfaction of having pinked the opposition in a vital spot. The ingrained American respect for the apparent objectivity of facts and figures could not be denied forever.

Willcox went on to enjoy a successful academic career, although he never achieved the reputation his excellent work should have earned him. The chief beneficiary of his initiative was George E. Howard, whose *History of Matrimonial Institutions* literally crushed the scientific opposition to divorce. Howard was a colorless scholar, who had taken his Ph.D. in Germany before becoming a professor of history at Stanford University. After more than twenty years of relative obscurity, he gained public attention through his involvement in the Ross affair. When in 1901 the volatile E. A. Ross was fired for defending free silver and opposing Chinese immigration, the academic world was irritated, if hardly surprised. But when the normally circumspect Howard spoke up for Ross and resigned rather than disavow statements he had made to students, more than a few eyebrows were raised around the country. The publication of his massive *History,* coming as it did on the heels of the Ross affair, marked Howard's final emergence as a public man. Howard never achieved the stature of a Ross or a Giddings, but he followed up his study with a stream of speeches and articles defending free divorce, which earned him a solid, if modest, reputation. No one who cared for the family could escape knowing about him, and his colleagues recognized his worth when they elected him to the presidency of the American Sociological Society in 1917.

Howard's *History* resembled Thwing's in many ways. It too was an exercise in institutional history, but Howard had been trained by masters in the art, and so his three volumes were highly craftsmanlike explications of ancient law and precedent. Howard was also a moralist—but a moralist in reverse. He took great pains to explain that the scientist's duty was to carefully examine the evidence, which would then speak for itself, but somehow he ended up by discovering an elevated moral quality in divorce that had hitherto escaped general notice. He also was opposed to selfish individualism, but divorce did not seem to him narrowly antisocial at all. Like Thwing he was a progressive of many years standing, but he saw divorce as part of a great forward movement. Not only was the new freedom raising the spiritual standards of home life, but there were countervailing forces, such as the growing suburbs and the shorter working day, that were serving to lessen domestic unrest.

Like many others, Howard found the roots of the problem buried deeply in economics, but this did not prevent him from believing that its solution was an educational matter. The apparent discrepancy between cause and cure troubled Howard not at all, for it was central to the whole progressive mystique that there was no social problem, no matter how tangled or complex, that could not be removed if only it were properly understood. Once an enlightened public opinion had been created through education, appropriate solutions would manifest themselves. Right thinking, coeducation, and eugenics would liberate the "vitalizing, regenerative power of a more efficient moral, physical and social training of the young."[5]

Howard was hardly more rapturous about sex than Thwing, but he saw it from another angle. Not divorce but traditional marriage exaggerated sexuality. The marriage of convenience, a staple of the old order, was simply an exchange of sex capital for security. Fortunately, the feminist movement was helping to eliminate this barbarous vestige of a more carnal age and preparing the way for purer and less commercial unions.

Nor was Howard concerned about the increasing power of the state. The traditional family had been narrow, exclusive, and antisocial. By breaking up these tiny units and blending the whole population into one great whole, the modern state not only freed the individual from family authoritarianism but transformed the family into a "spiritual and psychic association of parent and child based on persuasion."[6] Radicals were assisting in this great work, and in a long survey of their writings, Howard paid tribute to Robert Dale Owen, Mary Wollstonecraft, Mona Caird, Edward Carpenter, and numerous other feminists, socialists, utopians, and agitators. Howard was more than an admirer of radical

5. George E. Howard, *A History of Matrimonial Institutions* (3 vols. Chicago, 1904), 3, 225.

6. George E. Howard, "Social Control and the Function of the Family," Congress of Arts and Sciences, *Proceedings, 7* (St. Louis, 1904), 701.

commentators; he was deeply influenced by them. His ideas on the excessively sexual nature of marriages of convenience came, of course, from C. P. Gilman and Olive Schreiner. The socialists Friedrich Engels and August Bebel showed him how economics influenced family life. He admired these radicals because they aroused in the public mind "a loftier ideal of wedded life" and strongly favored the complete emancipation of women.

While Howard's orthodox methods hardly qualified him as an expert in the new sense, he had a respect for expertise that was far more characteristic of the twentieth century than the nineteenth. Accordingly, he was irritated by the clergy, who seemed to him unappreciative of

> the great constructive work of moral and social progress . . . being done by expert students of the realities of modern life, especially by the trained and fearless minds who are now making our colleges and universities radiant centers of helpful and honest thought.[7]

Equally characteristic of the Progressive era was the authoritarian view that ran beneath Howard's obvious libertarianism. If the progressives expanded the meaning of liberty to include freedom from many kinds of want and privation, which the Victorians regarded as inseparable from the human condition, they also carried over something of the moral absolutism of the previous age. This found expression in their favorite phrase,

7. George E. Howard, "Divorce and the Public Welfare," *McClure's Magazine, 34* (1909), 242.

"social control," which, with its straightforwardly coercive implications, is both more forceful and more candid than the euphemisms of later generations. Thus, Howard regarded the restriction of divorce as brutal and antisocial, but the restriction of marriage as simple good sense. Lax marriage laws, he declared, were anarchic and subversive of social order. Common-law marriages were even more dangerous and had to be suppressed, for it was better

> that the children of a delinquent minority should bear the stain of illegitimacy than that the welfare of the whole social body should be endangered. For the same reason the supposed rights of the individual must yield to the higher claims of society.[8]

Although his rhetoric and academic style were slightly dated, Howard was in many ways a strikingly modern figure. Eclectic, professional, and generally libertarian, he was closer in spirit to the efficient, pragmatic intellectuals of, say, the *New Republic* than most scholars of his generation. While he was not a scientist as the term is now understood, Howard made a science of the family possible for the first time by breaking the hold of Christian moralizers on family studies. Moreover, little was added to the social scientists' case for divorce for a generation after his *History*. Perhaps even more significant was his rejection of the apocalyptic vision that dominated Victorian discussions of divorce. It now became possible to contemplate the problem with some degree of objectivity and without the necessity of assuring

8. Howard, *History,* p. 184.

178

one's audience that civilization could be saved only by making marriage indissoluble. Unusually optimistic, even for a progressive, Howard managed to infuse some of this spirit into an area where pessimism had been fashionable.

Howard's books, scholarly papers, and popular articles made him *the* authority on divorce. But soon he was to share this distinction with James P. Lichtenberger, whose *Divorce: A Study in Social Causation* underlined and reinforced Howard's conclusions. Like Thwing, Lichtenberger had begun his career as a protestant minister; however, he went on to earn a Ph.D. in sociology under the brilliant Franklin H. Giddings, at Columbia University. Lichtenberger's study of divorce was important in two ways. First, it represented a shift away from the usual fields of history, law, and statistics. Lichtenberger summed up all that was then known about divorce, surveyed the position of the leading denominations, and drew the obvious conclusions. If Willcox and Howard had covered this ground before, they had not done so in Lichtenberger's concise, readable fashion. In addition, Lichtenberger's study appeared when the demand for such a work was being felt by social workers, counselors, and others who could hardly be expected to toil through Howard's massive opus.

Lichtenberger was probably most arresting for the vim and vigor with which he lambasted "the alarmist, the professional reformer and the moral and religious dogmatist."[9] In his zeal to discredit the Christian moral-

9. James P. Lichtenberger, *Divorce: A Study in Social Causation* (New York, 1909), p. 12.

ists he came very close to simply inverting their preachments. At the outset of his study he primly announced that it was based on the following assumptions: that the proper approach to divorce was inductive, scientific analysis, that marriage rested upon the inherent nature of society and was not the product of coercion, that society followed certain natural evolutionary laws, and that the scientist was not a reformer but a detached seeker after truth. If his credo seemed less than startling, that is because its tenets were already articles of faith among most sociologists. However, Lichtenberger needed to say these things, not only because the general public was not yet prepared to concede sociology its right to a scientific view of sexual questions, but because his own past as a clergyman might have told against him among social scientists.

Lichtenberger censured the churches for their failure to understand the economic and idealistic sources of the divorce movement. Divorce, he believed, was a temporary phenomenon produced by the industrial revolution and the emancipation of women. Once this transitional period was over, the family would be reconstructed on the basis of perfect freedom and equality. These great changes were both inevitable and desirable, and if theologians would only heed the words of Herbert Spencer, they would recognize the futility of attempting to obstruct progress with moral fulminations. Of course Spencer ranked considerably below Saint Paul in the world of American Protestantism, but Lichtenberger's remarks were probably intended for his fellow sociologists, who could be expected to read them, even as most clergymen could not.

A more potent blast against the churches was delivered by the irrepressible E. A. Ross. Divorce was not one of his major interests, but he had something to say about it, as he did about most controversial issues, and his views were important if only because Ross was. Thanks to his prominence, Ross was not confined to scholarly journals; when he decided to enlighten the public on this question he was able to do so in the *Century's* stately pages. Repeating all the usual liberal clichés about divorce, he predicted that its frequency was bound to diminish in the future, along with such unpleasant side effects as excessive individualism and selfishness. Insofar as divorce pointed up certain weaknesses in the family system, these were best dealt with by institutional reform, which would get to the root of the problem, and by an extensive program of sex and marriage education.

Ross thumbed his nose at the clergyman "who beseeches us to 'protect the poor from the evils of loose divorce statutes' and who evidently conceives permission to separate as a malignant entity which goes about rending harmonious households."[10] To those who were given to sentimental effusions over traditional marriage he said, "The loveless couples of the 'good old times' appear to have been held together by public opinion, religious ordinance, ignorance of a remedy, the expense of divorce, or the wife's economic helplessness, rather than by heroic fidelity to an ideal."[11]

By 1915, when Willystine Goodsell's *History of the*

10. E. A. Ross, "The Significance of Increasing Divorce," *Century, 78* (1909), 150.
11. Ibid., p. 150.

Family appeared, the liberal, scientific view of the family had reached the textbook level; thus only eleven years separated its first complete expression in Howard's *History* from its entombment as a new orthodoxy. Given the usual time lag that keeps novel ideas out of general circulation until they have become sufficiently stale, one can only conclude that the liberal case had become respectable in an astonishingly short period of time. Goodsell's book competed successfully with Thwing's text from the outset, and in the course of events replaced it. The largest part of his *History* was devoted to the usual soggy recitation of the family's varying fortunes from Neolithic times to the present, but his last 95 pages dealt with topical questions and judiciously culled out the distastefully radical from the appropriately liberal arguments. Indeed, he went so far as to classify "Current Theories of Reform" under three headings—radical, conservative, and moderate progressive, the last being, of course, the right one.

Goodsell's enthusiasm for the radicals was under such control that he was able to dismiss Shaw, Wells, Bebel, and especially Edward Carpenter with the remark that "they offend not only our finer feelings but also our intelligence."[12] Ellen Key's elevated pronouncements, on the other hand, delighted him, and he was even prepared to concede that C. P. Gilman had her points. He gave short shrift to the conservatives by citing only the Roman Catholic position, which he criticized as too harsh and authoritarian. The moderate progressives,

12. Willystine Goodsell, *History of the Family as a Social and Educational Institution* (New York, 1915), p. 506. Goodsell was on the faculty of Teachers College, Columbia University.

however, who favored welfare legislation, industrial reforms, and a cautious support of eugenics (Goodsell was later to become director of the Eugenics Society) had his complete respect.

Goodsell's support of political progressivism was tempered only by his faith in education, for he believed that legislation alone would never solve the family problem. He proposed a dual effort to improve the conditions of family life through various reforms, while at the same time raising its moral tone by better training in sex hygiene, and imbuing youth with a "fine spirit of idealism." This combination of sex education and traditional moral inspiration was a common recipe; Goodsell heartily agreed with the psychologist and educator G. Stanley Hall that good teaching, by raising standards and developing new interests in young people, tended to "draw off sex feeling" into safer and more constructive channels.[13]

Goodsell exemplifies the limits of the accommodation that respectable authorities were in the process of making to the New Morality. Although he did not acknowledge the importance of eroticism, as was later to become customary, he found it easy to approve of divorce as a necessary social mechanism. If much of what the New Moralists were saying was too bizarre for his taste, he had an unerring instinct for what was safe and assimilable—work for women so long as it did not jeopardize the domestic ideal, motherhood in the usual context, and social reforms that did not significantly alter the existing order. The process of defusing the radicals'

13. Ibid., p. 550.

moral bombshells was clearly well advanced, and Goodsell pointed the way which American society was to
follow in making—to paraphrase the remark of a contemporary educator—women safe for ideas.[14]

Interestingly enough, Elsie Clews Parsons, the only
woman scholar to write on the family with any authority,
was also the most original academician to study these
problems. Her father was the financier Henry Clews,
but she early proved that she was not just another rich
girl, by studying anthropology under Franz Boas and
earning a Ph.D. from Columbia University in 1899.
The first of more than twenty books she was to write in
her long and productive career was *The Family*, a study
outline and textbook for college girls.[15] Although in
every other respect it was typical of this class of texts,

14. One other historian of the family with whom I have not
dealt because his work appeared too late to influence the debate
was Arthur W. Calhoun, *A Social History of the American
Family from Colonial Times to the Present* (3 vols. Cleveland,
1919). Although it remains the standard work on this subject,
it differed from the other histories only in that Calhoun was an
avowed socialist—a fact of which he was extremely proud, but
which had little influence on his scholarship. He was, however,
rather more optimistic than even his progressive colleagues. He
concluded his history with these words: "A new family is inevitable, a family based on the conservation and scientific ad-
ministration of limited resources, on the social ownership of
the instrumentalities of economic production and the universal
enjoyment of the fruits, and on a social democracy devoid of
artificial stratification based on economic exploitation. Such is
the promise of American life, of world life."

15. Elsie Clews Parsons, *The Family* (New York, 1906). In
1940 she was elected president of the American Anthropologi-
cal Association.

it gained a certain notoriety because Mrs. Parsons advocated trial marriages as a good way of putting the American family on a firmer footing. This one suggestion indicated the direction her thought was taking, for she was growing steadily more radical both politically and professionally. In a few more years she was to become a contributor to the *Masses* and other left-wing periodicals, and the author of several unique studies.

In *Fear and Conventionality* Mrs. Parsons argued that too much had been made of marriage as an economic and religious institution. "Is it not," she asked, "in the love of the habitual rather than in the love of property that marriage is rooted?"[16] Although herself a feminist, Mrs. Parsons rejected the feminist dogma which saw marriage as a form of economic exploitation. At a time when the social sciences were still largely pre-Freudian, she had made contact with the new psychology. It seemed to her, therefore, that marriage existed to protect both men and women from dangerous sexual passions and unsettlingly ambiguous personal relationships. In *Social Freedom* she emphasized the social and emotional stability that marriage provided.[17] Society resisted divorce, she contended, not primarily because it regarded divorce as immoral, or out of a heartless unconcern for the victims of bad marriages, but because it feared change and desired personalities to remain constant.

As Mrs. Parsons' observations fell outside the limits of conventional scholarship, they were not taken up by

16. Elsie Clews Parsons, *Fear and Conventionality* (New York, 1914), p. 147.

17. Elsie Clews Parsons, *Social Freedom* (New York, 1915).

her peers; since they went against the grain of most radical thinking about the family, they got little attention from the feminists and their sympathizers who ought properly to have constituted her audience. Few Americans had heard of psychoanalysis and so, while Mrs. Parsons was highly regarded by the advanced New York intelligentsia, her ideas on marriage and the family had little effect on the public debate. Perhaps if she had pulled her scattered ideas together they might have had a greater impact, but on the whole she had gone too far beyond the tolerable level of liberal dissent, represented by Goodsell, to obtain a sympathetic hearing. Thus, in a negative way, she also illustrated the process by which America was coming to terms with divorce and bringing the old orthodoxy into conformity with post-Victorian conditions.

With the obvious exception of Mrs. Parsons, most of the social scientists who dealt with divorce in the Progressive period were notably confident and optimistic. They believed that the family was in transition, but they were sure it would weather the storms of change and certain that in the long run most change was beneficial. E. A. Ross was characteristically assured that divorce worked for progressive ends, but his easy faith was not shared by one of his most eminent students, Charles A. Ellwood.

Ellwood had come under the influence of both Ross and Willcox as an undergraduate at Cornell before going to the University of Chicago, where he studied under John Dewey, W. I. Thomas, and Albion Small. He became the first American sociologist to investigate seriously the uses of psychology, and he was the only

major social scientist before World War I deeply interested in the sociology of the family. Ellwood was also
a devout Christian, and since sociologists were not conspicuous for their piety, his lifelong concern with the
Social Gospel and the relevance of Christian ethics to
social problems was to make him almost unique among
the leaders of his profession.[18]

Given his convictions, it was almost inevitable that
Ellwood would speak for the traditional view of divorce;
given his professional competence it was equally certain
that he would be unable to do so easily or simply. Ellwood enjoyed a curious position indeed. While his stand
was still endorsed by the great majority of middle-class
Americans, he was out of step with most of his own
peers. Having little new in the way of evidence or
method to offer, Ellwood found himself recapitulating
Thwing's arguments, but the popular sociology of 1887
was neither usable nor effective in 1910. Thus Ellwood
believed, with the friends of divorce, in the coming
emergence of a higher form of marriage and, with its
opponents, that contemporary family life was decaying.
He hoped for the limitation of divorces at the same time
that he endorsed the now general conviction that little
good could be expected from restrictive legislation.
These contradictions amply demonstrated the tensions

18. A man of unusual courage and constancy, he insisted
upon using sociology as an instrument of social reform long
after this attitude was frowned upon by his colleagues. Having
become a pacifist following the First World War, he remained
one even after Pearl Harbor at great cost to his reputation.
Harry Elmer Barnes, ed., *An Introduction to the History of
Sociology* (Chicago, 1948), p. 858.

induced by his marginal position while simultaneously exposing the intellectual poverty of the critics of divorce.

Just as Ellwood revealed the substantive bankruptcy of the scientific opposition to divorce, so did he demonstrate its technical inadequacy. Given the paucity of empirical evidence on either side of the question, Ellwood had the best of reasons for undertaking some kind of study which would buttress his feeble case. If such evidence could be found it would be all the more persuasive because of its uniqueness. However, in choosing a point to verify he lighted upon one of the less viable notions—the idea, which Ross had ridiculed only a few years earlier, that divorce was one of the causes of family instability. In 1909, shortly after a meeting of the American Sociological Society that had gone badly for the opponents of divorce, Ellwood wrote to the heads of state reform schools and similar institutions asking how many inmates were the products of broken homes. Naturally he learned that many of them were the children of divorced parents. On the strength of this electric discovery he argued that the restriction of divorce would in some way have a beneficial effect on the number of children in reform schools.[19]

Bereft of new ideas, barren of any usable methodology to advance his minority views, Ellwood occupied an unenviable position, made all the more awkward by his subscription to the liberal ideology of his day. Ellwood believed that the family was a progressive social force, and that history was characterized by the struggle to

19. Charles A. Ellwood, "The Instability of the Family as a Cause of Child Dependence and Delinquency," *Survey*, September 24, 1910, pp. 886–89.

transfer the altruism and solidarity of the family to larger social groupings. "The amount of altruism in every group has a very close relation to the quality of its family life," he insisted. The obvious incompatability of this conviction with his contention that divorce was destroying the family led Ellwood to view the growth of industrialization with something less than the equanimity of his colleagues. Since the growth of industry was thought to make divorces easier by providing women with new occupations, taking them outside the home, and making families less interdependent, Ellwood felt that a choice had to be made. "There can be no sane and stable family life," he wrote, "until we are willing to subordinate the requirements of industry to the requirements of the family."[20]

Having gone this far in questioning a fundamental tenet of the Progressive ethic, Ellwood could go no further. As a serious Christian, he was shocked by divorce, concerned with the future of the family, and suspicious of a social order whose real reforms and immense material gains seemed to produce no corresponding moral growth. As a sociologist, he was weighted down by the sentiment favoring divorce and inhibited by a body of assumptions and beliefs about the nature of society and the function of sociology which he could not wholly discard, but which he could not fully accept without doing damage to his essential convictions. A steady contemplation of the family problem would probably have driven him to despair, but he could take comfort from the gains of the Social Gospel in

20. Charles A. Ellwood, *Sociology and Modern Social Problems* (New York, 1913), p. 82.

189

these years. If he was unable to separate himself from the assumptions that helped make his judgment erratic and sometimes unreliable, he was at least sensitive to the inadequacies of social progressivism, and so, lacking the confidence and serenity of many of his colleagues, he remains rather more interesting than most of them.

The study of the family came of age in 1908, when the American Sociological Society devoted its annual meeting to it. This was only the third time that the ASS had formally convened, and the decision to focus on the family indicated a widespread concern over divorce, even as it foreshadowed a time when the sociology of the family, then hardly recognized as a separate field of study, would become the discipline's largest single branch. Since this meeting opened a new era for the social sciences, there was more than a little irony in the role of William G. Sumner as presiding officer. Sumner, the crusty, aging president of the ASS, was the pre-eminent figure of the old sociological order, the demise of which was in effect being celebrated. As the last and greatest of the old guard, Sumner took it upon himself to inform the convention as to just what these changes meant. His opening address, "The Family and Social Change," reviewed the history of the family and concluded somberly:

> The family has to a great extent lost its position as a conservative institution and has become a field for social change. This, however, is only a part of the decay of doctrines once thought most sound and the abandonment of standards once thought the definition of good order and stability. The

190

changes in social and political philosophy have lowered the family.[21]

We may be sure that Sumner did not control the program committee, for his funereal remarks were followed by a paper which embodied almost everything he loathed about the modern world. Charlotte P. Gilman set the tone for the meeting with a vigorous attack on the traditional family system. She was followed by Charles Zueblin, who called for greater economic freedom for women—a restatement of Mrs. Gilman's central point. One may well imagine Sumner's discomfiture as he listened to these polemics, but the next four papers must have been even more disturbing, for these severely factual reports on the Pittsburgh Survey illustrated in great detail how the factory system was affecting the traditional family. Here, laid out for anyone who cared to see, was graphic evidence that almost everything being said about marriage and the family was simply irrelevant. There is nothing in the record to suggest that this fact made any impression upon those assembled, but the Survey associates had made a start, and in time the sheer weight of evidence would prevail.

All this lay in the future, however; for the time being both sides rehashed their ancient arguments and bombarded one another with stale clichés and empty slogans. George Howard's paper, "Is the Freer Granting of Divorce an Evil?"[22] set off the liveliest debate of the

21. *Papers and Proceedings of the American Sociological Society, 3* (Chicago, 1909), 15. It is now the American Sociological Association.

22. Ibid., pp. 150–60.

meeting. Since Howard's remarks were taken largely from his *History,* they could hardly have stunned his audience. But judging by the angry response of his critics, time had not made them easier to take. Samuel Dike, head of the National League for the Preservation of the Family and the most respected lay authority on divorce, dutifully took issue with Howard. He was followed by a liberal clergyman from Philadelphia, who defended Howard by painting a lurid picture of innocent womanhood freed from the horrors of sexual enslavement by the kindly hand of divorce, until Howard must have wished him in the enemy camp. Fortunately Howard received more useful support from professors Ross and Lichtenberger.

The climax of this exchange came when Walter George Smith stepped forth to assail Howard on traditional religious grounds. Smith, a prominent Catholic layman and socially well-connected Philadelphia lawyer, was active in the movement to establish uniform marriage and divorce laws throughout the country. But twenty years of legal combat in the divorce wars had done nothing to refine his perceptions, much less his temper. He attacked Howard for condoning a social revolution that was destroying the divinely constituted order of things, and accused the scholar of having a "perverted chivalry" which was responsible for America's shockingly lax divorce laws. As if this were not enough, Smith charged him with degrading American civilization and perversely refusing to admit that, while women were made of finer stuff than men, the inequality of the sexes was a fact of nature. To all of which Howard mildly replied that marriage was a purely social institution, "to be freely dealt with by men according to human needs."[23]

The last word was had by Albion W. Small, the University of Chicago's distinguished sociologist, who summed up the three-day meeting with the statement that "this society regarded the American family as on trial with the presumption strongly against it."[24] To this conclusion Professor Small registered an angry dissent. But if Small was wrong in thinking the family's critics were hostile to the institution itself, it was true that from President Sumner on down the ASS believed the family was in serious trouble.

This third meeting of the American Sociological Society, then, indicated fairly clearly where the profession was heading. The meeting was composed of three major groups. The first, and least important, were those who were actively engaged in original research on family problems (although they played a very minor role in the ASS meeting, they were of course the wave of the future in sociology). The dominant group was made up of eminent figures like Howard and Ross, who favored divorce. They professed to be experts, but their expertise was really no greater than that of most well-read laymen. Their position on divorce was more polemical than scientific and, like the earlier emphasis on Christian morality and social order, it was based on personal prejudice rather than impartial research. Who could prove that the family was in transition, or that the divorce rate would decline, or that society benefited when the powers of the state were increased? Yet these notions

23. Ibid., p. 180.
24. Ibid., p. 190.

were repeatedly advanced to justify an optimism that owed more to the time in which they lived than to the research they undertook.

The real losers were, of course, the demoralized opponents of divorce, who found the shift from traditionalism to liberalism bewildering, if not actually sinister. Reporting to his supporters after the meeting, Samuel Dike stressed the importance of establishing a dialogue between the social scientists and the Christian men and women who yet hoped that something could be done about divorce.[25] Dike himself admired and respected the scientists who favored divorce, and long after the breach had become too great to heal he continued to hope for a reconciliation. But a more typical reaction was Walter George Smith's flat refusal to accommodate himself to the new consensus which was forming on the divorce question.

Smith had good reason to fear the teachings of the social scientists. He knew that the fight to secure restrictive legislation had been lost by 1914, even though it had the nominal support of most literate Americans. The change of attitude within the ASS meant that it would be impossible to renew the struggle at some future date. The sociologists probably had little to do with the failure of the legislative campaigns to restrict divorce, but they were beginning to have a significant effect upon public opinion. Slowly the public was coming to accept, not the desirability of divorce, but its inevitability. Partly this was because divorce continued to increase despite the overwhelming sentiment against it. Social scientists

25. Annual Report of the NLPF for 1909 (Boston, 1910).

were more responsible than any other group for the public's recognition of this fact.

The Progressive generation impresses us with its modernity, not because of its style, which was still Victorian in many ways, but because of its changing modes of thought. One of the things responsible for this new way of looking at the world was the emergence of the expert. The proliferation of knowledge and the great strides made in science and technology created new occupations, disciplines, specialties, which grew partly by meeting the needs of an enormous, industrialized population, and partly by absorbing some of the functions previously monopolized by the traditional all-purpose professions. This process, so well described by Richard Hofstadter, was especially hard on the ministry.[26] The clergyman, who had once been the sole arbiter of morality, was now forced to share his office with the social worker, the philanthropist and reformer, and, where the family was concerned, the sociologist. By condoning divorce, sociologists were in effect legitimizing it. However much the churches raged, divorce had been sanctioned by the appropriate authorities, with telling results.

The development of the divorce controversy during the Progressive era offers, therefore, a suggestive example of the way the social sciences influence public opinion. In this instance the change was accomplished by altering the context within which the debate took place. So long as traditional Christian morality was considered the appropriate yardstick for measuring the

26. Richard Hofstadter, *The Age of Reform* (New York, 1955).

effect of divorce, little could be done about the public resistance to it. But once it was conceded that the social effects of divorce were relevant, the opposition virtually disarmed itself. Since no one really knew what the social consequences of divorce were, the whole picture became a good deal murkier, while at the same time the moral absolutes which could be wielded by anyone were replaced by lines of reasoning with which sociologists were far more comfortable than their critics. The real victory won by the social scientists involved, then, not reversing public opinion on divorce, but moving the battle to ground of their own choosing, and thereby rendering the largest part of the traditional argument obsolete.

While claiming that divorce was really a technical problem that ought to be resolved by the appropriate experts, the social scientists also infused their arguments with a certain moral quality, which was not only inevitable, considering that in the Progressive period every public question was accounted to have a moral dimension, but doubtlessly effective as well. However, since other groups were defending divorce on moral grounds with no great success, the high moral tone of the scientific argument probably was not crucial.

The invocation of professional jurisdiction over sensitive public issues is now much more common than it was during the Progressive period, but the men who began this custom lived in a very different world from those who make such claims today. Particularly striking was their willingness to engage in the rough and tumble of public debate. They were confident that what they knew was a sufficient guide to policy and that what they studied was of immediate relevance to society's problems. Sociology was still more of a speculative than an empirical discipline, although the professional training of sociologists was hardly less exacting than it is now. Standard English was their instrument of communication, and so they were able, as well as willing, to make contact with the public in a direct and intelligible way that is closed to many contemporary scientists.

Finally, they were separated from us by almost half a century of experience. They could believe, as we cannot, in the perfectibility of society and the inevitability of its progress. Lacking the scars and inhibitions that afflict social scientists today, no less than other men, they enjoyed a clear and relatively simple faith in themselves and the possibilities of their age—an animating vision that war, the threat of war, and fifty scarring years of social change have made unimaginably remote.

The liberal rationale that evolved in the twentieth century owed a great deal to the scientific arguments constructed by Howard and company, but it had its own sources as well. It borrowed from both the scientists and the New Moralists, yet its advocates were more overtly moralistic than the scientists and more conservative than the sexual radicals. They were, in fact, often quite close in other respects to the critics of divorce, whom they resembled in more ways than they did the New Moralists. But they had, for reasons which seem unrelated to class, caste, or status, accepted a different view of the social consequences and ethical content of divorce.

7

THE CASE FOR DIVORCE

While the liberal defenders of the right to divorce were neither more intelligent nor more effective than their opposition, they presented a sharp contrast in several respects with the conservatives we have previously considered. Although few in number and completely unorganized, liberals were confident that the winds of change blew in their direction. Consequently their morale was good, their spirits high, and their polemical literature clearer and better integrated than the conservatives'. Since divorces were becoming more frequent without anyone's help, liberals had no need of defensive alliances like those the conservatives tried to form. We can, therefore, move directly to a consideration of liberal and other related opinions on the divorce question.

One would like to begin with an intensive study of the radical position on divorce, but, alas, radicals did not think much about divorce at all. Orthodox socialists were interested in winning elections, and there was no profit to be gained from espousing marginal and potentially explosive issues. Moreover, social democrats like Victor Berger and Morris Hillquit did not entertain ideas about sexual morality that were shockingly different from those of most Americans. The only people on the left who really thought much about sexual problems were the anarchists and the young rebels.

Neither of these two groups cared especially for divorce as an issue, because it seemed to them a part of the bourgeois social system that they proposed to wipe out altogether. Divorce was only a reform, an accommodation with a hopelessly corrupt institution. It took place in the same manner and within the same legal context as marriage. The reverse of marriage was not divorce but nonmarriage. No one argued this more forcefully than Emma Goldman, who maintained that sexual morality was only another instrument of capitalist exploitation. Prostitution continued because the exactions of the profit system forced women to sell themselves to live, while marriage condemned those who escaped the streets to breed and rear swarms of children to satisfy the hungry mills' insatiable appetite for fresh labor. Only free love, birth control, and the social revolution could break this vicious system and the degenerate Christian morality which supported it.

The anarchists made a brave attempt to practice what they preached; to create prototypes of the coming good society within the bad old one. Emma Goldman's own life triumphantly vindicated her principles, even though her contemptuous refusal to marry gave her a notoriety

199

which later helped the authorities extradite her.[1] However, most anarchists lacked her strength and resolution. Their attempts to shed the constraints of bourgeois morality were productive of the most bizarre confusions imaginable. Hutchins Hapgood, a journalist and aesthete with many friendships among American radicals, said of the Chicago anarchists:

> The unnatural idealism of the group made it obligatory on the part of the male not only to tolerate but to encourage the occasional impulse of the wife or sweetheart toward some other man, or, on the part of the woman a more than tolerant willingness to have her man follow out a brief impulse with some other woman.[2]

The result was that these people, who had what Hapgood called a "certain pathetic dignity," experienced not only the pangs of jealousy, but torrents of guilt inspired by the surfacing of such an archaic and antisocial emotion.

More influential than the relatively humorless and glamourless anarchists were the brilliant young partisans of what Henry F. May has termed the Rebellion. The attack on traditional art, culture, and morality

---

1. For a much fuller account, see Richard Drinnon's splendid biography of Miss Goldman, *Rebel in Paradise* (Chicago, 1961). A typical expression of her views is the pamphlet "Victims of Morality and the Failure of Christianity" (New York, 1913).

2. Hutchins Hapgood, *A Victorian in the Modern World* (New York, 1939), p. 202.

which centered in Greenwich Village was in full swing by 1912, and the rebels, with their glorification of instinct, spontaneity, pleasure, and personal freedom, were naturally attracted to free love and repelled by marriage. The fathers and mothers who feared that their offspring might be deflowered in the Village had good cause for alarm. But this was before narcotics and homosexuality came to Greenwich Village, and its affairs did have an essential innocence about them. The Rebellion had little use for chastity, but cared greatly about such things as honesty, fidelity, stable personal relationships, and revolutionary politics.

Led by the *Masses,* the rebels cheerfully flouted capitalist morality's most sacred tenets. Edited by Max Eastman and his assistant Floyd Dell, the *Masses* was as irreverent and unconventional as the censor permitted. Gay nudes danced through its pages, and, while the magazine lasted, prostitutes, birth control, and hedonism did not lack a champion, nor organized religion and the institution of marriage a foe. This occurred at a time when Anthony Comstock was driving Margaret Sanger out of the country, and had already suppressed an art students' magazine for reproducing an inoffensive academic nude. The *Masses* suggested, rather than articulated, its contributors' ideas on sexual freedom, but even so it strained community tolerance to the very limits.[3]

3. For a representative selection of the magazine's contributions to the revolution in morals see William L. O'Neill, ed., *Echoes of Revolt: The Masses, 1911–17* (Chicago, 1966); see also Henry F. May, *The End of American Innocence* (New York, 1959).

While the *Masses* was proclaiming its version of the New Freedom throughout the land, its editors were demonstrating by their own actions precisely what they had in mind. The Village had freed itself from wedlock only to replace the old slavery with a way of life that was sometimes hardly distinguishable from marriage itself, except for being a good deal more exacting. The idea was for a man and woman to live together as if they were married, while shunning the humiliating legal forms that turned love to bondage. Floyd Dell's three-year affair was the pride of the Village, for it justified the Rebellion's contention that free love could be fully as stable as marriage. When Dell finally married another girl and announced that he had been in favor of marriage all along, it was, Joseph Freeman later wrote, "almost as if William Z. Foster had come out openly in favor of private profit. It meant practically the sexual counterrevolution."[4] Freeman may have overstated the case, but undoubtedly many Villagers felt that Dell had let the cause down.

The Village understood that one had to live in the world, but the proper form for gracefully conceding to social pressure was to make clear that one was marrying out of necessity and not conviction. When Max Eastman married Ida Rauh, they informed the world that although they did not approve of marriage, they were too adult to make a fuss about it. The bride allegedly said that "it was with us a placating of convention, because if

4. Joseph Freeman, *An American Testament* (New York, 1936), p. 245. Dell himself vigorously denies this charge, claiming that his views on love and marriage did not change, and that his reputation as a proponent of free love was undeserved.

we had gone counter to the convention it would have been too much of a bother for the gain."[5]

The innocent Rebellion did not last very long, but by the time America entered the war in a frenzy of patriotism that destroyed both the Rebellion and the radical movement with which it was allied, the moral climate of America had been permanently altered. The anarchists and rebels may have had a negative effect on the cause of free divorce; they alarmed conservatives and embarrassed liberals, who had to continually dissociate themselves from the sexual left. On the other hand, it is possible that, by espousing free love, the radicals made divorce seem a comparatively mild response to the marriage problem. In any case, one cannot understand the struggles over divorce without bearing in mind that both liberals and conservatives were looking over their shoulders at the well-publicized, if usually misreported, activities of the radicals.

The cause of free divorce needed, as do all controversial proposals, the support of respected and conventional public figures. Such a man was Carroll D. Wright. His endorsement of divorce in 1891 was an event of some consequence, because of his prominence and because he voiced what were to become the principal themes of the case for divorce.

Wright was one of those able public servants whose reputations do not long survive their deaths. Despite obscure origins and an indifferent education, he was successively a Colonel of Volunteers in the Civil War,

5. Quoted from a newspaper interview by Max Eastman, *Enjoyment of Living* (New York, 1948), p. 380.

a State Senator, and then Massachusetts' first Commissioner of Labor Statistics before becoming the first United States Commissioner of Labor in 1885. His zeal and efficiency at a time when the government service was notably deficient in both made him something of a sacred cow. Running an honest and effective bureau was no mean feat in the Gilded Age, and Carroll Wright would merit the respect of posterity if he had done nothing else. But he has at least three other claims on our attention.

According to his biographer, Wright laid the foundations for much of the labor legislation of the Progressive era through his exhaustive statistical studies.[6] He was always sympathetic to labor's needs, and distinguished himself when he was appointed by Grover Cleveland to the commission investigating the great Pullman strike. While many avowed friends of labor were running for cover, Wright defended the strikers and got the only bad press of his life, even while he gained an honorable place in American history. And, finally, he was almost the first public man since Robert Dale Owen openly to defend the right of divorce.

There was little in Wright's background to explain his position on divorce. He was the son of a Universalist minister and became in time president of the Unitarian Association. But many Unitarians opposed divorce, and Wright was a friend of Samuel Dike and other critics of the institution. His supervision of the government report on marriage and divorce brought him close to the problem, however, and while the report drew no conclusions

6. James Leiby, *Carroll Wright and Labor Reform: The Origin of Labor Statistics* (Cambridge, 1960).

from its data, Wright did. He decided to defend divorce before the social sciences had made his position respectable. Curiously, he was not severely criticized for his stand, but he had no way of knowing in advance that he would not be injured for what he said. Indeed, it may have taken more courage for him to support divorce than to defend the American Railway Union.

Wright declared for divorce at the Unitarian convention in the summer of 1891. He argued that Jesus had not intended to forbid divorce; that the son of God was not a lawmaker but a formulator of general principles; that divorce was a secular institution and therefore the state's responsibility; and that the state had to deal with men as they were rather than as religion would like them to be. Wright spoke as a man of affairs as well as the first expert on divorce with scientific credentials, but he touched also upon matters of theology and church history. He accused Christianity of discriminating against women and demanded an end to the mischievous and degrading Pauline moral code. It was blasphemous, he said, to call "the union of a beast and an angel, or of two beasts, a sacrament on the ground that God hath joined them together."[7] Not God but man was responsible for bad marriages. A few years later he repeated himself at greater length and concluded with a rare burst of eloquence:

> The pressure for divorce finds its impetus outside of laws, outside of our institutions, outside of our theology; it springs from the rebellion of the human

7. Reprinted in Wilbur Crafts, *Practical Christian Sociology* (4th ed., New York, 1907), p. 451.

heart against that slavery which binds in the cruelest bonds human beings who have, by their haste, their want of wisdom, or the intervention of friends, missed the divine purpose as well as the civil purpose of marriage.[8]

In stressing the secular character of marriage and divorce, the irrelevance or erroneous interpretation of traditional Christian teachings, and especially the importance of divorce for women, Wright outlined what was to become the standard defense of divorce. He was not by any means the first person to articulate these ideas. For longer than most Americans could remember, Elizabeth Cady Stanton had stood for free divorce, having advocated it at a woman's rights convention as early as 1860. In 1861 she spoke before the New York Senate's Judiciary Committee and ceaselessly editorialized in her short-lived weekly paper, *The Revolution,* on behalf of freer divorce laws. She persevered in her campaign as opposition rose and the woman's rights movement split, until the Beecher-Tilton affair exploded in 1872 and forced a strategic retreat.[9]

8. Carroll D. Wright, *Outline of Practical Sociology* (New York, 1898), p. 176.

9. Blake, *The Road to Reno,* Chapters seven and eight, gives a full account of this scandal. Briefly, Henry Ward Beecher was having an affair with Elizabeth Tilton, the wife of Theodore Tilton, a liberal editor, friend of Mrs. Stanton, and supporter of more liberal divorce laws. The affair became public knowledge when the reckless and beautiful free-love advocate Victoria Woodhull struck back at her critics by writing a lurid account of Beecher's relations with Mrs. Tilton in her journal

Mrs. Stanton's conviction that women needed divorce was reinforced by this scandal, and she raised her voice again as soon as she could. When the populistic *Arena* was founded in 1890, she had at last an opportunity to say things the general press was reluctant to publish and the suffrage press afraid to touch. With her customary verve and eloquence she blasted the marriage contract as an instrument for the oppression of women, declared that incompatibility (a favorite target of conservatives) was the best reason in the world for getting a divorce, and scoffed at the conservatives who thought the whole institution of marriage was "about to topple on their heads" simply because "a new type of womanhood has been developed demanding larger freedom in the mar-

---

Woodhull's and Claflin's Weekly. Beecher's friends and admirers successfully defended him by smearing not only the vulnerable Mrs. Woodhull, but all her associates as well, including the militant suffragists like Mrs. Stanton. Although the conservative backlash retarded the cause of free divorce for several decades and may have handicapped the suffrage movement, Mrs. Stanton characteristically refused to blame Mrs. Woodhull. On April 1, 1872, she wrote her old friend and co-worker Lucretia Mott to explain why she refused to add her voice to the general hue and cry. "We have already women enough sacrificed to this sentimental, hypocritical prating about purity, without going out of our way to increase the number. Women have crucified the Mary Wollstonecrafts, the Fanny Wrights and the George Sands of all ages. . . . Let us end this ignoble record and henceforth stand by womanhood. If this present woman must be crucified, let men drive the spikes." Stanton and Blatch, eds., *Elizabeth Cady Stanton as Revealed in Her Letters, Diary and Reminiscences* (2 vols. New York, 1922), *2*, 27.

riage relation, justice, liberty, and equality under the law."[10]

Mrs. Stanton, never one to spare the churches' feelings (she thought Robert Ingersoll one of the greatest men of the century and embarrassed the suffrage movement by publishing an attack on Christianity called *The Woman's Bible*), took up her cudgels again shortly before her death in 1902. She attacked the movement for uniform divorce laws as an effort to eliminate divorce colonies, which indeed it was, and declared that the "states which have liberal divorce laws are to women what Canada was to the slaves before Emancipation." Observing that "we can trace the icy fingers of the Canon law in all our most sacred relations," she concluded: "Marriage should be regarded as a civil contract, entirely under the jurisdiction of the state. The less latitude the Church has in our temporal affairs, the better."[11]

Mrs. Stanton, although hardly a New Moralist, was nearly unique among Victorian women for her charitable view of the sexual habits of public men. During the Parnell affair she was appalled by the ignoble enthusiasm women displayed. It seemed to her that women damaged their own chances by insisting that chastity was indispensable to a useful career. She pointed out that by this standard they would have to disavow not only many of their greatest stateswomen, like Cleopatra

10. Elizabeth Cady Stanton, "Divorce vs. Domestic Warfare," *Arena, 1* (1890), 568.

11. Elizabeth Cady Stanton, "Are Homogeneous Divorce Laws in All the States Desirable?" *North American Review, 170* (1900), 405–09.

and Queen Elizabeth the First, but such notable contributors to life and art as George Sand, Frances Wright, Mary Wollstonecraft, and George Eliot. It was not by hounding men, she insisted, that women would establish a higher moral order, but by struggling to win their own freedom from ignorance and dependency. With many radicals, Mrs. Stanton believed that the conventional sexual morality was one of the means by which women were kept in their place, but she also had an appreciation for the vagaries of human nature far more characteristic of other centuries than the one in which she lived. "We are all," she observed, "what law, custom, and public sentiment have made us, alike fragmentary, some truth and some error bound up in every human soul."[12]

The *Arena's* pages were open to Mrs. Stanton because its editor, the volatile Benjamin O. Flower, was a passionate believer in divorce. Something of an eccentric, equally enthusiastic about psychic phenomena and social justice, he supported divorce for the same reasons he took part in the purity crusades which periodically agitated the American conscience.[13] Conservatives accused divorce liberals of being pleasure-mad sensualists, but in fact the reverse was more often true. Flower, like many feminists, saw divorce as a way of freeing women from sex rather than as a way of expanding their sexual horizons. With Mrs. Stanton he believed that the carnal

12. Elizabeth Cady Stanton, "Patriotism and Chastity," *Westminster Review, 135* (1891), 3.

13. For a biographical sketch of this curious figure see Allen J. Matusow, "The Mind of B. O. Flower," *New England Quarterly, 34* (1961), 492–509.

passions were inherited characteristics, and consequently the laws that forced women to remain married to lustful men and bear them children passed on the taint to each new generation. Liberal divorce laws alone could stop the production of these "children of lust."

Flower waged a constant campaign over the years to make woman "the Monarch of the marriage bed." Only by giving women power over their own bodies could the injustices perpetuated by "ignorance, thoughtlessness, and the weakness born of centuries of allegiance to false standards and low ideals, the all-pervading conspiracy of silence, and woman's inequality before the law" be ended.[14] Repeatedly he observed that prostitutes were freer than the wife who was compelled by law to endure nightly "the unholy passion of her master." Sex education and free divorce were the tools which would free women from sexual slavery and create a new generation of pure, healthy men and women.

While Mrs. Stanton was extraordinarily tolerant about the affairs of others, like many feminists she regarded sexual relations with a marked lack of enthusiasm. Her unmarried colleagues were celibate from choice as much as necessity, and in time their point of view became sufficiently respectable even for the circumspect *Good Housekeeping*. In 1914 that pillar of conventional morality allowed playwright Jesse Lynch Williams to ask of the unhappily married woman, "Is allowing herself to be owned body and soul by a man she loathes doing right?" Apparently it was not, for Williams went on delicately to suggest that "that seems

14. Benjamin O. Flower, "Prostitution Within the Marriage Bond," *Arena, 13* (1895), 68.

rather like a dishonorable institution more ancient than marriage."[15] It is a little amusing that the Victorians, who were in so many ways squeamish about things sexual, should have considered voluntary intercourse a radical notion, but in truth they did and so lent substance to the liberal contention that conservatives were the real sensualists.

This charge was most forcefully delivered by Theodore Schroeder in the *Arena*. Schroeder had been a Utah attorney for twelve years and achieved some disstinction as an antipolygamy crusader. Benjamin Flower thought that Schroeder's most original contribution stemmed from his familiarity with sex psychology— particularly with the writings of Ellis and Krafft-Ebing.[16] Schroeder's special interests led him to believe that the church fathers were victims of "erotophobia." He argued that asceticism and salaciousness flowed from the same source—asceticism being essentially an effort

15. Jesse Lynch Williams, "The New Marriage," *Good Housekeeping, 52* (1914), 184.

16. Schroeder was a single-taxer, free-thinker, and an amateur sex-psychologist. He was forced to leave Utah because of his assertion, among other things, that Joseph Smith was an abortionist. But he is best known for helping in 1911 to found the Free Speech League, of which he was the secretary and moving spirit. He was associated in this work with such men as Brand Whitlock, Lincoln Steffens, Bolton Hall, and Hutchins Hapgood. A believer in free speech as an absolute right, he defended the Wobblies, *Mother Earth,* and other radical organs, and was a devoted foe of Comstock and comstockery. During the First War he was, he says, a "philosophical slacker." Theodore Schroeder, *A New Concept of Liberty: From an Evolutionary Psychologist* (Berkeley Heights, N.J., 1940).

to make a virtue of emasculation. The Christian monks and nuns, he continued, suffered from erotic hallucinations that they interpreted as supernatural experiences and that were "accepted by the mob as a sign of the presence of God."[17]

Bringing the argument up-to-date, Schroeder wrote:

> This "asceticism with limited liability" is still popular among certain narrow purists. Its influence upon our president who is always verbally strenuous induced him to say that the "wilfully barren woman has no place in a sane, healthy, and vigorous community." Obsessed by the necessity of finding an excuse for any sensual indulgence, he forgets that the barren woman may do more good than her fecund sisters.[18]

These twisted motives influenced divorce restriction, Schroeder maintained, in that "sex-mad purists" wanted the grounds for divorce restricted to a single cause. Adultery as an infringement of sex monopoly was the only thing they recognized as destroying a marriage.

If most liberals came to support divorce because of their feminist sympathies, feminism was far less useful than the Higher Criticism in making a case for divorce. The social scientists may have been more influential in persuading Americans of the need for divorce, but it was essential that the opposition of most church leaders, theologians, moralists, and biblical scholars be undermined if divorce was to become legitimate. The handful

17. Theodore Schroeder, "The Impurity of Divorce Suppression," *Arena, 33* (1905), 143.
18. Ibid., p. 144.

of scholars who challenged the theological consensus rendered, therefore, an indispensable service to the cause. Aside from whatever intrinsic merit their arguments possessed, they made divorce seem more like a moot question on which experts disagreed than a hideous breach of moral discipline.

The most ambitious effort to show that Jesus had not intended to abolish divorce was made by Ernest D. Burton, a professor at the University of Chicago and the editor of *Biblical World*. Burton believed that one could make few definite statements about the position of divorce in Jewish society because of the scanty evidence. Divorce was probably comparatively rare, it was a private and not a legal process, and no one disputed the right of husbands to make use of it. Although the scribes disagreed on what was adequate cause for a divorce, the actual decision was the husband's to make. Apparently the right to remarry was recognized.[19]

After establishing these points, Burton went on to suggest the importance of the biblical precedents for modern students of divorce.[20] He prefaced these conclusions by saying that since the central doctrine of Christ's teaching was love, Christ could not have intended his apparent prohibition of divorce to be taken literally. What Christ must have meant was that the question of divorce and remarriage should always be decided in terms of what would produce the most good

19. Ernest D. Burton, "Some Biblical Teaching Concerning Divorce," *Biblical World, 29* (1907), 121–27.

20. Ernest D. Burton, "The Biblical Teaching Concerning Divorce II: New Testament Teaching," *Biblical World, 29* (1907), 191–200.

213

in each individual case. At this point Burton, seemingly without realizing it, had left the field of biblical scholarship and embarked on a discussion that owed more to George Howard than to Matthew, Mark, Luke, or John. In this vein he made five points which he thought should be applied to divorce: (1) The decision to divorce should be the husband's. (2) Divorce laws ought to provide for the care of the wife and children, as biblical laws did not. (3) Only "right ideals" could end divorce. (4) The effort of society ought to be directed toward the elimination of easy marriages. (5) Divorces should not be granted by the courts, but by boards of five men and women who would grant divorces according to the merits of each case. Burton concluded his remarks by expressing the conventional hope that education would prevent divorces.

A little earlier, while protesting against the "wave of virtue" that periodically swept the nation in respect to divorce, Norman Jones had argued that Christians were misreading the Bible when they attempted to use it to suppress divorce.[21] Jesus had not spoken against divorce; rather he objected to the Near Eastern custom of arbitrary divorce. Modern divorce was in no sense comparable to the evil Jesus deplored, because it was enshrined in the civil law and included safeguards for women which the Mosaic law did not. Much the same position was taken by "E. H. B." in the *Overland Monthly*. He cited Paul, Tertullian, Origen, and other church fathers to support his contention that Jesus had not intended to abolish divorce, but only to reform the

21. Norman Jones, "Marriage and Divorce: The Letter of the Law," *North American Review, 181* (1905), 597–602.

divorce laws of Israel, which permitted husbands to put aside their wives for trivial reasons.[22]

These arguments were by no means original. Thomas S. Potwin had written as early as 1892 that Jesus' statements on divorce could only be understood in terms of the audience to which they were addressed.[23] A careful reading of the Greek texts of Matthew had convinced him that Jesus had reacted against the ancient world's universal custom of arbitrary personal divorce. By "man" in the phrase "let no man put asunder," Jesus meant "husband." He had not established a new law of marriage, Potwin maintained, because he believed marriage was a human custom that had to be dealt with in human terms. Given the obscurity of the New Testament texts on this point, Potwin enjoined lawmakers to frame their ordinances in terms of the general welfare and not on the basis of what Jesus was thought to have said.

In 1904 the *North American Review* published a scathing attack on Bishop Doane's views by the classicist and Bible scholar William G. Ballentine. Ballentine was responding to an article by the Bishop in *Harper's Weekly* in which Doane had cited a biblical injunction against divorce. Ballentine pointed out that the same passage contained the admonition to "resist not evil." How, Ballentine asked, were Christians to know which commandment to obey and which to ignore? The truth was, he continued, that "even if all thoughtful Christian men were today united in a resolute

22. E. H. B., "The Bible and Divorce: What is the Teaching of Scripture Upon the Subject?" *Overland*, 25 (1895), 362–67.

23. Thomas S. Potwin, "Should Marriage Be Indissoluble?" *New Englander and Yale Review*, 56 (1892), 40–50.

purpose of conformity to the letter of Scripture the path of duty would be far from plain."[24]

Ballentine described the life of Jesus as a struggle against Talmudic literalism:

> During his whole life, he fought against the tyranny of mere words, and for the lordship of the present living spiritual man. In his discourse he suggested great truths by parables, by questions, by metaphors, by paradoxes, by hyperboles, by every device that could elude the semblance of fixed judicial formulas. It is the irony of history that such language should be seized upon for statute law.[25]

Ballentine concluded by observing that Jesus often broke his own "hyperbolic" prescriptions and that he was in the habit of forgiving what the modern legalists were unable to excuse. Ballentine warned Bishop Doane and the other prohibitionists not to compress the great spiritual truths of Jesus' teachings into mere law.

The effect of this attack on the literal application of the New Testament was to persuade some Christians that divorce was not contrary to the teachings of Jesus. Edward Sandford Martin, magazine editor and essayist, was one such man. In the early nineties Martin had aligned himself with the divorce conservatives. Later, however, he published a volume of essays appropriately titled *In a New Century* (1908), in which he reversed himself on divorce. By this time he had come to believe

24. William G. Ballentine, "The Hyperbolic Teachings of Jesus," *North American Review, 179* (1904), 452–53.
25. Ibid., p. 447.

that Jesus only meant that divorce was a morally inferior solution to marital difficulties, not an immoral solution. Jesus, he now saw, recognized that all men were not of sufficient strength to obey his prescription, and American divorce laws were in harmony with Jesus' desire for charity and justice.

Despite the assistance that they received from some ministers and theologians, many liberals remained critical of Christianity in general and the Catholic Church in particular. The anti-Catholicism of these liberals was a natural response to the Roman Church's leadership in the struggle against divorce. In 1908 the Papal decree *Ne Temere* became effective in the United States, provoking fresh outbursts from liberal Protestants. In 1912 Lewis Stockton of the Episcopal Church described the decree in these terms:[26]

> The *Ne Temere* decree is said to have been enacted as a measure designed to check abuses and to safeguard the sacredness of marriage, but it would seem that its effect would inevitably be, in countries not wholly Roman Catholic, to lead to the waging of a covert war against human liberty in its most intimate private relation.[26]

Although Stockton objected to the decree because he believed it was not in keeping with American principles of civil liberty and the separation of church and state, he also resented its use of the sacramental theory. Marriage, he contended, was made sacred by the love of the

26. Lewis Stockton, *Marriage: Considered from Legal and Ecclesiastical Viewpoints* (Buffalo, 1912), p. 31.

married couple. Its sacramental character was not, as Catholics believed, inherent in the ceremony itself.

Liberals sometimes accused Catholics of prohibiting divorce in order to strengthen the power of the Church. Others questioned the consequences of Catholic doctrine rather than the motives behind it. Roland D. Sawyer, for example, believed that the countries where the Roman Church had successfully banned divorce were the most immoral in the world.[27] Although criticisms of the Roman Church's position on divorce were often voiced by liberals, most of them (with the exception of Benjamin Flower) refrained from the xenophobic attacks on foreigners and Catholics that were common during the 1890s and early 1900s. Liberal criticisms were usually directed against the Christian Church as a whole, which they considered to be oppressive and reactionary on the divorce question. Many agreed with Flower that marriage was an essentially secular institution.

Dr. Woods Hutchinson, a leading eugenicist, believed that the Christian Church was only one of a number of institutions responsible for the unnatural rigidity of marital customs: "Institutions and morals are the result of experiences and are both rational and plastic, like everything else that is alive; the moment the law or the Church crystallizes them fossilisation sets in."[28] Eugeni-

27. Roland D. Sawyer, "The Failure of Organized Religion in the Treatment of the Marriage Institution," *Arena, 39* (1908), 681–84.

28. Woods Hutchinson, "Evolutionary Ethics of Marriage and Divorce," *Contemporary Review, 88* (1905), 398.

cists, like all the others, disagreed on the divorce question.[29] But Hutchinson was not alone in blaming "churchly fanaticism" for the rigidity of contemporary divorce laws. The trouble with marriage was not that too many people were getting divorces; rather too many people were marrying at the behest of "fat-witted priests" instead of in response to obvious racial needs.

A physician, public health expert, and pioneer medical publicist who was to become president of the American Academy of Medicine, Dr. Hutchinson believed that marriage was a biological institution, whose purpose, the efficient rearing of children, was corrupted by religious dogmatizing. Himself a Quaker, he urged women not to practice "the slave virtues of forbearance, long-suffering and other such dog-like qualities" when they were married to an undesirable. "Any woman," he continued, "who willingly and knowingly bears a child to a drunken or criminal husband is herself committing a crime against the race."[30]

The divorce laws that made it difficult for women to shed partners with mental, moral, or physical weaknesses seemed to Hutchinson uneugenic and subversive of the real interests of the race. He held the church responsible for this miserable state of affairs, as did an anonymous writer in the *Forum* who charged that the church had originally been opposed to marriage altogether. However, marriage's continuing popularity forced the church to take it over and convert it into a

29. For a criticism of divorce on eugenic grounds see Jirah D. Buck, *The Soul and Sex in Education, Morals, Religion, and Adolescence* (Cincinnati, 1912), p. 150.

30. Hutchinson, "Evolutionary Ethics," p. 409.

sacrament, thereby making men so miserable that Martin Luther had to rise up and free them from it.[31]

Elizabeth Carpenter resented the Christian Church because she believed it was a reactionary force in the world. Replying to one of Bishop Doane's attacks on divorce, she chided him for failing to see that the most important truth of modern life was the "large, sane sense, of an ever-progressing moral ideal in the great world." She contrasted the Church's continuing efforts to oppress the individual with the state's recognition of the social utility of divorce—a recognition based on the experience of centuries. Miss Carpenter's more-in-sorrow-than-in-anger tone and her assumption that divorce was justified by the "proven tendency of man to continually elevate and refine his physical, mental, moral and spiritual condition" were shared by many liberals.[32]

Nothing so divided liberals and conservatives as the relationship of happiness to marriage. As we have already seen, conservatives invariably felt that happiness, if it came at all, was a bonus which no one had a right to expect. In this they reflected the Calvinist belief that real happiness came from doing one's duty, for once married, one's duty was to stay married at all costs. Nothing was more revolutionary about the liberals' defense of divorce than their insistence that happiness was a necessary condition of marriage. This was not just a technical quibble about the meaning of scriptural passages, but a challenge to the central thesis of the old morality. If

31. "Our Incestuous Marriages," *Forum, 54* (1915), 641–60.
32. Elizabeth Carpenter, "Marriage and Divorce From a Lay Point of View," *North American Review, 181* (1905), 123–24.

unhappiness was a good reason for divorce, why was it not a good reason for changing sexual partners with or without marriage? Indeed, conservatives were quite right to think that there was almost no area of life which would remain unaffected if such a frankly hedonistic moral standard became acceptable. Most liberals had no intention of bringing down the temple; they were not New Moralists, but few things better prepared the ground for the new sexual norms than this particular argument.

Here again Carroll Wright led the way by asking "What is marriage for, if not for happiness, the divine end of all institutions, when sought in its broadest outlines?"[33] Wright believed that unhappy marriages frustrated the purpose of the institution, and he assured his readers that in some cases the divine end was better achieved by a divorce than by attempting to prop up a ruined marriage.

Many liberals believed that under certain circumstances divorce could be a highly moral act. However, this approval was not as often extended to remarriage. Where remarriages were concerned, the most common argument was that if divorced people were not allowed to remarry, many of them would fall into sin. The *Independent* repeatedly advanced this thesis. In 1910 it editorialized against the Episcopal Church's House of Bishops for attempting again to secure a prohibition of remarriage and congratulated the House of Deputies for refusing to allow such a revision. Noting that "marriage is an institution created for the benefit of man:

33. Carroll D. Wright, *Outline of Sociology*, p. 170.

not man for the sake of marriage," the *Independent* warned against laws which encouraged immorality. "Even for the guilty party it is safer for society that he should be held by such restraints as marriage can provide than that he should be left an utter menace to society."[34]

A few months later the *Independent* printed an article by an Episcopal clergyman reflecting the thinking of many in the House of Deputies, which had consistently refused to support the bishops' efforts at prohibiting remarriage. The Reverend William E. Barton insisted that Christ's words on the subject did not amount to legislation. He pointed to the many successful remarriages he was familiar with, and reminded his readers that "remarriage is better than fornication."[35] The *Independent's* attitude toward the whole issue was summed up by its editors in 1916, when they observed:

> The American rate of one divorce for twelve marriages is deplored and denounced on all sides. Yet when one knows intimately the causes which impel any particular couple to separate he usually comes to the conclusion that it would be wrong to themselves and to the community for them to continue living together.[36]

The moderate tone of these statements is a little misleading, since they were written at a time when it was

34. The *Independent* first supported divorce in 1870. Blake, *The Road to Reno,* p. 110; "Divorce," October 20, 1910, p. 941.

35. William E. Barton, "The Minister's Attitude Toward Divorce," *Independent,* December 29, 1910, p. 1454.

36. "Divorce Evil," *Independent,* May 1, 1916, p. 161.

becoming clear that the campaign against divorce would fail. Earlier, when the campaign against divorce was at its height, the *Independent* had spoken with a louder voice and a sharper tongue. In 1900 the magazine condemned prohibitions against divorce as "anti-scriptural" and said they tended to "encourage license and immorality." A few months after this the Committee of Twelve at the Episcopal Church's triennial convention recommended that the canon on divorce be revised to forbid all remarriages, and the *Independent* explosively described this proposal as "unjust, tyrannical and wholly vicious."[37]

With this argument the sober *Independent* found itself in strange company. The proposition that prohibition encouraged immorality had earlier been advanced by America's most famous skeptic, the redoubtable Colonel Robert Ingersoll. Writing in the *North American Review's* first divorce symposium in 1889, Ingersoll had blistered the prohibitionists for stimulating vice, penalizing virtue, and weakening America's homes. Appealing to that robust ethnocentrism which has always marked this country's approach to social problems, Colonel Ingersoll asked his readers whether or not those countries which prohibited divorce and remarriage (Ireland, Spain, etc.) exhibited a more refined moral sense than the United States.

Theodore Schroeder achieved the same effect by turning his pre-Freudian spotlight on the divorce prohibitionists. He caustically observed that anyone not warped

37. "Forbidding to Marry," *Independent,* May 25, 1900, p. 1271; "Forbidding to Remarry," *Independent,* November 22, 1900, p. 2818.

by "sex-inversion" would be able to see that keeping couples together after the marriage had been destroyed was a form of prostitution, while forbidding remarriage incited concubinage and other vices. Calling for a wider public understanding of the principles of sex psychology, Schroeder urged his readers to unite for a defense of the right of everyone to a happy life through easy divorce and remarriage.

A month after Schroeder's observations the *Arena* published a more restrained statement of this position by a southern professor of education. Professor H. G. Hawn wrote that sex was the major reason for marriage and that the Episcopalian convention in Boston had ignored this point in urging ministers not to remarry divorced persons. A divorce, he insisted, was more holy than a bad marriage.[38] This was also the position of Hugo Munsterberg, Harvard's great psychologist, who wrote of divorce:

> The case lies in the democratic spirit of self-determination which wants to loosen bonds that individuals no longer freely recognize. It might be said that this is a higher individual morality which ends marriage when it has lost its inner sanctity.[39]

Another way of giving priority to happiness in marriage while at the same time evading the hedonistic implications that most Christians still found disagreeable was to focus on romantic love. The Reverend

38. Harry Gaines Hawn, "The Divorce Problem: A Suggestion," *Arena, 33* (1905), 262–66.
39. Hugo Munsterberg, *The Americans* (New York, 1904), p. 523.

Minot J. Savage, in his little book *Men and Women* (1902), argued that the essence of marriage was love and that when both parties ceased to love each other they had every reason to get divorced. He qualified this rule by adding that when there were children, or when an innocent party continued to love the other, divorce was mere selfishness and should not be allowed.

A more ambitious presentation along the same lines was made by the Reverend John Haynes Holmes. Holmes was the pastor of New York's Church of the Messiah, active in civic and reform movements, and a well-known spokesman for liberal Christianity. An active civil libertarian, Holmes expressed his personal creed when he wrote that "the highest individualism, which must be the goal of all progress, is to be secured only through the widest and firmest extension of democratic social control."[40] His book was an effort to find a middle way between what he regarded as the extremes dominating the divorce controversy.

The conservative sacramentarians seemed to Holmes superstitious and irrelevant, while the libertarian position tended toward free love. A happy mean between these two poles could be found by establishing love as the standard of a good marriage. Accordingly, Holmes declared that when love ended the marriage was over and divorce only formally recognized what was a matter of fact. Separation without divorce was no solution, because it was a form of eternal punishment and therefore repugnant to humane men. If one substitutes happiness for love in this disquisition, its sense is hardly altered.

40. John Haynes Holmes, *Marriage and Divorce* (New York, 1913), pp. 9–10.

We have already seen that divorce liberals usually offered a few suggestions toward reducing the divorce rate. Carroll Wright expressed what came to be liberal dogma when he wrote in his *Outline* that it was not divorce but marriage laws that needed to be stiffened. Wright went so far as to say that the state ought to be made an interested party in all divorce suits, a principle which was later utilized by those cities which adopted the divorce proctor system. George Howard's vigorous restatement of Wright's arguments persuaded countless liberals, and Howard seems to have been the most influential publicist of this point of view.

Another idea which met with considerable approval was the feminist contention that the state ought to subsidize divorced mothers for the sake of their children. A variation of the subsidy theme was developed by Alden Harden when he inquired if it might not be possible to tax the divorces of the rich in order to finance the divorces of the poor. The money collected would not go for court costs, but would be used to subsidize the cost of rearing the poor children of divorce.[41]

A more controversial proposal was the one made by Mona Caird that marriage contracts be written for a specific length of time, at the expiration of which either party could elect not to renew the contract. This suggestion received some support from respectable circles as early as 1888.[42] The idea emerged periodically but achieved particular prominence in 1904 when George

41. Alden Harden, "Getting Divorced," *New Republic,* August 12, 1916, pp. 42–43.
42. Dr. E. D. Cope, "The Marriage Problem," *Open Court,* November 22, 1888, pp. 1320–24.

Meredith advocated it in a letter to the *London Daily Mail*. Meredith had refined the idea a bit by suggesting that provision for the raising of children affected by nonrenewals could be assured by a compulsory state insurance system.[43] This notion was close to the trial marriage idea, later to be identified with Colorado's Judge Ben Lindsey. As we have seen, the proposal drew a storm of criticism when Elsie Clews Parsons made it in 1906.

Other liberal proposals were designed to facilitate or rationalize the process of getting a divorce. The most popular of these was Elizabeth Cady Stanton's demand that marriage and divorce be made strictly legal enterprises. The liberals who maintained this position denied that the marriage contract was more sacred than any other contract. Others, like Robert Ingersoll, believed that marriage was sacred under certain conditions, but that the couples themselves were the best judges of whether or not their marriages were so blessed. These liberals hoped to see simple contractual arrangements established that would eliminate the need for society to make decisions on the basis of religious criteria.

Anna Garland Spencer, a noted feminist and minister, wanted the state to accept the fact that neither the church nor the family could adequately control marriage. She thought the first step in the state's new perception of itself ought to be the establishment of a uniform civil marriage service that would be required for a legal marriage. Along with eugenic laws, Mrs.

43. See "Leasehold Marriage," *Living Age,* November 5, 1904, pp. 377–79, for an exceptionally stuffy response from the *Spectator.*

Spencer looked forward to an extension of the domestic relations courts and the abolition of divorce lawyers who, she thought, deliberately complicated matrimonial affairs for their own advantage. She believed that the state should make itself responsible for the children of divorce, and place them in institutions if necessary. Mrs. Spencer, like most feminists, was encouraged by the movement of society in this direction. She gave credit to the prostitute for awakening the state to its duties, and she heartily endorsed the tendency of modern nations to establish the legal identity of women. Mrs. Spencer concluded by decrying the activities of alarmists who were attempting to give a false impression of the imminent collapse of the American family. Actually, she said, divorce strengthened the home.[44]

In all of these arguments one finds faithfully reflected the sometimes facile optimism of the years before the First World War. If the liberals possessed no great intellectual advantages over their conservative opponents, they had at least a more generous humanitarianism. The difference between conservatives and liberals seems to have been partly a matter of temperament. Both groups had their share of distinguished, as well as silly and vapid, men and women. But the liberals were marked, as a group, by a concern for the human element in marriage, a greater tolerance for individual error and weakness, and a substantial hostility to the churches if not to religion itself.

More important, perhaps, were the different perspec-

44. Anna Garland Spencer, "Problems of Marriage and Divorce," *Forum, 48* (1912), 188–204, and *International Journal of Ethics, 19* (July, 1909), 443–65.

tives from which moral conservatives and moral liberals viewed the past and the future. As we saw earlier, conservatives tended to idealize the homely virtues of the past and to distrust the future. Liberals, on the other hand, faced the future with confidence and assumed that history represented the progressive realization of liberal values. At bottom liberals and conservatives were separated not so much by class or interest as by matters of belief and principle. The conservatives stressed tradition and community, and the liberals emphasized charity and individual freedom. In this way the struggle over divorce represented at times a conflict between the classic forms of liberalism and conservatism—something which has not often occurred in a country where, as Louis Hartz has reminded us, most traditions are liberal.

In the long run, one suspects, the influence of the freethinking proponents of divorce, like Ingersoll and Mrs. Stanton, was less substantial than the arguments of religious liberals. Mrs. Stanton was unsurpassed, of course, in vigor, wit, and clarity of discourse, but she had been speaking on divorce for such a long time that it was possible to disregard her. On the one hand, she gained a certain immunity from attack, but at the same time the public, having grown accustomed to her voice, catalogued and filed away her arguments without listening to them. This is one way democracies neutralize dissent, as the position of Norman Thomas in our own time demonstrates.

But, except for the social scientists and freethinkers, most of the prominent spokesmen for divorce had strong religious connections. Some, like Carroll Wright, were active laymen; more were professional ministers or theologians. The testimony of figures like William Ballentine and Anna Garland Spencer (the only woman minister of her time to serve on the faculty of a school of theology) did not outweigh the arguments of those Higher Critics who opposed divorce, but it did neutralize them to a considerable extent, and created doubt where only certainty had reigned. Nor could the teachings of practicing ministers like Savage and Holmes be ignored, for they showed that the Social Gospel did not point in any one direction on crucial moral questions. A careful reader of the literature on divorce could not escape learning, therefore, that the clergy was divided on the question, while most social scientists supported the right to divorce. Together the liberal ministry and the liberal professoriat reinforced each other and constituted an intellectual one-two punch of formidable dimensions.

The struggle over divorce was not, however, waged solely with words. It had a political character as well, and the political setbacks that the enemies of divorce experienced did more to demoralize them than almost anything else. Liberals remained very much a minority in the country, and while social scientists had given the intellectual foundations of the old orthodoxy a fatal wound, it might well have survived in practice for generations on sheer momentum alone. But political defeats could not be shrugged off or ignored like rhetorical losses. The traditional ways of containing divorce—a hostile public opinion and social pressure—had demonstrably failed by the end of the nineteenth century, which left political action as the only hope of moral conservatives.

Chapter

8

THE POLITICS OF DIVORCE

The crucial struggles over divorce took place in Congress and the state legislatures. The most publicized and dramatic of these involved the periodic crusades launched by conservatives against the Western divorce colonies. These curious enclaves, created by state sovereignty in the field of marriage and divorce, have existed throughout most of our national history. Moral conservatives, however, never accepted them as a permanent feature of American life.[1]

In the early 1890s Sioux Falls, South Dakota, was the best known divorce colony in the United States. In 1889 both North and South Dakota had been admitted to the Union, and they retained Dakota Territory's generous ninety-day residence requirement. Sioux Falls, the larg-

1. See Blake, *The Road to Reno,* for the early history of the divorce colonies, and for a more extensive treatment of divorce politics.

est and most accessible town in the two states, soon developed a sizable divorce trade. In the peak year of 1892 there were about 400 divorces awarded in South Dakota, most of them to out-of-staters, and perhaps half of them in Sioux Falls and its environs.[2] Room and board cost a minimum of five dollars a day and legal fees ranged from $250 to $3,500. The average monthly income for the town from divorces must have been around $8,000.[3]

Despite the enthusiasm of the business community for this profitable state of affairs, the days of Sioux Falls as a divorce colony were numbered. The popular base for a campaign against divorce was provided by the Farmers Alliance, whose power in South Dakota was demonstrated by the election of James H. Kyle to the United States Senate in 1890. The Alliance was known to be hostile to divorce, but the catalyst needed to translate discontent into action was provided by Bishop Hare of the Episcopal Church. Bishop Hare, whose missionary work among the Indians in Dakota Territory had earned him the sobriquet "Apostle to the Sioux," returned from a stay in Japan in 1892. Alarmed by South Dakota's notoriety as a divorce state, he launched an

2. "Divorce in South Dakota," *Nation*, January 26, 1893, p. 61.

3. These figures are for Fargo, North Dakota, for 1896, adjusted to the lower volume of divorces in Sioux Falls. Given the similarities in the cost of living for the two towns they are reasonably accurate and correspond to the estimate of a Sioux Falls newspaper cited by Blake. *New York Times*, May 10, 1896, p. 25.

immediate attack on the state's divorce laws, which received national attention.[4]

Bishop Hare had more than the usual hatred of divorce and divorcees. He wrote his daughter-in-law that he despised "people who trifle with marital relations so intensely that the moral nausea produces nausea of the stomach."[5] Hare's distaste for divorce was strengthened by his contact with the divorcees of Sioux Falls, but his passionate convictions on marriage antedated his Dakota experiences. Although his wife died in 1867, when he was not yet thirty, he never remarried. He may, like many strong-willed people, have found it impossible to believe that other men's capacity for self-denial was less than his own.

Hare began his campaign on January 11, 1893, with a pastoral letter condemning divorce as "consecutive polygamy." He declared that divorce could hardly be called the refuge of the poor and the oppressed when it was defended by florists, jewelers, and other businessmen who dealt in luxury goods and services.

> Does not this increase in this particular business indicate that lovers are about, and that not compassion for wronged and broken-hearted husbands

4. M. A. DeWolfe Howe, *The Life and Labors of Bishop Hare* (New York, 1912). For press comment see "Divorce in South Dakota." The *Nation* was interested in Dakota divorces, and this particular article is noteworthy because it attacked the widespread habit of treating divorce colonies as objects of humor. Earlier the *Nation* itself had been guilty of this offense. See "Divorce as a State Industry," May 5, 1892.

5. Howe, p. 356.

and wives is chiefly needed, but denunciation of those who, in the language of Scripture, "creep into houses and lead captive silly women."[6]

Hare denied that divorce was good for business. He attempted to show that it actually discouraged investment, since some believed that the state's determination to attract divorce applicants indicated its poverty. A state's wealth, he declared, was measured by its schools, credit, and homes—not by its divorce rate.

Bishop Hare then presented a petition to the legislature asking that the South Dakota's residence requirement be extended from ninety days to six months. With Alliance support a bill to this effect was pushed through, and in 1895 an attempt to restore the old requirement was defeated by the Hare forces. In 1908, a year before his death, Bishop Hare launched another campaign, and succeeded in extending the residence requirement to one year. As a result of his successes, he acquired a national reputation, which strengthened his position in the Episcopal Church's triennial struggles over the divorce canon. In 1906 he was appointed a delegate to the National Divorce Congress. Unlike Bishop Doane, whose sectarianism alienated both Protestants and Catholics, Hare enjoyed the respect of all believers.

With the end of easy divorce in South Dakota, Fargo, North Dakota, became the leading divorce colony. Here the pattern of events was the same as in South Dakota. The newspapers, which devoted an extraordinary amount of attention to divorce colonies, ground out the same tired stories about sensational doings in care-

6. Ibid., p. 361.

free Fargo as had been printed about Sioux Falls.[7] The divorce rate was rising in these years, and Fargo's divorce business was probably greater than Sioux Falls' had been.[8] In 1896 the *St. Paul* (Minnesota) *Dispatch* estimated that there were 150 applicants for divorce residing in Fargo, and that their business added from ten to seventeen thousand dollars a month to the coffers of local merchants.[9]

North Dakota conservatives made several efforts to limit divorces by extending the residence requirements to six months. In 1897 the State Senate defeated one such attempt, provoking the *Outlook* to speculate, wrongly no doubt, that this was probably because foreigners outnumbered natives in North Dakota.[10] The leader of the antidivorce coalition was the Catholic Bishop Shankley, who reacted vigorously to this defeat, declaring: "I hereby enter my protest against this hell-born social enemy and I call on all Christian people in this state to aid me in the war of extermination which now, God helping me, I declare against it."[11] Two years later the Bishop's appeal was answered, when the state legislature extended North Dakota's residence requirement to six months, destroying the migratory divorce business.[12]

7. E.g. the *New York Times,* January 10, 1896, p. 15.

8. Another cause of this increased business was the New York offices established by Western divorce lawyers beginning in 1896. *New York Times,* May 10, 1896, p. 25.

9. *New York Times,* January 10, 1896, p. 15.

10. *Outlook,* April 17, 1897, p. 1013.

11. Ibid.

12. Blake, *The Road to Reno,* p. 127.

The hardest struggle over state divorce laws occurred in Nevada during the years 1913–15. Nevada became a divorce state after the elimination of the Dakota divorce colonies. Other states had residence requirements as generous as those of Nevada (six months), but Reno, because of its location, good transportation, and climate, became the divorce capital of the United States. The additional business strengthened Nevada's narrow economic base, but the notoriety surrounding a divorce colony was most unwelcome. In 1913 conservatives, led by militant women, induced the newly elected Democratic Legislature to pass a law extending Nevada's residence requirement to one year.[13]

The triumph of good over evil in Nevada was short-lived. In 1915 the old residence requirement was reestablished after a stormy series of legislative debates, attended by an estimated one thousand out-of-town partisans.[14] Reno's career as a divorce colony indicated the changes that were taking place in the national attitude toward divorce. The Western divorce colonies catered largely to New Yorkers fleeing the oppressive laws of the Empire State. In the nineteenth century the colonies were small and offered reasonably inexpensive divorces to people who shunned publicity. Although the press attempted to play up the lurid and sensational aspects of life in Sioux Falls and Fargo, there was little

13. Blake has a full discussion of Reno's history as a divorce colony. See also the *New York Times,* February 8, 1913, p. 24; February 18, 1913, p. 8.

14. *New York Times,* February 4, 1915, p. 1; February 19, 1915, p. 8.

raw material for it to exploit. Sioux Falls was dry, and neither of the two towns had much to offer those accustomed to the more sophisticated pleasures of the East.

Reno, though small and provincial, attracted a different clientele. Reno divorces were at least twice as expensive as Dakota divorces had been (because of the longer residence requirement and higher transportation costs), but the Reno divorce colony in 1913 was four times as large as Fargo's in 1896.[15] The town of 12,000 people had 460 automobiles—a high figure for the times. Reno's riding stables were always busy, and hunting and fishing were available in the nearby Sierra Nevada for the more adventurous. Reno even had a night life of sorts, although it was modest enough by later standards. The relative affluence of the Reno divorce colony is one indication that divorces were becoming more respectable as well as more frequent.

This history of the divorce colonies during this period suggests two things about the nature of America's response to divorce. In the first place, the continuous existence of these colonies illustrated the workings of the law of supply and demand. The piecemeal prohibition of divorce in various parts of the country created a need which the divorce colonies in their imperfect ways attempted to meet. Given the diversity of American customs and mores, this was a natural and, in many ways, a healthy situation.

Secondly, the efforts to abolish the divorce colonies pitted conservatives against, not liberals, but merchants. Conservative leaders like Bishop Hare believed that

15. *New York Times,* January 11, 1914, Section 5, p. 5.

these struggles were between morality and the forces of private greed. There were almost no liberal moralists in the underpopulated Western states to dispute this point. But if free divorce lacked spokesmen, it was not without defenders. The forces of local business enterprise were not always strong enough to resist indignant moral conservatism, and most of the battles to retain easy divorce laws were lost. However, there were always communities willing to pick up the fallen banner, and so there was usually a divorce colony to which the maritally oppressed could repair.

Of greater significance was the movement that developed during this period toward uniform marriage and divorce legislation. This goal was pursued in two ways. One method was to seek uniformity by means of a constitutional amendment giving Congress exclusive jurisdiction over marriage and divorce. Another was to increase uniformity through voluntary state action.

The campaign for uniformity followed the movements of public opinion, waxing and waning as interest in divorce rose and fell. The first attempt to secure a constitutional amendment came in 1892, a little over two years after Carroll Wright's report was issued. The attempt was made by Senator James H. Kyle, of South Dakota. Senator Kyle seems to have been one of the better men in Congress, but he was interested in education, conservation, and other subjects which lacked the attention-getting qualities of the causes championed by his fellow Populists.

On February 3, 1892, Senator Kyle introduced S.R. 29, a joint resolution which read in full: "The Congress shall have the exclusive power to regulate marriage and divorce in the several states, Territories, and the District of Columbia."[16] Kyle spoke briefly on its behalf. He began by noting that the era of great wars and revolutions was over and that history was now largely concerned with sociological questions. He believed that no social problem was as pressing as that of the family, and he made the usual conservative statements about the family's role as the foundation of society. He listed the following reasons for a divorce amendment: it was desired by Samuel Dike and the whole nation (in this he was wrong since Dike did not favor such an amendment); the National Bar Association wanted it in order to simplify the nation's legal codes; it would rationalize the position of Americans married to foreigners; it would prevent states like Utah from legislating customs repugnant to the rest of the nation; it would eliminate divorce colonies, especially those in his own state; it would permit the concentration of all the best state laws in one statute; and finally, it "would preserve the family and the home, and thus lay a broad foundation for the perpetuity of the nation."[17]

Senator Kyle's resolution was sent to the Judiciary Committee, where it died. A similar fate befell later attempts to obtain a constitutional amendment on marriage and divorce. In 1914 Senator Joseph Ransdell, of Louisiana, produced a Joint Resolution calling for the abolition of divorce. Ransdell argued that only prohibition would protect the home, which he described as "the

16. *U.S. Congressional Record,* 52 Cong., 1 Sess. (February 3, 1892), p. 791.
17. Ibid., p. 792.

239

greatest protection from anarchy, the strongest defense against socialism, and the chief bulwark of society."[18] Senator Ransdell's resolution was doomed to failure, for, as the *Times* pointed out, it was "utterly out of harmony with the spirit and tendency of the age."[19] Moreover, as Senator Shortridge observed a few years later at one of the Senate Judiciary Committee hearings on a similar resolution, most Congressmen felt that the situation was not grave enough to justify increasing the power of the federal government at the expense of the states.[20]

Other efforts to obtain a constitutional amendment failed in both the House and Senate.[21] Because of these failures, and because many people doubted the value of federal action, efforts were made throughout this period to construct a model statute to which the states would voluntarily subscribe. The most persistent of these were the products of the National Conference of Commissioners on Uniform State Laws. This organization met yearly, in connection with the meetings of the American Bar Association, to frame model codes on a wide range of subjects. It was created as the result of a recommendation by the Bar Association in 1889; the first state commission was appointed by New York in

18. *U.S. Congressional Record,* 63 Cong., 2 Sess. (February 4, 1914), p. 2863.

19. *New York Times,* February 7, 1914, 10.

20. *Senate Judiciary Committee* "Hearings on S.J. Res. 31" (November 1, 1921).

21. See "Report on S.J. Res. 9," *Senate Judiciary Committee* (June 5, 1906); "Hearings on H.J. Res. 48," *House Judiciary Committee* (April 12, 1916); "Hearings on H.J. Res. 187" (Oct. 2, 1918).

1890. In 1892 the organization was founded as the Conference of Commissioners on Uniform State Laws. The State Commissions and their members were usually appointed by the governors, but a few commissions owed their existence to state legislation.[22]

The commissioners drafted a total of seven statutes on marriage and divorce. These statutes reflected the practical concerns of the American legal profession, and they dealt essentially with procedure. The commissioners' 1889 model divorce law, for example, provided for a two-year residence requirement, delivery of notice to the defendant, open hearings, and remarriage for either party. The causes for which divorces might be granted were not specified.[23]

By 1916 only a few states had enacted any of the model laws. Accordingly, the commissioners appointed a committee to ask the state bar associations why so little had been accomplished. The committee (which included the ubiquitous Walter George Smith of Philadelphia) reported that apparently three causes were responsible for the failure of state legislators to enact the model statutes. Because of the variety of opinion on the subject, most legislators preferred to leave well enough alone. In addition, legislators who were interested in uniformity preferred to concentrate on bills that were easier to pass. Finally, the committee declared that the "subject of marriage and divorce is in many of the states con-

---

22. "Secretary's Memorandum," *Proceedings of the 26th Annual Meeting of the NCCUSL* (New York, 1916).

23. "Uniform Divorce Bill," *Public Opinion,* Oct. 26, 1889, p. 527.

sidered to be a strictly local question."[24] The *Independent* had earlier attempted to explain the failure of voluntary uniformity by blaming the machinations of divorce lawyers in the state judiciary committees.[25] Although this accusation cannot be entirely discounted, it could have applied only to those few states that monopolized the migratory divorce business. The model acts would not have reduced the divorce rate elsewhere.

The weakness of voluntary state action was demonstrated also by the failure of the National Divorce Congress in 1906. The Congress was the result of action by Bishop Doane's Inter-Church Conference, which succeeded in persuading President Theodore Roosevelt to request a new census study of marriage and divorce. The study was authorized by Congress, and the discussion aroused by its authorization moved Governor Pennypacker of Pennsylvania to take responsibility for a national conference to draft model uniform legislation on divorce. The National Congress on Uniform Divorce Laws was the most ambitious effort to advance the cause of uniform divorce legislation ever attempted. Its delegates included representatives from 42 of the 45 states in the Union, although its second session included only 21 delegations.[26]

The delegations were composed largely of conservative lawyers and clergymen, many of them with experi-

24. *Proceedings of the 27th Annual Meeting of the NCCUSL* (unpublished, 1917), p. 263.

25. "Uniform Divorce Legislation," *Independent,* September 4, 1902, pp. 2150–52.

26. See Blake, pp. 140–45, for a more complete description of the Congress.

ence on the State Commissions for Uniformity. The first session, held at Washington, D.C., in February 1906, established the framework of the proposed statute. The November session in Philadelphia approved the final draft. There was ample discussion at the Philadelphia session, although there ought to have been little left to discuss. The efforts of a few moderates to liberalize the bill's provisions were, however, ineffectual. Walter George Smith, as Chairman of the Committee on Resolutions, conducted the session, and he skillfully pushed the bill through exactly as it had been written. Bishop Doane had the last word. In his closing prayer he commended the Congress for its "strong, clear, conservative position" and expressed his hope that "the Conference in Philadelphia agrees with the Conference in Washington, in urging that where there are few causes [for divorce] they shall not be increased, and where there are many, they should be reduced in number."[27]

Despite Bishop Doane's brave words and the conservative inclinations of most delegates, the Congress settled on a compromise bill that was not significantly different from the model act drawn up by the State Commissioners. Moreover, the moderation of the bill and the extensive publicity accorded the Congress failed to move more than a few state legislatures to enact the proposed statute. The failure of this effort meant, in effect, the failure of uniformity. The movement never collapsed entirely, but it was becoming clear that uniformity was a lost cause.

---

27. *Proceedings of the Adjourned Meeting of the National Congress on Uniform Divorce Laws* (Harrisburg, 1907), p. 150.

The failure of the movement for uniformity is all the more interesting when measured against the apparent enthusiasm for it. Both divorce liberals and conservatives supported it, or at least gave it lip service, although conservatives were the most enthusiastic. The Federal Council of Churches endorsed the idea in its Executive Committee's first annual report. At the same time it praised the work of Bishop Doane and the Inter-Church Conference. Because of the diverse views represented in the Federal Council, it was unable to do more.[28] In subsequent years the Federal Council repeated its statements on behalf of uniformity, but its Committee on the Family became less and less active and in some years failed to issue a report at all. In 1921 the Council's Secretary was forced to admit that the Council had no official position on uniform divorce laws.[29]

Many conservatives saw uniform legislation as a way of making divorces more difficult to obtain. The *Nation,* for example, ended one of its attacks on Sioux Falls with the observation that such scandalous conditions showed the need for uniform laws.[30] William Howard Taft believed that "we ought to have a general uniform law on the subject that stiffens up and makes sacred the Marriage Tie."[31] The *New York Tribune* hoped for a uniform divorce law that would extend the blessings of

28. *First Annual Report of the Executive Committee of the Inter-Church Conference on Federation* (New York, 1908).

29. "Hearings on S.J. Res. 31."

30. "Divorce in South Dakota," January 26, 1893.

31. "How Shall We Solve the Divorce Problem?" *Hearst's Magazine, 21* (1912), 2393.

New York's ban on all but adultery suits throughout the land.[32]

The conservative hard line on uniformity was articulated as late as 1909 by Dr. George Clarke Houghton, who told the *New York World* that "there is no instance of life where divorce may be called justifiable. Those who get it for any reason are committing a great sin."[33] Dr. Houghton concluded with the customary observation that he saw "very little difference between the way in which our divorce system is tending and the way of free love."[34] In the same spirit, the *Nation* declared in 1894 that a national divorce law was needed to prevent some states from giving "what is really a state of concubinage the appearance of a real marriage."[35] Some conservatives thought that such legislation would end the great danger posed to public morals by Utah polygamy.[36] President Roosevelt shared many of these feelings, and his message to Congress in 1905 called for uniform legislation in unmistakably conservative terms:

> The institution of marriage is, of course, at the very foundation of our social organization, and influences that affect that institution are of vital concern

32. "Reform of Divorce Laws," *Public Opinion,* November 9, 1889, pp. 103–05.

33. "Is Freer Divorce an Evil?" *Current Literature, 47* (1909), 63. See also E. J. Phelps, "Divorce in the United States," *Forum, 8* (1889), 350–64.

34. "Is Freer Divorce an Evil?" 63.

35. "The Marriage Scandal," *Nation,* May 18, 1899, p. 369.

36. R. W. Taylor, "Marriage and Divorce," *Harper's Weekly,* June 8, 1901, p. 573. Taylor was referring to a constitutional amendment.

to the people of the whole country. There is a widespread conviction that the divorce laws are dangerously lax and indifferently administered in some of the states, resulting in a diminishing regard for the sanctity of the marriage relation.[37]

George W. Norris of Nebraska, then in the House of Representatives, subscribed to President Roosevelt's ideas on divorce. He demonstrated his feelings by introducing a resolution to appropriate money for the travel expenses of delegates to the Divorce Congress. Norris, like many political progressives, was a conservative on the divorce issue. He did not believe that divorces ought to be eliminated—only reduced—and he thought that uniform laws would accomplish this feat. He opposed the constitutional amendment method of securing uniformity because it would weaken the state governments.[38]

Norris' position on uniformity demonstrated the inability of many divorce conservatives to see the political realities confronting the movement. Most conservatives insisted that divorce was a menace threatening the very pillars of civilization. But at the same time they opposed the only method which could be expected to lower the divorce rate—a constitutional amendment. Perhaps few of them really believed divorce was as dangerous as a literal reading of their comments would suggest. Conservatives were torn between their hatred of divorce and

37. Bureau of the Census, *Marriage and Divorce 1867–1906*, p. 4.

38. "Divorce and the Means of Diminishing It," *Editorial Review* (December, 1911). From Johnsen, ed., *Selected Articles*.

their fear of strong federal action, and they wanted to believe that uniformity could be achieved painlessly through voluntary cooperation.

A typical example of this attitude occurred in 1912 when the New York State Marriage and Divorce Commission met to discuss uniformity. The meeting was essentially conservative in tone, thanks to the presence of Felix Adler and other advocates of strict divorce laws. Although the Roman Catholic Church was not officially represented, Catholic laymen did attend and the meeting had the blessing of New York's Cardinal Farley. Most of the talking was done by the Reverend Francis M. Moody, a leader in the Western uniform divorce movement, who argued that only a federal law would secure effective uniformity. Members of the Commission expressed the usual objections and voiced the usual hopes for voluntary state action. Moody answered simply that "not in a thousand years could you move some of those Western States to reform their divorce laws."[39]

The whole history of the uniform divorce movement testified to the accuracy of Moody's observation. But many conservatives, especially those at the New York meeting, were unable to see this. Samuel Dike was one who could. Shortly after the publication of the Wright report he pointed out some of the implications of uniformity. Dike assumed that everyone was in favor of uniform laws, but he emphasized the limitations of statute law. In the first place, only a small proportion of divorces were migratory, and uniform laws would al-

39. *New York Times,* January 15, 1913, p. 9.

most certainly enlarge the number of causes for divorce in some states and increase the divorce rate. He guessed that "many would think this too dear a price to pay for uniformity."[40] Dike believed that divorce alone would not be the subject of a constitutional amendment, for Congress would probably also gain control of the whole range of family legislation, with unpredictable consequences.

Dike pointed out that constitutional amendments did not always have the intended effect. The failure to achieve racial equality in the South proved this. States could frustrate the intentions of an amendment when the people were determined to resist it. "The trouble is that we cannot easily reach behind the States to the social hostility that nullifies the aims of the law."[41] Dike concluded that the constitutional amendment method was too dangerous to experiment with, and he recommended that voluntary state action be attempted first. Dike was not sanguine about this alternative, because he recognized its difficulties better than most men.

The New York *Times* was an early and consistent critic of compulsory uniformity. The *Times* insisted that a constitutional amendment would be "contrary to the whole theory of the constitution and subversive of the principles upon which the distinction between State and Federal jurisdiction is founded."[42] For many years the *Times* maintained that the proper approach to uniformity was through support of the National Divorce

40. "Uniform Marriage and Divorce Laws," *Arena, 2* (1890), 401.
41. Ibid., p. 404.
42. *New York Times,* February 7, 1897, p. 16.

Reform League and the various bodies attempting to secure voluntary uniformity. This method commended itself to the *Times* on the grounds that a federal law would probably be more lax than New York's, and because any law which conflicted with local customs would be evaded.[43] The *Times* continued to urge voluntary uniformity even after its confidence in the superiority of New York's divorce law declined.[44] The paper finally adopted a fatalistic attitude toward the whole issue. It concluded in 1919 that "the origin of the modern evil of divorce is too deep to be touched by any body of legislation, however uniform, however scientific. It is largely economic."[45]

Although the *Nation* advocated federal legislation on divorce, its contributors were by no means agreed on this point. D. M. Means argued that federal legislation on divorce could not succeed because "legislation can promote morality only when it is in harmony with a substantially unanimous public opinion—which would perhaps be as effective without legislation as with it."[46] The *Outlook* opposed federal action because it would

43. *New York Times,* March 12, 1899, p. 18; March 4, 1900, p. 22.

44. Compare the *Times'* defense of New York's law (November 11, 1900, p. 18), with its repudiation of Senator Ransdell's proposed amendment (February 7, 1914, p. 101). In the latter editorial the *Times* noted approvingly that "most countries nowadays consider . . . that, bad as is divorce, there are things which are worse, more degrading to individuals, and more harmful to society."

45. *New York Times,* September 7, 1919, p. 1.

46. D. M. Means, "The Statistics of Divorce," *Nation,* June 18, 1891, pp. 493–94.

create "more lax" conditions in states like New York and South Carolina.[47] The *Outlook* was not insensitive to the constitutional dangers posed by federal action in this area. Moreover, it felt that little could be achieved through voluntary action.[48]

Bishop Doane rejected the whole idea of uniformity for reasons similar to the *Outlook's*. Because of the great interest in uniformity around the turn of the century, Doane apparently found it expedient to make a few concessions. In 1904 he suggested that the Inter-Church Conference might be able to support uniformity if the standards of New York or South Carolina were used as guides. Such a development was, of course, quite impossible, and Bishop Doane knew it, but the suggestion did make his position seem more in harmony with the mood of other divorce conservatives.[49] During the National Divorce Congress he grudgingly gave his blessing to the movement, with the understanding that uniformity would not mean changes in the statutes of New York and South Carolina.

Liberal enthusiasm for uniformity was tepid and irregular. The *Independent* evinced some interest in uniformity through state action if it was understood, "as Dr. Dike has often said, that for a divorce law we must not go to Leviticus or Matthew or Paul; but fol-

47. "Protection of the Family," *Outlook,* November 24, 1906, p. 691.
48. "Polygamy and Divorce," *Outlook,* January 5, 1901, p. 2; "The Recent Divorce Decisions," *Outlook,* May 18, 1901, pp. 141–42; "Degrading Marriages," *Outlook,* August 26, 1911, pp. 909–10.
49. *New York Times,* March 27, 1904, p. 7.

lowing our Lord in his escape from Biblical edict to the first principles of the family."[50] A few years later, the *Independent* observed blandly that the failure of state efforts at uniformity might make a constitutional amendment necessary. This thought did not excite the *Independent,* but its editors believed that shoddy divorces ought to be prevented and some order brought out of the chaos of state divorce laws.[51] The magazine later declared itself against uniformity.[52]

Liberal statements on uniformity were usually hostile. William Snyder's position on this issue anticipated Samuel Dike's, for he too was aware that, while everyone wanted uniformity in principle, it was impossible to get in practice. The constitutional amendment notion was dangerous, he felt, because it would extend the power of Congress to an unhealthy degree.[53] H. H. Gardner, in the *Arena,* protested against uniformity because it would make divorces more difficult for women to obtain. He was disturbed by the efforts of the movement's partisans to make uniformity a religious issue and mockingly observed:

> We do not drag religion into the inter-state commerce debate; when a bill comes up for street-paving nobody inquires what kind of stone St. Paul was interested in having put down. When the

50. "Better Divorce Laws," *Independent,* January 10, 1901, p. 112.

51. "Uniform Divorce Laws," *Independent,* October 29, 1903, pp. 2591–92.

52. "The Divorce Evil," *Independent,* May 1, 1916, p. 161.

53. William L. Snyder, *The Geography of Marriage* (New York, 1889).

Chinese bill is before us it is not necessary to know what St. Sebastian thought of the laundry business. Their views may have been sound; but they do not apply.[54]

Minot J. Savage argued that divorce was a private matter and no concern of the states. He complained that some people seemed to think that appropriate legislation could solve all their problems. Savage thought the real issue in the uniformity question was the proper role of the state, and he did not believe that its duties extended as far as most reformers seemed to think. The attempt to establish religious criteria for legislation violated the separation of church and state and constituted an intolerable invasion of personal rights. Savage concluded that even if such laws were possible they were undesirable because they would only increase immorality.[55]

Further examples of these viewpoints could be offered indefinitely, for uniformity was the single most talked-about solution to the divorce problem. The history of the movement for uniformity illustrated the intractability of the divorce problem. In an editorial at the height of public enthusiasm for uniformity, *Harper's Weekly* pointed out how unrealistic the whole movement was.[56] The constitutional amendment approach was out of the question because it was an invasion of states' rights, and thus would meet with general hostility. The campaign

54. H. H. Gardner, "Divorce and the Proposed National Law," *Arena, 1* (1890), 421.
55. "Matrimony and the State," *Forum, 10* (1890), 115–23.
56. "Our Chaotic Divorce Laws," *Harper's Weekly,* October 17, 1903, p. 1657.

for voluntary uniformity, although widely applauded, was doomed from the start because different religious groups with differing ideas on divorce dominated enough state legislatures to prevent the passage of model laws.

To this analysis *Harper's Weekly* might have added that the divorce trade was sufficiently attractive to businessmen and lawyers in some states to bring them out in opposition to important changes in the divorce laws. Moreover, many politicians were reluctant to become involved in struggles over laws that could not possibly help their careers and that were likely to antagonize the growing percentage of voters interested in obtaining divorces. In this way inertia, greed, religious dissension, and political calculation combined to block the conservatives. They found themselves in the frustrating position of advocating measures which, though apparently enjoying widespread support from civic and religious leaders, could not be translated into effective legislation.

Chapter

9

CONCLUSIONS

It should be clear that the debate over divorce and the political efforts to restrict divorce were quite separate movements. Outside of New York State, those who wrote about divorce and those who struggled with the law seem to have operated independently. Since little real change in the legal status of divorce took place during these years, we can assume that what people said about divorce is more useful to us than what they did about it.

If the volume of periodical literature on divorce is a reliable gauge of public interest, there were two periods during the thirty years with which we are concerned when the problem received most attention. The first period lasted from about 1889 to 1894, and the second roughly from 1904 to 1914.[1] Public concern was most

1. James H. Barnett, *Divorce and the American Divorce Novel, 1858–1937* (Philadelphia, 1939), p. 34, lists the refer-

intense during the years 1909–12, when about a third of the books on marriage and divorce that appeared between 1889 to 1919 were published. Thereafter interest in the problem declined rapidly, not to be renewed until after World War I. By then draconian solutions to the marriage crisis were obviously impossible.

A number of events occurred around 1912 which further justify our calling this the critical period in the divorce controversy. Samuel Dike's League for the Protection of the Family had begun to wane even before his death in 1913, but it collapsed altogether within two years of his passing. Even more revealing was the history of the Committee on Family Life, established by the Federal Council of Churches in 1911. By 1913, the Committee had yet to meet and was still without a budget. This condition lasted through the war, and in 1919 the Committee was not listed at all in the Council's annual report.

Similarly, the movement for uniform legislation bogged down, and while there was some talk of constitutional amendments throughout the period, nothing came of it. Walter George Smith admitted in 1914 that the public was uninterested in uniform marriage and divorce laws, regardless of the method employed to obtain them.[2]

The changing outlook on the legitimacy of divorce can be seen in the national magazines, which not only

---

ences to divorce in the standard periodical indexes which support this point.

2. Walter George Smith, "Ethics of Divorce," in Johnsen, ed., *Selected Articles*.

carried more articles defending the right to divorce but also began editorially to treat divorce as a morally neutral and sometimes even morally positive act. In 1909 the *Chautauquan's* editor straddled the issue, whereas only a few years earlier anything but condemnation from a family uplift magazine would have been unthinkable.[3] In January 1910 the *World's Work* announced that the "True View of Increasing Divorce" was that the divorce rate was not alarming and divorces should not be further restricted. *Current Literature* took up the same theme in a lengthy article summarizing the views of numerous experts as well as laymen on the value of divorce. Professors Lichtenberger, Thomas, and Howard were heard from, as was former Justice Brown of the Supreme Court, who wrote:

> It is not perceived why the partnership created by marriage should so far differ from a commercial partnership that one may be dissolved at pleasure while the other is indissoluble.[4]

Although the *Outlook* continued to oppose divorce, its editorial position was modified in 1910 when it admitted that cruelty, drunkenness, and life imprisonment were probably legitimate grounds for divorce.[5] Previously the magazine had insisted that adultery was the only possible ground. Ida Tarbell also changed her

3. "The Divorce Problem Again," *Chautauquan, 56* (1909), 8–10.

4. "The Most Difficult Problem of Modern Civilization," *Current Literature, 18* (1910), 59.

5. "Just Grounds for Divorce," *Outlook,* November 23, 1910, p. 602.

mind. In a 1914 article on the Chicago Court of Domestic Relations, she wrote that "if there be one thing more than another that the daily revelations of this courtroom demonstrates it is the righteousness of divorce."[6] Even the *Nation* concluded that divorce was a necessary evil. Criticizing the failure of Parliament to enact a moderate divorce bill, the *Nation* compared Britain unfavorably with Sweden: "Sweden makes the law coincide with the undeniable facts, instead of pretending that the facts fit the law—a British habit that has just been reaffirmed by action of Parliament."[7] The *Nation* went on to brand the opponents of the divorce bill as "enemies of freedom." The *Nation's* about-face reflected a change of management as much as a change of heart, but it was of a piece with the general movement away from orthodoxy.

It is hardly a coincidence that the shift in American attitudes toward divorce took place during the period Henry F. May has identified as "the end of American innocence." The whole of American society and culture was undergoing a change in the years immediately before American entry into the Great War: the Victorian synthesis was fragmenting, and new modes of thought and behavior which we recognize as distinctively our own were coming into being. We would not expect divorce to evolve independently of its social context, and in fact it was very much a part of the cultural revolu-

6. Ida Tarbell, "A Municipal Court of Marital Hope," *Current Opinion, 17* (1914), 263. From the *Contemporary Review*.
7. "They Shall Not Pass," *Nation,* May 15, 1920, p. 640.

tion discussed by May. Divorce, therefore, has implications that deserve mention even though they go beyond the limits of this study.

We saw at the outset that divorces began to increase as America came to grips with the machine age. The dynamics of an industrialism that regarded human beings not as members of families or even as individuals but simply as "hands" inevitably affected traditional relationships. Great social energies were released in the process and, as science and technology were making old assumptions untenable, prophets arose to establish new ones. Few subjects escaped re-examination, and the people I have called New Moralists stepped forth to do for divorce in particular and sex in general what the social scientists were doing for the other areas of human experience.

As society became ever more dense and intricate, new professions developed, and divorce became the province of sociologists who were themselves far more under the influence of the new morality than was the general public. The combination of sociology and the new ideas about morality proved to be both potent and crucial to the evolution of the divorce controversy. The tradition-minded opponents of divorce were compelled to fight on ground not of their own choosing. Orthodox Christianity had once seemed an impregnable bastion in which moral conservatives could hold out forever. But by the turn of the century sociologists were simply bypassing Christianity, and if the conservatives proposed to fight they had to attack divorce on the basis of its social inutility. But by engaging the enemy on his own terms conservatives made a fatal, if inescapable, mistake, for they were in no position to challenge the professional credentials and equipment of the sociologists.

Conservatives were disarmed by their obligatory shift from moral to practical grounds, dismayed by their inability to retard the divorce rate, and more than a little disillusioned with the culture responsible for their plight. One can see, therefore, the beginnings of the great attitude change which was to occur after the First World War taking shape well before American entry. One of the major features of nineteenth-century American thought had been what Professor May calls it "inveterate optimism." But by the turn of the century, only moral liberals could be optimistic about the family. Thus we find liberals making sanguine prophecies about marriage and the family that conservatives simply could not accept, even though most of them had always been squarely in the mainstream of American thought—optimism included.

Moreover, since the relaxation of the prohibitions against divorce was billed as a "reform," conservatives had even more reason for distrusting the liberal, reformist values of the Progressive era. In their worst moments conservatives reacted to the dilemma by witch-hunting and scapegoating. But more importantly, their disenchantment over the movement for divorce prepared them for the greater disappointments to come. In this manner the discontent which is so prominent a feature of modern conservatism and the conservatives' disposition to see America's moral fiber as badly in need of stiffening probably owe something to the pre-World War I experience.

Another aspect of contemporary conservatism, its

emphasis on individualism, may also be related to the struggle over divorce. As we have seen, the critics of divorce consistently accused those who obtained divorces, and those who defended the practice, of espousing a dangerously antisocial individualism. Indeed, their major objection to socialist doctrines was that they believed socialism put the rights of individuals ahead of the needs of society. They distrusted big government not because it suppressed individualism but because it exalted the individual by breaking down the local and familial associations that had previously checked his antisocial impulses. Today, of course, conservatives argue just the opposite. Senator Goldwater's presidential campaign in 1964 was proclaimed as an effort to obtain greater rights for the individual. At the same time, however, Goldwater was obviously the champion of moral as well as political conservatism, and his candidacy illustrates what has happened to moral conservatism in the past fifty years.

A moral conservative in 1904 would certainly have been opposed to divorce, prostitution, erotic literature, and unwed motherhood, but he would have been just as likely to favor unemployment insurance, the Social Gospel, and generous immigration policies. He would not have thought these inconsistent beliefs, because all of them could be justified on the grounds that they promoted social order and advanced the general welfare. Conservatives continue to insist upon social order and to demand the suppression of direct action and civil disobedience programs because, like crimes of violence, they are thought to be subversive of public harmony. However, conservatives have soured on the general welfare and no longer recognize it as an important object of good government.

To explain the contemporary emphasis on individualism would require an examination of the political history of the past half century. The adoption of individualistic values foreign in spirit to traditional conservative doctrines was in part a matter of expediency. A concern with individual rights is deeply embedded in the American experience, and its enduring popularity made it helpful in the defense of property rights threatened by zoning laws, fair housing ordinances, taxes, regulatory commissions, and the whole apparatus of public control that has evolved in recent years. Moreover, the failure of the Communist bloc to protect individual rights gave political conservatives another valuable argument and a further reason for using it.

But if individualism has been useful to political conservatism, it remains a problem for moral conservatives faced with a continuing sexual evolution that derives its strength from the very American belief in the pursuit of happiness. One cannot easily proclaim the rights of every man to dispose of his property as he sees fit while denying him the right to use his body in the same manner. The dilemma confronting moral conservatives in 1904 has, therefore, become much more acute in our time. The older divorce critics were in most respects sympathetic with the progressive, optimistic assumptions of their age. But to the degree that they believed that divorce was destroying the moral and social underpinnings of the national life, their confidence and faith in American culture was being undermined. One sees in them the beginnings of that alienation which is so marked a feature of modern conservatism. In 1904 or 1914 moral conservatives, however frustrated by their inability to retard divorce, could still believe that most Americans maintained the same moral standards as themselves. By 1924, much less 1964, this was obviously no longer true. Divorce, which once seemed so flagrantly immoral, is now obscured by things like pornography and promiscuity, which have become, not the vices of a few, but the pleasures of the many. The commercialized exploitation of sex is no longer a furtive, underground business, but a mainstay of American capitalism. One can understand, then, why moral conservatives have become so profoundly disaffected, so estranged from the mainstream of American culture, that it has become possible to run for president by indicting the moral character of the nation.

However, by abandoning their traditional anti-individualism, conservatives have only compounded their difficulties. Whatever they may have gained politically by adopting individualistic arguments, they have lost emotionally and intellectually by having to use one set of standards for economic problems and another for social and sexual ones. We have already seen how the relatively mild conflict between a progressive, optimistic view of American history and society on the one hand, and a pessimistic view of marriage and the family on the other made moral conservatives cranky and irritable at the turn of the century. How much more reason there is for the conservatives of our time, torn between moral authoritarianism and economic liberalism while at the same time experiencing a much more profound sense of isolation and alienation, to be peevish and intemperate.

The position of the moral liberals seems to have been in some ways less difficult. Not only was their optimistic, progressive view of divorce in keeping with the spirit of their age, but they were in the enviable position of those who win without effort. Throughout these years divorces increased, and conservatives were driven back without liberals having to lift a finger. Since history was working with them, they could afford to be relatively even-tempered. Perhaps for these reasons liberals were less prepared for the shocking denouement of the Wilson era and the plunge into normalcy. Certainly the future proved very different from what they had imagined it would be. Many of those who had urged divorce as a way of freeing women from sex lived to see the open adoration of sexuality in the jazz age, while most of the sociologists who believed that the divorce rate would level off and family cohesion increase had to wait a long time for their hopes to be realized.

Yet despite their predictive failures, liberals very well may have had the best of it. If divorce failed to live up to their expectations, neither did it produce the disasters anticipated by conservatives. We know today that divorce has not grown at the expense of marriage and the family. Not only do Americans now marry more often than in the recent past, but they marry earlier and have larger families. The institution of marriage has changed somewhat in the past half century, yet the changes do not seem to have noticeably decreased the sum total of human happiness or imperiled the structure of society.

In the long run those who defended divorce for libertarian reasons found themselves on the safest ground. For one thing, since civil liberties are primarily a matter of principle, they are not subject to revision on the basis of experience. For another, there is no question that easier divorce has strengthened women's rights, even if it has not improved their social position, and from a libertarian point of view such a result is self-justifying.

However, while many did support the right to divorce for libertarian reasons, their case was far from free of the manipulative and authoritarian undercurrents which marred the advanced thought of their age. As Christopher Lasch has recently pointed out, progressive intellectuals like Jane Addams and Randolph Bourne (whom he somewhat misleadingly calls new radicals) had a definite bias against the family, which they regarded as oppressive and tyrannical.[8] Their attitude helped inspire a certain distrust of the family on the part of sociologists like George Howard, who, while certainly not overtly antifamilial, rejoiced in the modern tendency of the state to view its citizens as individuals rather than as members of family units.

One clear advantage of this proposition was that it made social control much easier to accomplish. The patriarchal family seemed balky, awkward, and resistant to change. The streamlined contemporary family, on the other hand, was considered to be susceptible of intelligent handling and consequently far less of a problem to aspiring social engineers. Thus it was possible for a radical sociologist like Arthur W. Calhoun to call in

8. Christopher Lasch, *The New Radicalism in America* (New York, 1965).

one breath for a more democratic society and in another for tighter controls over marriage and the suppression of newspaper stories about divorce, ending with a crude appeal to the self-interest of capitalists and managers:

> The spread of the "scientific management" movement for economic efficiency should have a large bearing on the problem of divorce. Employers are coming to recognize the importance of family troubles as an element in inefficiency. The influence of divorce upon the productivity of adults and the development of children and thus upon the interests of property must be very considerable. In general the burden and expense of divorce and of its consequences is a noteworthy reduction of social efficiency that should direct the attention of administrators to the economics of the problem.[9]

The intellectual gulf between conservatives and liberals was not, therefore, quite so wide as their emotional differences might suggest. Liberals did not commonly regard individual rights as inviolable, although they attached more weight to them than conservatives did, and both sides unhesitatingly advanced coercive solutions to problems which did not easily lend themselves to permissive alternatives. Since both factions were committed to many of the same principles and were composed in many cases of individuals from similar social backgrounds, the precise differences between them were sometimes far from obvious. The essence of the ideological conflict was, after all, that while they started from

9. Calhoun, *A Social History of the American Family, 3,* 281.

265

essentially the same position, their understanding of what was at stake and their moral reference points came in the end to be very different.

Of crucial importance was their reaction to the feminist thrust. The critics of divorce were almost all anti-feminists; its defenders invariably sympathized with the woman movement. It is surely no accident that Richard Hofstadter, in his brilliant and influential analysis of the Progressive era, *The Age of Reform,* pays virtually no attention to feminism. If one wishes to prove, as Hofstadter does, that the Progressives were conservative counterrevolutionaries motivated by status anxieties, then obviously one cannot spend much time on the feminists, for they are not so easily fitted into this pattern as some of the other people we have examined.

But the feminists and liberals are interesting precisely because they do reflect the moral fervor in Progressive thought that Hofstadter feels has been overemphasized. While some Progressives, such as Felix Adler and Margaret Deland, called for a return to the patriarchal family and the old social order, others hoped for newer and more flexible arrangements. The feminist vision of a free and equal marriage prepared for by sex education and based on equal employment opportunities commanded impressive support among advanced progressives. Even the modest statements by social scientists that a substantial divorce rate was no danger to society indicated an outlook on social change that was more forward-looking than reactionary.

Divorce was a moral and ideological issue which cut across class and interest lines. It might be said that the campaign for free divorce reflected the status anxieties of the new middle-class business and professional women, but it was believed that free divorce accelerated the breakdown of the traditional family system, and its proponents hardly can be described, therefore, as conservative counterrevolutionaries. The liberal ideologists of the feminist movement—Schreiner, Gilman, Dorr—were deeply committed to many aspects of the changing morality, of which divorce was only the most conspicuous part. Those who defended or advanced the new sexual norms did so for reasons that cannot be explained in terms of the social groups to which they belonged. Feminists wished to see mores changed to conform to the position of educated women in an industrial society, and some attorneys may have supported them because divorces were good business. But the reasons that impelled the professoriat and the liberal clergy to defend the new morality would seem to owe more to ideology than to status or interest.

It could be argued also that divorce as an issue was peripheral to the mainstream of Progressivism. No party platform called for divorce reforms, although leading politicians sometimes did. In this respect the relationship of divorce to politics in the Progressive era was something like the relationship of juvenile delinquency to politics today. To the extent that there is a difference between liberals and conservatives on juvenile delinquency, the tendency of liberals is to argue that delinquency can be dealt with best by eliminating the conditions that breed it. Conservatives, on the other hand, are more likely to call for direct action against delinquency itself. The contemporary liberal sees the delinquent as a social casualty; the conservative sees him as a criminal. The same pattern of responses marked the progressives' approach to divorce. Liberals like E. A. Ross and moderates like Samuel Dike insisted that divorce was symptomatic of more serious problems, which could only be solved by changes in the social order. Conservatives demanded legal action against divorce. Liberals saw the divorcee as a helpless victim of circumstance bravely facing a difficult future; conservatives saw her as a wilful hedonist, selfishly and irresponsibly warping the structure of society.

The divorce controversy illustrates the difficulties in trying to interpret the social reforms of this century in terms of status politics. Ideology is not just a rationalization of the needs of particular groups but an expression of values that are themselves motivating forces. The divorce controversy was not waged between two sets of groups with contradictory status anxieties, for most of the protagonists on both sides of the issue belonged to the same social groups. The real conflict was between those who wished to maintain the traditional family structure and those who supported the newer, more egalitarian family that they believed was coming into existence. The difference was between those who argued that the needs of society took precedence over those of the individual, and those who believed the reverse— that marriage was made for man. The traditional conservative insistence on order was set against the historic liberal appeal for freedom.

The moral transformation which was getting under way in the Progressive era owed relatively little to previous American experience. It was this radical expectancy in advanced Progressivism that distinguished it from most earlier reform movements. The feeling that the old moral and cultural order was being overthrown was not confined to the urban avant-garde. Kenneth Rexroth has remarked that society today bears little resemblance to the world which his parents' generation assumed was coming:

> People like my parents had a moral confidence in the future that is incomprehensible today. They and everyone like them believed soon all life from clothing design to a game of chess was going to change for the better. It wasn't a political attitude as we understand the word today; in fact, nobody I knew until after my minority was over thought politically in the present meaning of the word.[10]

The misty notion of a time when art, culture, and a frank, healthy (though moral) relationship between the sexes would transform the style of middle-class life obtained in Elkhart, Indiana, and Davenport, Iowa, as it did in New York and Chicago.

Any interpretation which ignores the changing moral climate of the Progressive era does less than justice to the period. Certainly these moral alterations and Progressivism were not identical developments. This became clear in the 1920s, when one withered and the other flourished. But the two were bound together by more than their temporal coexistence. What united them was their utopian quality, and this is exactly what was missing from the new sexual standards of the 1920s and the political reforms of the 1930s. The hard-boiled,

10. Kenneth Rexroth, *An Autobiographical Novel* (Garden City, 1966), p. viii.

269

pragmatic, not to say opportunistic, reformism of the New Deal was as remote from the airy hopefulness of Progressivism as the careless sexuality of the Lost Generation was from the high-minded innocence of the pre-war rebellion. Both the political reforms and the moral changes of the Progressive years were sustained by a belief in the relative perfectibility of society. The death of this vision in the trenches of France and the conference halls of Versailles did not mean the end of political reform and moral change. But reforms and reformers were never quite the same again.

This is not to say that confidence and optimism were unique to the Progressive era. The whole difficulty in dealing with recent historical periods is that they share many of our own attributes. The progressives were not so greatly different from ourselves that we cannot understand them. Quite the contrary, the problem is that because they were much like us we tend to ignore the subtle distinctions that, taken as a whole, made the feel and texture of their life and the flavor of their thought unlike our own. That the future will be better than the present has been an article of faith in America since before we were a nation. But the intensity with which this was believed, the sense of what the present was like and the future ought to be, and the areas where progress was expected have changed repeatedly. Thus, in the 1830s and 40s the Transcendentalists and Utopians dreamed of a radically different future that had little connection with their own day, while the Jacksonians visualized a society very much like the one they lived in except that opportunity would be broader and the corrupt institutions of privilege contained or destroyed.

In our time we are inclined to see the future as a direct extension of the present. Winning the war on poverty means that everyone will live in tract houses or high-rise apartments. Tomorrow will be like today, except more so. We can understand why high school graduates who are sending their children to college believe in progress, but once we go beyond this limited perspective, if we find anything at all, it is a kind of forced, nightmarish, technological futurism. Buckminster Fuller proposes to solve the Harlem problem by erecting gigantic hive cities atop the existing slums.[11] The future development of San Francisco is to be effected apparently by leveling the hills and filling in the bay. Lewis Mumford is almost alone in calling for a city that meets man's spiritual and aesthetic needs.

But Mumford is a living reminder of a way of viewing the human condition that was once quite common. It is not that his ideas are in any way dated or old-fashioned. They are, in fact, tougher, tighter, and more sophisticated than anyone could fashion who had not experienced the continuing crisis of these past fifty years. It is the contour, not the content, of his social thought that is suggestive. At the turn of the century technical improvements were welcomed by the visionary, but they were understood to be instruments of progress and not progress itself. People like Ellis and Carpenter and Mrs. Gilman were concerned principally with human beings rather than the physical environment. They were vague about the mechanics of the good society, but they had a fairly clear idea of the kind of people they wanted to live

11. J. Meyer, "Instant Slum Clearance," *Esquire, 63* (1965), 108–11.

271

in it. As the twentieth century wore on, however, it became harder and harder to sustain the simple faith in human nature that had animated the prophets and reformers of the prewar era, and so we have come to rely upon techniques and technologies that are constant and reliable in ways that fractious humanity can never be.

History has operated in America, and most other developed countries as well, to diminish our faith in man and to preserve the least agreeable aspects of late nineteenth-century social thought. The technocratic elitism of Wells marches on, while the hopes of his colleagues for a new man and woman in a new world have long since been forgotten. As with everything else, sex and marriage have become objects of investigation and manipulation. We do not concern ourselves with the broad social context in which these things function, but rather view sexual inadequacy, marital breakups, and the like as discrete problems to be studied, experimented with, and prescribed for as if they were simply mechanical breakdowns. We are in consequence deluged with handbooks on sexual intercourse, proposals for divorce bureaus and marital counseling services, endless studies of behavioral patterns, and the whole varied output of the sex and marriage industry.

By this I do not mean to suggest that there is something inherently wrong with explicit directions and scientific studies, but rather that our preoccupation with style and technique at the expense of a large concern for the future of society is, as much as any other single thing, what makes us different from the Progressives. Many of them were technicians and manipulators, and the whole idea of the reformer as expert, for example, dates from this period, but the new moralists' great interest in the quality of life, the meaning of human relationships, and the social atmosphere in which people function is alien to us.

The failure of divorce to justify either the expectations of liberals or the fears of conservatives is, therefore, part of the whole process by which their system of attitudes and ideas has been replaced by our own. What was once a moral issue has become increasingly a clinical problem. That we have not solved it any more than the Progressives did is probably less important than our abandonment of their utopian stance. We are different from them because we have become more sophisticated about the mechanics of social change, and less hopeful of its possibilities.

BIBLIOGRAPHY

Public Documents

Meyer, Harmann H. B., Chief Bibliographer, Library of Congress, *List of References Submitted to the Committee on Judiciary, U.S. Senate, 63d Cong., 3d Sess., 1915, in Connection with S.J. Res. 109, A Resolution Proposing an Amendment to the Constitution Relating to Divorce.*

U.S. Bureau of the Census. *Marriage and Divorce 1867–1906: 1909,* Vol. 1.

———. *Marriage and Divorce 1916, 1919.*

U.S. *Congressional Record.* Vols. 23, 51.

U.S. Senate, Committee on the Judiciary. *Hearings on S.J. Res. 31, A Joint Resolution to Amend the Constitution to Authorize Uniform Marriage and Divorce Laws, November 21, 1921.* 67th Cong., 1st Sess., 1921.

Biographical Dictionaries

Cattell, Jacques, and E. E. Ross, *Leaders in Education,* Lancaster, The Science Press, 1948.

Directory of the American Sociological Association, New York, New York University, 1959.

Johnson, Allen, and Dumas Malone, eds., *Dictionary of American Biography,* New York, Charles Scribner's Sons, 1928–36.

National Cyclopaedia of American Biography, New York, James T. White & Company, 1904–62.

Primary Books—Scientific and Scholarly

Bailey, William B., *Modern Social Conditions,* New York, The Century Co., 1906.

Calhoun, Arthur W., *A Social History of the American Family From Colonial Times to the Present,* 3 vols. Cleveland, The Arthur H. Clark Company, 1919.

Colcord, Joanna C., *Broken Homes: A Study of Desertion and Its Social Treatment,* New York, Russell Sage Foundation, 1919.

Dealey, James Quayle, *The Family in its Sociological Aspects,* Boston, Houghton Mifflin Company, 1912.

Ellwood, Charles A., *Sociology and Modern Social Problems,* New York, American Book Company, 1913.

Gillette, John M., *The Family and Society,* Chicago, A. C. McClurg, 1922.

Goodsell, Willystine, *A History of the Family As a Social and Educational Institution,* New York, Macmillan, 1915.

Hall, Fred S., Elisabeth W. Brooke, *American Marriage Laws in Their Social Aspects: A Digest,* New York, Russell Sage Foundation, 1919.

Howard, George Elliott, *A History of Matrimonial Institutions,* 3 vols. Chicago, University of Chicago Press, 1904.

Lichtenberger, James P., "Divorce: A Study in Social Causation," Vol. 25 in *Studies in History, Economics, and Public Law,* New York, Columbia University Press, 1909.

Marvin, Donald M., *Occupational Propinquity as a Factor in Marriage Selection,* Philadelphia, University of Pennsylvania Press, 1918.

Nearing, Scott, *Women and Social Progress,* New York, Macmillan, 1912.

Parsons, Elsie Clews, *The Family,* New York, Putnam, 1906.

———, *Fear and Conventionality,* New York, Putnam, 1914.

———, *Social Freedom: A Study of the Conflicts between Social Classification and Personality,* New York, Putnam, 1915.

BIBLIOGRAPHY

Patten, Simon N., *The New Basis of Civilization*, New York, Macmillan, 1912.

Ross, Edward Alsworth, *Changing America*, New York, Century, 1912.

————, *Social Control: A Survey of the Foundations of Order*. New York, Macmillan, 1901.

Spencer, Herbert, *The Principles of Sociology*, 3d ed., 2 vols. New York, Appleton, 1892.

Thwing, Charles F., Carrie Thwing, *The Family: An Historical and Social Study*, 2nd ed., Boston, Lee & Shepard, 1913.

Ward, Lester F., *Dynamic Sociology*, 2 vols. New York, Appleton, 1883.

Willcox, Walter F., *The Divorce Problem: A Study in Statistics*, vol. 1 in *Studies in History, Economics and Public Law*, New York, Columbia University Press, 1897.

Wright, Carroll D., *Outline of Practical Sociology*, New York, Longman Green, 1898.

Primary Books and Pamphlets—General

Abbott, Lyman, *Christianity and Social Problems*, Boston, Houghton Mifflin, 1896.

Adler, Felix, *Marriage and Divorce*, New York, Appleton, 1915.

Barnes, Earl, *Woman in Modern Society*, New York, B. W. Huebsch, 1912.

Bebel, August, *Woman and Socialism*, New York, Socialist Literature Co., 1910.

Buck, Jirah D., *The Soul and Sex in Education, Morals, Religion, and Adolescence: Scientific Psychology for Parents and Teachers*, Cincinnati, Steward and Kidd, 1912.

Byrd, William, *The London Diary (1717–21) and Other Writings*, Louis B. Wright and Marion Tinling, eds., New York, Oxford University Press, 1958.

Carpenter, Edward, *The Intermediate Sex: A Study of Some*

277

Transitional Types of Men and Women, New York, Mitchell Kennerley, 1921.

————, *Love's Coming of Age: A Series of Papers on the Relations of the Sexes,* London, Swan Sonnenschein, 1903.

————, *My Days and Dreams: Being Autobiographical Notes,* 4th ed., London, George Allen & Unwin, 1921.

Carson, William E., *The Marriage Revolt,* New York, Hearst's International Library, 1915.

Cook, Joseph, ed., *Christ and Modern Thought: The Boston Monday Lectures, 1880–81,* Boston, Roberts Brothers, 1881.

Crafts, Wilbur, *Practical Christian Sociology,* 4th ed., New York, Funk and Wagnalls, 1907.

Crane, R. Newton, *Marriage Laws and Statutory Experiments in Eugenics in the United States,* London, Eugenics Education Society, 1910.

Dell, Floyd, *Women As World Builders,* Chicago, Forbes and Company, 1913.

Dike, Samuel W., *Some Fundamentals of the Divorce Question* (Special Issue of the National League for the Protection of the Family), Boston, Fort Hill Press, 1909.

————, *A Survey of the Chief Points of the U.S. Marriage and Divorce Report of 1909* (Special Issue of the National League for the Protection of the Family), Boston, Fort Hill Press, 1909.

————, *The Theory of the Marriage Tie.* (Special Issue of the National Divorce Reform League), Boston, Everett Press, 1893.

Dorr, Rheta Childe, *What Eight Million Women Want,* Boston, Small Maynard, 1910.

Ellis, Edith, *The New Horizon in Love and Life,* London, A. & C. Black, 1921.

Ellis, Havelock, *Little Essays of Love and Virtue,* New York, George H. Doran, 1921.

BIBLIOGRAPHY

————, *Studies in the Psychology of Sex,* 6 vols. Philadelphia, F. A. Davis, 1925.

Fielding, William J., *Sanity in Sex,* New York, Dodd Mead, 1920.

Gilman, Charlotte Perkins Stetson, *The Home: Its Work and Influence,* New York, McClure Phillips, 1903.

————, *The Living of Charlotte Perkins Gilman,* New York, Appleton Century, 1935.

————, *Women and Economics: A Study of the Economic Relation Between Men and Women as a Factor in Social Evolution,* Boston, Small Maynard, 1898.

Lecky, William Edward Hartpole, *History of European Morals: From Augustus to Charlemagne,* New York, Braziller, 1955.

Nystrom-Hamilton, Louise, *Ellen Key: Her Life and Her Work,* translated by A. E. B. Fries with an introduction by Havelock Ellis, New York, Putnam, 1886.

Henderson, Charles Richmond, *Social Duties: From the Christian Point of View,* Chicago, University of Chicago Press, 1909.

————, *Social Elements: Institutions, Character, Progress,* New York, Scribner, 1898.

Holmes, John H., *Marriage and Divorce,* New York, B. W. Huebsch, 1913.

Howe, M. A. DeWolfe, *The Life and Labors of Bishop Hare, Apostle to the Sioux,* New York, Sturgis & Walton, 1912.

Johnsen, Julia E., ed., *Selected Articles on Marriage and Divorce,* New York, H. W. Wilson, 1925.

Key, Ellen, *Love and Marriage,* New York, Putnam, 1911.

Kenney, Abbot, *The Conquest of Death,* New York, n.p., 1893.

Lawton, Robert O., *The Making of a Home,* Boston, Sherman French, 1914.

Martin, Edward Sandford, *In a New Century,* New York, Scribner, 1908.

————, *Windfalls of Observation,* Scribner, 1893.

279

Mathews, Shailer, *The Social Teachings of Jesus,* New York, Macmillan, 1909.

Munsterberg, Hugo, *The Americans,* New York, McClure Phillips, 1904.

Northcote, Hugh, *Christianity and Sex Problems,* Philadelphia, F. A. Davis, 1907.

Peabody, Francis Greenwood, *Jesus Christ and the Social Question,* New York, Macmillan, 1903.

Pearson, Karl, *The Ethic of Freethought,* London, Unwin, 1888.

Quilter, Harry, ed., *Is Marriage a Failure?,* London, Swan Sonnenschein, n.d.

Ringrose, Hyacinthe, *Marriage and Divorce Laws of the World,* New York, Musson-Draper, 1911.

Rogers, Anna B., *Why American Marriages Fail,* Boston, Houghton Mifflin, 1909.

Roosevelt, Theodore, *Realizable Ideals,* San Francisco, Whitaker and Ray Wiggin, 1912.

Savage, Minot J., *Men and Women,* Boston, American Unitarian Association, 1902.

Schreiner, Olive, *Woman and Labor,* New York, Frederick A. Stokes, 1911.

Schroeder, Theodore, *A New Concept of Liberty: From an Evolutionary Psychologist,* Berkeley Heights, N.J., Oriole Press, 1940.

Snyder, William L., *The Geography of Marriage: Or Legal Perplexities of Wedlock in the United States,* New York, Putnam, 1889.

Stanton, Theodore and Harriot S. Blatch, ed., *Elizabeth Cady Stanton as Revealed in Her Letters, Diary and Reminiscences,* 2 vols. New York, Harper, 1922.

Stockton, Lewis, *Marriage: Considered from Legal and Ecclesiastical Viewpoints,* Buffalo, Huebner-Bleistein Patents Co., 1912.

Ward, Harry F., *The Social Creed of the Churches,* New York, The Abingdon Press, 1914.

BIBLIOGRAPHY

Whitney, Henry C., *Marriage and Divorce,* New York, John E. Potter, 1894.

Secondary Sources

Ariés, Philippe, *Centuries of Childhood: A Social History of Family Life,* New York, Knopf, 1962.

Barnes, Harry Elmer, ed., *An Introduction to the History of Sociology,* Chicago, University of Chicago Press, 1948.

Barnett, James Harwood, *Divorce and the American Divorce Novel 1858–1937: A Study in Literary Reflections of Social Influences,* Philadelphia, University of Pennsylvania Press, 1939.

Blake, Nelson Manfred, *The Road to Reno: A History of Divorce,* New York, Macmillan, 1962.

Bogardus, Emory S., *The Development of Social Thought,* New York, Longman Green, 1957.

Bridenbaugh, Carl, *Myths and Realities: Societies of the Colonial South,* New York, Atheneum, 1963.

Cahen, Alfred, *Statistical Analysis of American Divorce,* New York, Columbia University Press, 1932.

Calder-Marshall, Arthur, *The Sage of Sex: A Life of Havelock Ellis,* New York, Putnam, 1959.

Calverton, Victor F., *Sex Expression in Literature,* New York, Boni & Liveright, 1926.

Cargill, Oscar, *Intellectual America: Ideas on the March,* New York, Macmillan, 1921.

Christensen, Harold T., ed., *Handbook of Marriage and the Family,* Chicago, Rand McNally, 1964.

Cremin, Lawrence A., *The Transformation of the School: Progressivism in American Education 1876–1957,* New York, Knopf, 1961.

Degler, Carl N., "Charlotte Perkins Gilman on the Theory and Practice of Feminism," *American Quarterly, 8* (Spring, 1956), 21–39.

Deland, Margaret, *Golden Yesterdays,* New York, Harper, 1940.

Dell, Floyd, *Intellectual Vagabondage: An Apology for the Intelligentsia,* New York, George H. Doran, 1926.

Ditzion, Sidney, *Marriage, Morals and Sex in America,* New York, Bookman Associates, 1953.

Dodge, Mabel, *Intimate Memories,* New York, Harcourt Brace, 1936.

Drinon, Richard, *Rebel in Paradise: A Biography of Emma Goldman,* Chicago, University of Chicago Press, 1961.

Eastman, Max, *Enjoyment of Living,* New York, Harper, 1948.

Freeman, Joseph, *An American Testament,* New York, Farrar and Rinehart, 1939.

Fremantle, Anne, *This Little Band of Prophets: The Story of the Gentle Fabians,* New York, Macmillan, 1960.

Friedan, Betty, *The Feminine Mystique,* New York, Norton, 1963.

Goode, William J., *After Divorce,* Glencoe, Free Press, 1956.

————, *The Family,* Englewood Cliffs, N.J., Prentice-Hall, 1964.

————, *World Revolution and Family Patterns,* Glencoe, Free Press, 1963.

Grosskurth, Phyllis, *The Woeful Victorian: A Biography of John Addington Symonds,* New York, Holt Rinehart, 1965.

Hardy, Florence Emily, *The Later Years of Thomas Hardy,* New York, Macmillan, 1930.

Harris, Frank, *Bernard Shaw,* New York, Book League of America, 1931.

Hobman, D. L., *Olive Schreiner: Her Friends and Times,* London, Walls & Co., 1955.

Hofstadter, Richard, *The Age of Reform: Bryan to F. D. R.,* New York, Knopf, 1955.

Hapgood, Hutchins, *A Victorian in the Modern World,* New York, Harcourt Brace, 1939.

Jacobson, Paul H., *American Marriage and Divorce,* New York, Rinehart, 1959.

BIBLIOGRAPHY

Kephart, William M., *The Family, Society, and the Individual,* Boston, Houghton Mifflin, 1961.

Koster, Donald Nelson, *The Theme of Divorce in American Drama, 1871–1939,* Philadelphia, University of Pennsylvania Press, 1942.

Lader, Lawrence, *The Margaret Sanger Story: And the Fight for Birth Control,* Garden City, Doubleday, 1955.

Lasch, Christopher, *The New Radicalism in America, 1889–1963: The Intellectual as a Social Type,* New York, Knopf, 1965.

Leiby, James, *Carroll Wright and Labor Reform: The Origin of Labor Statistics,* Cambridge, Harvard University Press, 1960.

McKinley, Donald Gilbert, *Social Class and Family Life,* New York, Free Press of Glencoe, 1964.

Masters, William H. and Virginia E. Johnson, *Human Sexual Response,* Boston, Little Brown, 1966.

May, Henry F., *The End of American Innocence,* New York, Knopf, 1959.

Morgan, Edmund S., *The Puritan Family,* Boston, Trustees of the Public Library, 1944.

————, *Virginians at Home: Family Life in the Eighteenth Century,* Williamsburg, Colonial Williamsburg, 1952.

Nethercot, Arthur H., *The First Five Lives of Annie Besant,* Chicago, University of Chicago Press, 1960.

Neumann, Henry, *Spokesmen for Ethical Religion,* Boston, Beacon, 1951.

Newcomer, Mabel, *A Century of Higher Education for American Women,* New York, Harper, 1959.

Odum, Howard, *American Sociology: The Story of Sociology in the United States through 1950,* New York, Longmans Green, 1951.

O'Neill, William L., ed., *Echoes of Revolt: The Masses, 1911–1917,* Chicago, Quadrangle, 1966.

Parker, Robert Allerton, *Yankee Saint: John Humphrey*

Noyes and the Oneida Community, New York, Putnam, 1935.

Purcom, C. B., *A Guide to the Plays of Bernard Shaw,* New York, Crowell, 1963.

Rexroth, Kenneth, *An Autobiographical Novel,* Garden City, Doubleday, 1966.

Robertson, John M., *A History of Freethought in the Nineteenth Century,* London, Watts & Co., 1929.

Smuts, Robert, *Women and Work in America,* New York, Columbia University Press, 1959.

Victorian Ideas of Sex, London, Sylvan Press, 1950.

Young, G. M., *Victorian England: Portrait of an Age,* Garden City, Doubleday Anchor, 1954.

Reports and Proceedings

American Sociological Society, *Papers and Proceedings of the Third Annual Meeting: The Family,* Chicago, University of Chicago Press, 1909.

Dike, Samuel W., *Annual Reports of the National League of the Protection of the Family.* Published annually from 1885 to 1912, first as reports of the New England Divorce Reform League, then as reports of the National Divorce Reform League, and finally as reports of the NLPF.

Federal Council of Churches of Christ in America, *First Annual Report* of the Executive Committee of the Inter-Church Conference on Federation, New York, 81 Bible House, 1906.

————, *Annual Reports* of the Executive Committee from 1912 to 1920, New York, unpublished, undated.

McCullough, James E., ed., *The Call of the New South:* Addresses delivered at the Southern Sociological Congress, Nashville, Southern Sociological Congress, 1912.

National Conference of Commissioners on Uniform State Laws, *Proceedings of the 26th Annual Meeting,* Chicago, unpublished, 1916.

BIBLIOGRAPHY

———, *Proceedings of the 27th Annual Meeting,* Saratoga Springs, New York, unpublished, 1917.

National Congress on Uniform Divorce Laws, *Proceedings of the Adjourned Meeting Held at Philadelphia, Pa., November 13, 1906.*

Powell, Aaron M., ed., *The National Purity Congress: Papers and Proceedings of the First National Purity Congress,* New York, American Purity Alliance, 1896.

Rogers, Howard J., ed., *Congress of Arts and Sciences Universal Exposition, St. Louis, 1904.*

Miscellaneous

Allen, Grant, *The Woman Who Did,* Boston, Roberts Brothers, 1895.

Hardy, Thomas, *Jude the Obscure,* London, Macmillan, 1929.

Library of Congress, Samuel Warren Dike Papers. Twenty-six boxes of unsorted material including letters to Dike, manuscripts of articles and reports, published material, and a forty-two page autobiographical statement in draft form.

McFarlane, James Walter, ed., *The Oxford Ibsen,* 6 vols. London, Oxford University Press, 1961.

Shaw, George Bernard, *Complete Plays with Prefaces,* 6 vols. New York, Dodd Mead, 1962.

INDEX

287

293

INDEX

INDEX